This Ain't Brain Surgery

How to Win the Pennant Without Losing Your Mind

Larry Dierker

To Roberto with
Aloha!

Larry Dierker 49

UNIVERSITY OF NEBRASKA PRESS
LINCOLN AND LONDON

Library of Congress Cataloging-in-Publication Data
Dierker, Larry.
This ain't brain surgery: how to win the pennant without losing your
mind / Larry Dierker.
p.   cm.
Originally published: New York: Simon & Schuster, c2003.
ISBN 0-8032-6651-0 (pbk.: alk. paper)
1. Dierker, Larry.   2. Baseball players—United States—Biography.
3. Baseball managers—United States—Biography.   4. Sportscasters—
United States—Biography.   5. Houston Astros (Baseball team)   I. Title.
GV865.D47A3   2005
796.357'092—dc22   2004022359

To Judy, my inspiration, and Katie, my voice coach

Contents

This Ain't
Brain Surgery

Introduction

Well, I'll tell you, young fella, to be truthful and honest and frank about it, I'm eighty-three years old, which ain't bad. To be truthful and honest about it, the thing I'd like to be right now is an astronaut.

—CASEY STENGEL

IN SEPTEMBER OF 1996 I was suffering. I had spent a good part of the baseball season in the hospital. First it was surgery on a torn ligament in my right thumb; then it was pericarditis, an in-flammation in the lining of the sac that contains the heart; then it was surgery again for a bone infection where the first surgery had been performed on my thumb. All told, I was in one ward or an-other for three weeks and under anesthesia four times. The last time, I left the hospital with a bottle of prednisone, a medicine so powerful that it changes your personality and makes you into a trencherman of mythic proportions. I came out of the hospital weighing 215 pounds and a month later tipped the scales at 240. What's worse, I was doing a lot of the eating in the middle of the night, interrupting my sleep. I was so hungry I couldn't make it through the night without a meal. By September, most of my health problems were under control. The only lingering reminder of my personal travails was the cast on my right hand that had forced me to keep my scorebook left-handed while broadcasting

1

all year long. I couldn't wait for season's end, but I sure didn't want it to end in free fall.

Everyone with the Astros was suffering to some extent. The team had fallen out of the race and was in the midst of a nine-game losing streak that would give the Cardinals the Central Division title on a platter. It is so discouraging to tough it out for five months and over 125 ball games only to plummet like a stone thrown into a lake; but that's exactly what we did. I was determined to float down the Guadalupe River on an inner tube when the season ended, soaking my right hand in the cool water and enjoying a beer or two along the way, but first we had to finish the schedule and it was on the next to last road trip of the season that I uttered a line that has had a major impact on my life. It happened near the end of the losing streak, during a game with the Marlins. Florida didn't have a very good team that year but they were making us look like Little Leaguers.

We were way behind, maybe 9–2, in this particular game. Our cameras panned the dugout and it looked like a morgue. "You know what's wrong with this team, Brownie?" I asked my partner Bill Brown.

"Well, we're not hitting," he offered.

"No, it's not that," I said.

"Well then, what is it?"

"Not enough Hawaiian shirts," I said.

"Hawaiian shirts?"

"Yeah, Hawaiian shirts," I repeated. "Everyone in that dugout looks like someone in their family has died. You have to have some spirit to win games. This team looks dead. Did you ever see someone wearing a Hawaiian shirt that wasn't having a good time?"

"Well, no," he answered. "But where's yours?"

"I'll wear it tomorrow night," I said, not knowing how difficult it would be to find one, even in Miami.

The next day I canvassed the mall and came away with a shirt that had flowers on it—not really a Hawaiian shirt, but close. I didn't tell our producer or director that I was going to wear it for fear they would insist on our normal coat and tie policy. We lost again, but the words had been spoken. We talked about Hawaiian shirts during that broadcast and the next two in Atlanta, and by the time we got back to Houston, it was general knowledge among our faithful fans.

I called my boogie-boarding brother, Rick, and asked him to send me a couple of shirts. One of them was decorated with vintage woodie station wagons from the 1940s, a popular surfer car when I was in high school. The woodies on this particular shirt had surfboards hanging out the back windows or mounted on top. I wore it to the ballpark, just for grins. About half an hour before the game, I had a devilish idea. I was working radio with play-by-play man Milo Hamilton that night and I was almost sure he didn't know that the term "woody" was current slang for an erection. When Milo was out of earshot, I told our engineer and several young interns to listen closely. "I'm going to get Milo," I said. "Just wait."

When Milo came back into the booth, I pointed to one of the woodies on the shirt and said, "Hey, Milo. You know what this is?"

"Uh, a station wagon," he ventured.

"No, this is a woodie, man. You should know that. It comes from your era. These things were the rage when I was in high school in California. They were surfer cars."

"I didn't know they called them that," he said.

We went on the air and after he got all the preliminary information out, and with plenty of time in the inning to talk, I asked, "Hey, Milo. How do you like my new Hawaiian shirt?"

"You mean the one with all the woodies on it?" He took the bait. I could imagine all the middle-aged and younger fans in our audience getting a mental image of a shirt full of hard-ons.

"Yeah," I said. "When you were a young man, did you ever have a woodie?" I hadn't planned that line. It just came out.

"Oh no," he said. "We were much too poor."

"Boy, that's really poor," I said, stifling laughter, and looking back behind me where the others in the booth were sitting. One intern bolted from the booth. I imagine he couldn't contain himself. The rest of them were giggling in silence.

The next day, word of the interchange swept through the Astrodome like a brushfire. It was especially funny because Milo is a proud man, to say the least. He is not the type of person who can admit a mistake, let alone laugh at himself. Thinking about him discussing erections on the air gave rise to convulsions of laughter as it spread from office to office throughout the building. It continued for several days and Milo never knew it. I wore the shirt and got him a few more times before the season was over.

Although we were mourning the loss of our playoff hopes, we were also obligated to finish the schedule, and in this type of situation humor helps. If the players could just share in our glee, they would be better off. But they showed no outward signs of shedding the burden of choking in the clutch.

Nobody was happier to see the season end than I was. I was in Austin the night we finished, staying with friends for a few days. The next evening, when I came in from floating on the river, there was a message to call my wife, Judy.

She told me that the president of the Astros, Tal Smith, had called and he wanted to see me in his office at ten o'clock the next morning and that it was urgent. I grudgingly drove back to Houston, wondering what could possibly be so important.

A computer-tone version of "Take Me Out to the Ballgame" announced my arrival as I walked through the glass doors of Tal Smith Enterprises. "Let's sit out here on the balcony where we can relax," Tal suggested. Seven stories below, shoppers perused the many offerings of the Galleria, as Tal came characteristically to the point. "If you had to trade Bell [Derek] or Kile [Darryl] to make budget, which one would it be?"

"Well, we all know you don't win without pitching," I replied. "But Bell is a star and he could get better. I guess I would have to let Kile go, even though I wouldn't want to." As it turned out, we did not part with either player, and Kile, not Bell, got better.

Our conversation continued along these lines. Before long, we had discussed just about every player on the team. "Sounds like you've got a pretty good grasp of where we are and where we need to go," Tal said. "Maybe you should manage the club."

"Well, I'll tell you," I said. "I've been trying to think of a way to get away from Milo, but that would be rather extreme."

Tal laughed so loud that shoppers way down below looked up to see what was happening. It was all in the spirit of kidding from my standpoint. He had another perspective.

"I've taken the liberty of ordering some sandwiches," he said. "We can have lunch here."

"Fine," I said. I looked back toward Tal's longtime secretary Judy Vieno's desk and spotted Astros general manager Gerry Hunsicker.

"Let's go in here where we have more room," Tal said. "Gerry is going to join us if you don't mind." This is when I sniffed a hidden agenda. I couldn't imagine it to be anything that was personally threatening, and I always enjoyed talking baseball with Tal and Gerry, so I said an internal "what the heck" and chomped into a turkey sandwich. As we continued the evaluation, I was asked what I would do differently if I were running the team. "Well, I'd get some left-handed hitters and some pitching depth," I replied.

After we discussed relative strengths and weaknesses and commiserated over budget constraints, Tal and Gerry came to the heart of the issue.

"What did you think about Terry's performance last year?"

I paused.

Terry Collins, the manager of the Astros, had grown unpopular with the players as most managers eventually do. I am not a big fan of his hyperkinetic style, but I regard him as a smart baseball man, an energetic worker, and a keen competitor. I knew he was on the hot seat, but I had heard that the club would not eat the last year of his contract.

"I think he does a good job," I said. "I don't always agree with him, but that's what the game is all about."

"What about the clubhouse?" I was asked. "Did you get any feedback from the players?"

"Well, I know they aren't wild about him. But they liked him just fine and he seemed like a better manager in '94," I said. "We had a better team and we were winning more then. It makes a big difference."

"They say he's lost the clubhouse."

"It's a long winter. He can get it back."

At this point I realized that I was being interviewed for the manager's job. They hadn't really said that Terry was going to be fired but that's what I heard. My head was spinning like the Wheel of Fortune, but I knew I had to stay calm. It was like being on the mound, with a thousand thoughts crossing your mind while you try to concentrate on just one or two.

"How do you feel about statistical information?" Tal asked. "Do you think you can get an edge by getting favorable match-ups?"

"Sometimes," I said. "When a guy has hit a certain pitcher, year after year or vice versa, it is worth noting. I do think, however, that managers use statistics too much. If a guy is 3-5 against a particular pitcher and another guy is 0-4 that means very little to me. The sample is too small. In that case I would favor my instincts. If the pitcher is a sinker, slider guy, I would play the guy who is the best low-ball hitter. That type of thing."

I knew Tal to be a number cruncher; he relies on statistics to present his arbitration cases. I was relieved when he said, "I agree. I think a lot of managers fail to play hunches and use their instincts."

Whew, I thought. I cleared that hurdle, still not knowing if I wanted to clear it. At this juncture, I was competing for the job and wasn't sure why except that it is my nature to try difficult things. I guess I sensed this chance might not come again.

"Any manager in today's game has all the numbers he needs," I said. "And he would be a fool not to use them. But the most important thing is the combination of players a manager has available, the way he deploys them, and the effort they give. If you don't have the horses you can forget it. If you have horses that can run together, you have to cue them up right. Get the right batting order, get them enough playing time. Then you have a chance, but only if they want to run. Let's face it, a team is only as good as it thinks it is. Confidence is critical."

At that point, I brought up the importance of pitching, citing our division championship years in the 1980s. "The most important aspect of confidence is pitching," I continued. "You simply can't win a championship without good pitching. You can make it if your fielding and hitting is only adequate, but you must have a good bench because you'll have to deal with injuries."

"What would you do about Bagwell [Jeff] and Biggio [Craig]?"

This question stunned me. "Bagwell and Biggio?" I said. "Nothing. I'd just write their names in the lineup and let them play. I can't imagine those two guys being a problem."

"You might be surprised," Tal said. "They carry a lot of weight in the clubhouse and they brought it to bear on Terry."

I thought for a moment. I had heard that Biggio and Bagwell were unhappy with Terry. "Remember the story about Joe McCarthy when he took over the Red Sox?" I said.

Tal remembered it, but I doubted that Gerry did, so I elaborated.

"When McCarthy was with the Yankees, he was a stickler for appearances. He felt that it was important for the Yankees to maintain their classy image by dressing in a suit and tie whenever they were together. When he went to Boston, the writers jumped him about his dress code. 'What are you going to do about Ted Williams?' they asked. Well, everyone knew that Williams refused to wear a tie. And McCarthy wasn't stupid. 'That's easy, boys,' he said. 'If Ted doesn't want to wear a tie, he doesn't have to. If I can't get along with a .400 hitter, I should be fired.' "

This is the way I felt about Bagwell and Biggio. I don't know how Terry got crosswise with them; they certainly didn't do anything on the field to cause him trouble—quite the opposite. They played hard and smart; they played hurt; they played every day. I don't know what happened behind the clubhouse doors, but if I had players like that I would find a way to get along with them. Perhaps they wanted to run the team—to dictate who played, or what the batting order should be. This type of criticism is common with star players and it could either be a problem or it could be a solution. Players like Bagwell and Biggio have a lot of good ideas. I would listen to them, and if I didn't want to use their suggestions I would tell them why. Throughout my thirty-seven years in baseball, I had heard manager after manager say that there was one set of rules, not two. But in actuality, the stars got more than their share of favors. I got the star treatment myself for a few years and I didn't believe in one set of rules. I believed in the elasticity of a few rules. Playing hard and winning is the only real answer. When you do that, nobody cares about how the rules are applied.

"Look, I'm tired of this Bagwell and Biggio shit," I said. "Bagwell and Biggio will not be a problem, believe me."

I now believe that this statement is the one that got me the job. It also proved to be false.

One more thought on Biggio and Bagwell. In the spring of 1996, it was suggested that these two fine ballplayers, who had played with uncommon valor in the Wild Card race the previous September, should be made sort-of unofficial team captains and accept a leadership role in the clubhouse. This seemed a good idea, but it didn't work out. Bagwell cares deeply about the team, but his leadership talents are mostly nonvocal. Biggio is a team guy too and he likes to talk. But he is a driven man, a perfectionist. It works well for him, but leaves him intolerant of those who are less motivated. He may make a good leader as the years soften his edge, but in 1996 he wasn't ready. I didn't expect problems with these two guys because I would not ask them to work overtime. I would not ask them to be captains. I would address team problems myself, acting as policeman if necessary. I would ask Bagwell and Biggio to do just one thing: Play.

About this time I peered through the glass door of Tal's conference room and saw our owner, Drayton McLane.

This is it. Today's the day, I thought. I wonder if they will offer it today and I will have to say yes or no. The prospects were both exciting and frightening. I thought about all the things that could go wrong. What if I got fired in an unfriendly way? If that happened, I probably couldn't get my broadcast job back. What then? I thought about Judy, my daughter Julia, and my son, Ryan. They would like it, I was pretty sure of that, but would it cut into my time with them? What time? I have been a lot like my dad, working all the time. They haven't gotten much from me anyway. Perhaps in this role my influence would be greater. Maybe they would come to the games more often and we would have things to talk about and the kids might actually listen to me. I didn't see a red flag in the family department. I guess the only thing that truly scared me was my health. With everything that had happened that summer, and the underlying possibility of anxiety, managing could take a heavy toll. What the hell, I thought. I've had enough bad health this year to last for a while. I'll just have to get into good shape, something I had planned to do anyway.

Drayton came in, smiling like a practical joker. "How are things going so far?" he quipped. "Do we have ourselves a candidate?" We all smiled and Tal said that we had covered a lot of ground. "He clearly knows this team better than anyone we could get from the outside. He seems to have a good grasp on the issues too."

I felt like a champion, which is just the way Drayton wants everyone to feel. His two favorite expressions are "Thanks for your leadership" and "Do you want to be a champion?" I was ready. I wanted to be on the team.

"So, what is your theory of leadership?" he asked.

Drayton is a motivator, a self-described cheerleader, so this was a tricky question because I knew that I couldn't do it the way he does. I would have to have my own style. I knew some of his slogans, like "A leader is a guy who will take you to a place you wouldn't go on your own." I had read some books about successful big league managers and their theories, and had seen seven of them operate firsthand. I would have to act naturally, do it my own way, take the strong steady approach. Not too much bullshit, just clear instructions and common sense. Not too high, not too low, but doggedly persistent.

"My high school coach used to say you can lead a horse to water but you can't make him drink," I said. "The first thing is to identify the ones that will drink." I tickled myself with that statement. It just sort of came out that way and when Gerry and Tal started laughing, Drayton did too.

"Seriously, if you have to make players do things, you're

in trouble to begin with. You have to have players who are self-motivated. The next part is tricky; you have to make them believe you can lead them. In my case, that will be the biggest challenge. They know I played; they think I'm a good guy; but they also want to win badly, and they don't want some rookie manager who makes an ass of himself. I'll have to win their respect with my judgments and it will take time. I feel like I can accomplish this because we have good players. Winning creates the atmosphere of success and that feeling rubs off on everyone, including the manager.

"Afterward, we'll have a few drinks," I said. I couldn't resist.

We talked in this vein for another hour and everything went well. The meeting lasted so long that I had to call Judy and arrange for her to pick Ryan up from school. He is seventeen years old now and can drive, but did not get one of the few parking passes allotted to juniors. He can also walk and it is less than a mile to his school. But that's another story, which is more about his mother.

Anyway, when our meeting was finally over, I was told that Gerry would call me with the salary and the particulars later that night. He would expect my final decision and there would be a press conference tomorrow.

I went to Ryan's fall league baseball game with Judy that night and we sat in the stands and watched. We exchanged pleasantries with friends and acquaintances. I knew I was the Astros manager and so did Judy. It was our secret.

The press conference came the next day. I had so many butterflies I thought I might lift off until I realized that the weight of the world was upon me. I had some serious buyer's remorse. Had I compromised myself for the fame and fortune? I didn't need fame, would just as soon do without it, but like everyone, I could find a good use for more money. Why be so greedy? I asked myself. You don't need the money. You just want it. Is it pride that is pulling you? Or is it the affirmation that you are a real baseball expert with skills that go beyond performance?

That's it, I told myself, and that's exactly the way Judy put it when I told her. "It's about time they realized how much you know and what you can do. You deserve it," she said.

What she didn't know is that a lot of other guys deserved it more: guys who had slaved away in the minor leagues, guys who had spent years as bench coaches in the big leagues. Guys who were fully apprenticed and clearly capable and better prepared than I. Of course, I was prepared for the Fox broadcast job that went to Giants coach Bob Brenly, who was better prepared to manage. It's a crazy world, I thought. You have to take it as it comes. Don't worry. Everything will be all right.

I was terrified.

I was teetering on the edge of anxiety before attending the press conference. I felt the tingle on every nerve ending. It had happened so fast that I had almost no time to prepare my thoughts. In the end it was like pitching on opening day. You worry yourself to death and then the game starts and you are fine.

Gerry was introduced by our PR director, Rob Matwick. He walked to the microphone in front of the little Astros theater and spoke to about fifty media representatives. "The Astros have relieved Terry Collins of his duties," he said as the murmur in the room fell to a hush, "and the next Astros manager is in this room." That was a great line. Reporters were scanning the room, but nobody guessed it. When I was brought forth, the murmur returned. There was a sense of giddiness and it spread to a shared grin. I was one of them: I had not only broadcast the games for eighteen years, I had written a weekly column for the *Houston Chronicle* for ten. This was either a great joke or a great story. Either way, it was more than they expected.

Tal came up and made a short speech on the reasoning of the move. Drayton told the story of our meeting and how surprised I was. Finally, I was up there holding my first press conference. It went rather well, I thought.

"Is this your dream job?"

"No, I just gave up my dream job. This will be a lot harder."

"Whatever possessed you to take it?"

"I don't know," I said. "I guess it's like someone gave me an opportunity to be an astronaut and go to the moon. At first I would think of all the excuses why I couldn't do it. I'm too tall to get into the capsule. I don't know how to fix rocket engines. I'm claustrophobic. I have a dental appointment next week. None of the excuses were any good. I realized I had a chance to do something bold and exciting. Something offered to only a select few. If it didn't kill me it would be an unforgettable experience."

"What about the downside? You know you're going to be fired?"

"Yes, I know that. But my only regret is that as a player I never made it to the World Series. Now I have a chance to go—in uniform—this is a pretty good ball club. In the end, the lure of the competition was too much. I said the hell with safety. Fire up the engines!"

If I hadn't taken the job, I would never have forgiven myself. I would have felt like a coward. Sure, I was scared, and I realized that I might be making a colossal mistake, but I had to do it. I just had to.

After the press conference, it came easier. The TV stations sent reporters to my house to do interviews for the six o'clock news. Ryan was jumping up and down behind me waving his hands so his friends would see him on television. That night, he had another ball game. I sat in the stands with Judy, just like before, but this time I was signing autographs and answering questions the whole time. I felt like the same guy, but people, even our friends, were treating me differently—like a hero. I haven't even won a game, I thought. This is amazing.

It also had a dreamlike quality that made me feel uneasy. As I traveled around Houston, people recognized me more often; they usually called me Coach. This appellation bothers most baseball managers. It is an affront because the coaches work for the manager in professional baseball. Most people, especially in the South, don't know enough about professional baseball to call you "Skipper." And they feel uncomfortable calling you by your name if they don't know you. So, when they called me Coach I was irritated but I understood their frame of reference and reacted as if they had said Skipper.

In college, the head coach does a lot of teaching, but I would do very little, if any, teaching. My job would be to organize and orchestrate the activities of the team. I suddenly realized that I had no experience doing these things. I knew what I wanted the team to look like and I had some definite thoughts about plays and strategies, but I had no idea how to bring these things about.

The one thing I did know is that I would need a good bench coach and I asked if Bill Virdon was available, knowing him to be a close friend of Tal's. Everyone thought Bill was a good choice and he took the job, which made me feel a whole lot better. Bill had won more games than any Astros manager and he had been named Manager of the Year a couple of times. His presence gave me instant credibility. He was tough-minded, didn't put up with a lot of bullshit, and he knew how to run the game. I filled out my staff with former Astros: Vern Ruhle (pitching coach), Alan Ashby (bullpen coach), and Jose Cruz (first base coach). Gerry knew Mike Cubbage and Tom McCraw from his days with the Mets. We interviewed them and hired them as third base coach and hitting instructor, respectively.

With that assemblage of coaches, I started jotting down thoughts of spring training as I remembered it as a player. It had been eighteen years since I was on the field. As an announcer, I never came out early to watch the workouts. I talked with Bill and Cubby on the phone and learned that the routine was about the same as far as the workouts. But a lot of other things would be different. I had just entered another world.

CHAPTER 1

Spring Training

I hate the cursed Oriole fundamentals . . . I've been doing them
since 1964. I do them in my sleep. I hate spring training.

—JIM PALMER

FOR THE ARDENT BASEBALL FAN, the beginning of spring training is a cause for celebration. It is a renewal of sorts—a sign that old man winter has been pushed aside by the exuberant rush of youth, and that the boys of summer are on the way. Many a baseball writer has been inspired by the smell of new-cut grass, by the invigorating crack of horsehide against Northern white ash.

For most adult fans, a spring training vacation is a kind of reverie—a lyric journey back through time to the seamless days of youth when one more inning was better than Mom's home cooking.

I still remember those days.

"Larry, come in, it's time for dinner."

"One more inning, Mom. We're all tied up."

These thoughts don't enter my mind much anymore, especially at spring training. My view from the inside isn't rose-colored, but black and white. For me, spring training means traversing the monotonous Florida landscape playing exhibition games that are as dull as dirt. What is dull now was shiny then. In fact, my fondest memories of spring training go back more than thirty years, to the days of the Beatles and the Beachboys.

During my playing days, the Astros had a complex of fields in Cocoa, Florida, a short distance but a far cry from their current facility in Kissimmee where the team moved in 1985. I was broadcasting at that time and I'll never forget my first trip from the Orlando airport to our new spring home, the "Fantasy World Villas"—no kidding. It was late in the afternoon when I exited Interstate 4 and headed south on Highway 535 to Highway 192, where there is chaos of neon at night and chaos of architecture by day. The businesses along this strip have sprouted recently, fast as weeds and just as ugly. They are there to serve the families who have barely enough money to spend on the many splendors of Disney. On 192, they can get their T-shirts, fast food, and motel rooms at half the price and get their film developed overnight. Such a deal. One of the businesses, however, is different. It was owned by an old gentleman by the name of Bruce Muir, and it's such a deal that it scares all but the most intrepid tourists away.

Bruce grew up in Michigan, went away to Dartmouth, fought in World War Two, and finally headed south many years later after selling his inheritance, the Muir Drug Stores. The bar he opened in Kissimmee was only one of many watering holes along 192, but it had an authentic style that the others lacked. The other lounges and package stores were close to the highway and sported loud neon signs. But Bruce's place crouches inconspicuously away from the highway and the maze of plaster and plastic buildings that litter the strip. The structure is cinder block, and the parking lot is either dirt or mud, depending on the weather.

The Big Bamboo is right where Highway 535 dead-ends into Highway 192. Go right and you are on your way to the Fantasy World Villas, and further down, the Disney theme parks. Turn left and go about ten or twelve miles and you are at the Astros' spring training headquarters, Osceola County Stadium. Back down 535, on the north side of Interstate 4, you get Lake Buena Vista, a

Disney complex of hotels and first-class commercial buildings, shops, restaurants—places where you can unwittingly spend a lot of money.

Although the Bamboo occupies a choice location in a hot real estate market, you can't spend all that much money there. I learned that right away. As I rounded the turn from 535 south to 192 west, I noticed the Big Bamboo sign and pulled in. I didn't have to be at my villa at any particular time and a cool beer sounded awfully appealing. I noticed that the "boo" part of the sign had broken away and was relocated—I should say tacked—below the "Big Bam." From the road it looked like a hovel. I said to myself, "This is either a redneck joint or a nice little watering hole." I made the hard right into the dirt and pulled up alongside the only other car that was parked there.

When you walk in through the screen door, the strains of Glenn Miller greet you. Thousands of artifacts grab your eyeballs in a dizzying trip back through time and across many tropical lands. You feel like you have stepped into a bar in the South Pacific during World War Two.

"Good afternoon, young fella," Bruce said as I took a seat at the bar. "What'll it be?"

I saw a Red Stripe back behind the bar along with some old standbys like Budweiser and some exotics, like Ngoma, an African malt liquor. I opted for the Red Stripe and began to look around. There was only one other patron and he was hunched over his beer, as if in prayer. I talked to Bruce, taking in the scenery, which was eclectic at least and fascinating at best. The place was crawling with souvenirs Bruce and his wife collected in the Caribbean, where they sojourned for five years after selling the drugstores. How they came to this spot in Central Florida I'll never know, but how I came to them, I'm certain: It was fate. I was the only guy on the team who would take a chance on a place like the Boo without an invitation.

As the years went by, I became a regular. I liked the big band music. I liked Bruce and his sidekick, Ray Guenther. I liked the idea of wearing Hawaiian shirts, which was the standard uniform of the bartenders. And I grew to like Ngoma, which at the time came in a twenty-ounce bottle with drums painted on the label that said

"Catch the Rhythm, Feel the Beat." Three Ngomas was a snootful and that was my limit before I heard that the record was five and proceeded to drink six. I spent about four hours doing it and I was still sloshed. Later I learned that an Australian (wouldn't you know it) had consumed eight. I let him have it! I can't pitch anymore and I can't drink that way either. But I can have a few—and what a place to have them. When you are by yourself a lot, as I was after my playing days, it is nice to find a place where the atmosphere is convivial and the likelihood of finding interesting colloquy is great. One day it's a Disney artist; another day it's a chef. Ray studied literature, and we talked about books when the crowd was small enough to allow him time to talk. Sometimes there were a handful of customers. Sometimes it was standing room only.

Through my seventeen years in Kissimmee I was only harangued by a knucklehead four or five times. The Boo is so serene that I don't recall anyone so much as raising his or her voice in anger or impatience. And it is possible to become impatient, as the service is notoriously slow. Although I never found a confederate in the media or among the staff in Kissimmee, my propitious discovery of the Big Bamboo did not go unnoticed. A lot of staff people started going there and I bumped into them once in a while. The writers spent some time there too. I saw them more often, as I tended to get there later than the front office workers, who had to go to work early. The only player I ever saw there was Dale Berra, who stopped in on a hunch just like I did. Later on, after I started managing the team, we had a team party there at the end of training camp. It was the only time any of us on the staff had drinks with the players. The players have their places and they prefer privacy just as they did when I played. The only difference for me was that I always had a running buddy when I played and I never had a sidekick after my playing days were over.

Several years ago, when Bruce turned seventy, there was a fine celebration. One of the regulars, Big Jim, who at 6'9", 300 pounds was one of the largest set designers ever, designed a 1940s-vintage airplane guidance tower for the parking lot. All of us at the party participated in pulling the big telephone poles upright with four or five long ropes. On top of the poles there was a small hut with a corrugated tin roof. The big band music from the bar was wired to the tower so that you could get in the mood before entering. Up top, there was a revolving amber light and further up on a flagpole, "Maggie's drawers," a pair of bloomers, were flapping in the breeze to serve as a wind sock. The efficacy of the tower was obvious from the wrecked carcass of a World War Two vintage airplane that was pushed into the vegetation alongside the parking lot as if it had crashed there. I wrote a song for Bruce on the occasion. It goes like this:

> There's a crazy little bar down in Kissimmee
> Hunkered down in the shadow of Walt Disney
> Well, I've been all around and I'm telling you
> There ain't no place like the Big Bamboo
>
> Oh Big Bamboo, I'm so bamboozled
> By your Island charm
> And your big band music
> By your artifacts
> Odd and amusing
> C'mon let's go
> Let's go bamboozing
>
> Yes, I've been all around and I'm telling you
> There ain't no place like the Big Bamboo
>
> Oh Big Bamboo, ever so humble
> You're my hideaway
> In the neon jungle
> And your clientele
> Odd and amusing
> C'mon let's go
> Let's go bamboozing
>
> There's a crazy little bar down in Kissimmee
> Hunkered down in the shadow of Walt Disney
> Well, I've been all around and I'm telling you

There ain't no place like the Big Bamboo
No, there ain't no place like the Big Bamboo
My magic kingdom is the Big Bamboo

Bruce died a few years ago and now the heirs want to sell the place. Last I heard there was a "Save the Big Bamboo" campaign going on in Kissimmee, complete with Web page. I'm not sure if Bruce would be proud of, or appalled by, all the fuss. He was quite a character. Meanwhile, Ray took over operations, and the place became, of all things, a chess bar. You had to see it to believe it. Two or three chess games where you would least expect them.

Long before my Bamboo days, I was introduced to a similar haunt just down the street from the Astros' training facility in Cocoa, Florida, in March of 1965, my first spring training. I was weaned on beer in that hut, which was appropriately called The Hut. It was a shanty, just like the Boo, and I liked it principally because they let me drink beer there before I was twenty-one. It had some rustic charm but it wasn't nearly as inviting as the Big Bamboo. I wasn't a connoisseur of taprooms at the time. I was just happy to be served.

I recall passing the old baseball complex in Cocoa in 1997 on the way to Viera to play the Marlins. Seeing Cocoa Stadium and the dormitory we nicknamed the "Hofheinz Hilton" after the Astros' first owner, Judge Roy Hofheinz, sure brought back memories. Luckily, I was with the big league team from the start, affording me luxury status in the dorm. I had my own small room with a dresser and a photograph of the Astrodome on the wall. There were no telephones or televisions in the rooms to distract us, and there was only one bathroom for every two rooms. The rooms had a distinctive, but not unpleasant smell, kind of like a new car smell but not quite the same. If you blindfolded me and took me there I would immediately know my whereabouts. On the far side of the building, minor league players were stacked in bunk beds, four to a room. Eight men with only one sink and one toilet. That combination led to more than a few fights.

I loved Cocoa, even though it was a dump. It seems like the

Dark Ages compared to the modern facilities of this era. The locker room was not air-conditioned. It was steamy and stinky. It had a unique smell too—a smell that prevented us from lingering too long. Water from the showers ran out into the locker room. Half the time we were walking around in puddles. A printed sign over the pisser read: "Please do not throw gum or cigarette butts into the urinal. Would you like to clean it?" Below that sign was the handwritten reply of Doug Rader, "Yes, because I'm scummy!" Our sweat-drenched undergarments hung on a line outside the locker room to dry, but they weren't laundered very often. There was only one clubhouse attendant, one washer and no dryer.

Cocoa was a sleepy little town, but Cocoa Beach was a bee-hive. Most of the action was launched from Cape Kennedy, the headquarters of the space program. We trained by day and chased girls by night, while trying to out-drink the astronauts, which was no small task. Turk Farrell and Jim Owens took me to some of the joints down there and introduced me to the seductions of the nightlife. They knew all about it. While drinking and carousing, they occasionally packed a pistol. As young, hard-throwing pitchers with the Phillies, they joined Seth Morehead in a trio that became known as the Dalton Gang. Of the three, Farrell had the best career. He was one of the strongest players I have ever known. His left calf muscle was shriveled by a childhood case of polio, but he didn't seem to notice it. During pitchers' batting practice, he often turned around and hit left-handed. Even in the cavernous As-trodome, he could hit the ball out of the park both ways. Owens later became my pitching coach. He was preaching to a different kind of choir. His kind—the type that meets every morning before workouts to pass the Visine around from one pitcher to the next.

I think Judge Hofheinz thought that he could keep us isolated from diversions by building the camp and dormitory fifteen miles inland from the nightlife on the beach. It didn't work. More than a few times, we raced down the toll road leading back to the dorm, flying through the tollbooth without slowing down. If you don't think an automobile can cover fifteen miles in ten minutes you're sadly mistaken. That was the era of 424-cubic-inch engines and we beat the twelve o'clock curfew every time but once. That time Mark

Schaeffer got a speeding ticket. We appointed him to drive because he had already lost his license and therefore had nothing to lose. Turned out he was a two-time loser. He was fined by the ball club and the state of Florida; the rest of us were only fined by the team.

One rookie pitcher suffered a meaner fate. He was late and missed curfew too, but in his haste to beat the deadline, he raced down Friday Road in front of the dormitory and overshot the driveway. Slamming on his brakes, he screeched to a stop, waking most everyone in the building. Then he threw it in reverse, squealing backward for fifty yards or so, and slammed on his brakes again. He peeled into the driveway and then fishtailed into a parking spot. The only problem was that he was going too fast and he plowed over the curb, through a flower bed, and into the side of the building, just outside Paul Richards's room. Richards was the general manager of the team and he didn't think it was funny. The next day this guy looked like a bloodhound and reeked of vinegar. We nicknamed him Crash, then said goodbye. He was moved to the minor league clubhouse and never returned.

The funniest thing I have ever seen in Florida happened way back in 1965, in Cocoa at my very first spring training. Turk Farrell brought his baby alligator (about a two-footer) to the ballpark one day and barricaded it in the whirlpool basin. We had an outfielder by the name of Mike White that spring and everyone called him Snuffy because of his speech impediment. Snuffy was trying to rehab from knee surgery and we didn't have a lot of fancy exercise machinery back then, so he was sitting on the training table, doing leg raises with a ten-pound weight strapped to his foot. This was after the workout and everyone was in the locker room. Well, just as Snuffy was raising his leg, the alligator took a shit and it stank to the high heavens, overpowering the typical everyday stench that we were accustomed to. Snuffy started retching and cursing Farrell at the same time. He came stumbling off the table with the weight tied to his foot, hobbling through the locker room, heading for the bathroom trying not to throw up too soon. "Nod nammit, Turk," he said. "You thun of a bits."

• • •

When it comes to spring training, I had the best duty—starting pitcher. I got to leave after my work was done, usually about noon or one o'clock on days I wasn't pitching. As I reached veteran status, I was able to plan my rotation with the pitching coach so that I wouldn't have to make many road trips, a luxury I afforded my veteran starting pitchers when I managed the Astros. With ample free time, I lowered my handicap and caught quite a few fish in the Indian River. I bought a seventeen-foot motorboat in Houston and pulled it down to Florida with all my belongings inside under a tarp. Then I unpacked the boat and took it to a marina where it was moored, awaiting adventure.

One day I went fishing with five other starting pitchers, all sizable gents. We had a great day, emptying a large cooler of beer to slake our thirst, and refilling it with speckled trout. We arrived at an unmanned tollbooth, sunburned and sloshed, wedged into my compact station wagon shoulder to shoulder, with the cooler in the back. Everyone reached for his pocket in search of a quarter. We were so jammed in that none of us could slide a hand into his jeans. Jim Ray, sitting in the back seat, brought forth a fish from the ice chest, which he casually tossed into the coin receptacle. "That ought to be worth a quarter," he said. I floored it, right on through the red light, setting off a siren, and we all burst out in laughter. From time to time, I tell this story and still wonder what the next driver coming through the toll station thought when he saw that trout staring back at him.

I suppose baseball is like the army in the sense that the best stories occur on weekend pass rather than on the battlefield. Still, there are battles to fight and preparing for them can be tedious. Relievers are required to stay for the game most days even though they don't always get a chance to pitch, and position players have the same responsibility. For the first two weeks of games, the starting players only play about half the game. When they come out, they have to run a few sprints. And that's no big deal. The only disadvantage to being a starting pitcher is that you have to run sprints after you pitch. I hated those sprints because I had already spent my physical and emotional capital on the mound. Though I ran with a mission on nonduty days, my legs felt like logs when I tried to run after pitching, but because we ran in the outfield during the game, it was hard to get away with laziness.

I suppose we all had a gripe or two about spring training, but most of us could grin and bear it. Having oddballs like Doug Rader around helped a lot. One day, during a televised interview, Doug was asked what a young player could do to improve his game. "Eat baseball cards," Doug said, matter-of-factly. "Get yourself some duplicates of Willie Mays, Sandy Koufax, Luis Aparicio, and guys like that. Then eat them. I used to eat a lot of Brooks Robinson and Eddie Mathews cards because I'm a third baseman."

One year Doug was late for spring training and the team was unable to ascertain his whereabouts. His wife, Jeanette, was worried when the team called because she thought he was in Cocoa. On or about the third day of his absence, he strolled into the clubhouse after the workout, wearing tattered clothing, a beat-up straw hat, and sporting an unruly week-long growth of red hair on his face. He told us that he had been detained by a game warden in Orlando and had spent a couple of days in jail. Many springs later, after he had quit his coaching job with the Marlins, he showed up in Viera as we prepared to face the Marlins. He looked a little better, but not much. He was following the scent of the big game again, taking a break to visit his buddies and watch a ball game.

"What have you been doing with yourself?" I asked.

"Killing things," he replied. "Animals and fish."

About the fourth inning I was taking a break from the microphone and I saw him on the telephone in the press box.

"Latch [Rene Lachemann, the Marlins' manager], you hoo, this is Dougy. How ya' doing, Latch. Not so good I imagine with those dogs you got down there."

Silence.

"Yeah, it's me. I'm up here telling all the writers and broadcasters about the mistakes you're making."

"No, I can't have a beer after the game. I gotta get up to Daytona to kill some things."

"Yeah really, I'm outta here. I told the little Marlins all I knew last year and guess what? They're not any better. You can have them. Toodle-oo."

I'm glad he never came out to see me manage. I'd have to hold my calls in the dugout.

I'll never forget something Doug told me one spring in Cocoa. It was his plan for reporting for duty, and it went something like this: "I'm going to have a good year and hold out," he said. "Then on the day of the first game, I'm going to parachute onto the field with my glove and my uniform on and push whoever is playing third base back into the dugout." He never made good on that promise but the only reason he didn't do it was that he never had a good enough year.

One day, a decade or two later, the diminutive Casey Candaele acted up around the batting cage, flexing his mini-muscles and swinging from his ass and falling down. "Roid rage," he announced, screaming like a maniac, referring to steroids and poking fun at the guys with the really big muscles. When the batting practice pitcher threw one inside, Casey hit the deck and came up shaking his bat as if he were going to charge the mound. He kept the act going for the entire ten minutes of his hitting group, swinging like a mad mama when he was in the cage, huffing and snorting when he was awaiting his turn to bat. He actually hit a couple of balls over the fence while he was at it, flexing, posing, and challenging the pitcher to throw another strike so he could rip it into the lake beyond the right field fence. By the time he finished, the guys in his hitting group were laughing so hard they could hardly swing.

Luis Gonzalez was a lot like Casey, always stirring the pot. One day in 1997, my rookie season at the helm, we had a trip to Port St. Lucie to play the Mets. When we arrived at the clubhouse, the lineup looked like opening day, with all the star players going on the long trip. The bus was ready to go, but the players were grumbling. Gonzo broke the ice. "What is this, the great grudge match?" he yelled. "Cubby, did you sleep in your uniform?" (Mike Cubbage had been fired by the Mets after the '96 season along with our hitting coach Tom McCraw.) "You're the one who's behind this, I know. You and Mac. You're going back to your old stomping grounds and you want to kick ass. I just figured it out."

"I didn't make out the list, he did," Cubby said, pointing at me.

"I just did it the way you told me," I said, hamming an innocent expression.

"Where's Mac?" Gonzo asked. "He's not getting out of this one."

"He's already down there," I said. "He can't wait to get at 'em."

"All I know is this is horseshit," Gonzo said. "Making everyone take a long trip just so you can show off for your friends."

The guys were getting a pretty good laugh. Once again, I was grateful to have Luis, the live wire, on our team. We lost more than a ballplayer when he went to the Cubs, we lost a whole clubhouse atmosphere. Gonzo gets along with everyone. Because he speaks Spanish, he's great at getting the Latino guys involved, and he fits right in with the blacks and whites as well. How the Cubs could let him go, I don't know. We got him back for a million dollars, which was a bargain. He didn't really blossom until after he left us again and ended up with the Diamondbacks, but he helped us immeasurably, way beyond his steady work on the field.

I had all the regulars on the trip that day for a couple of reasons. There is a league rule that you have to take at least four frontline players (excluding pitchers) on every trip. Usually I set the schedule for the regular players and told them what trips they would make before we started playing games. The numbers dictated that they all had to make half the trips. On this particular day, I took the players who had missed the last long trip and added a few more who were coming off injuries and needed to play. Was it "horseshit"? I don't think so. "Horseshit," by the way, is the number one word in baseball—has been for the whole of my thirty-seven years on the scene. It is an arcane expression now, but we in the baseball industry are sure to keep it alive, especially when we have long bus trips in the spring.

It was difficult to persuade the veteran players to make long trips. They thought the four-player rule was ridiculous. Some of the teams cheated and we did it ourselves a time or two when we had injuries. One piece of advice here: If you're planning a spring training vacation and want to see your favorite players, get tickets for the home games.

For the most part I followed the rule, not because I thought the players needed to take the trips, but because I was responsible for enforcing the rule. However, that edict only reinforces my personal opinion that spring training is too long. The only guys who need six weeks are the starting pitchers and even they could get ready faster if they had to. They proved that in 1995, when a long strike was finally settled and each team had to get ready to play in three weeks. Even if they aren't ready to pitch nine innings after four or five outings, they should be able to throw 100 pitches, which is about what they do in most games anyway, even in the middle of the season.

My broadcast routine was way better than my duties as manager (and the coaches have it just as bad). The field staff, which includes several minor league managers along with hitting, pitching, and fielding coaches, typically get to the ballpark at 7:00 A.M. The workout usually starts at 9:30 or 10:00, and the game is over by four o'clock most days. Between interviews and postgame meetings, it was usually about six o'clock before I left the ballpark after a home game, and much later when we traveled. This goes on for a solid month, with only one day off. Since there are no off days leading up to the regular season games, the whole enchilada amounts to about forty-five days' work with only that one day away from the ballpark. As a manager, I went to the park on that one off day every year because we had a pitcher working a minor league game and I had to observe his work. I didn't have to spend a long day, but I still had to be there. My main responsibility at spring training was to evaluate talent. I had a lot of input regarding the final composition of the team, but even in this area there was some discomfort. Do you value a player's track record during seasons past, even if he looks bad in Florida, or do you go on what you see in March?

The evaluation process made the games more tolerable than they were when I was broadcasting. Even so, I didn't like spring training much. Who wants to play games without the desire to win? I hesitate to complain, however. Every job has its downside and ours isn't all that bad. During the off-season we enjoy almost five months of freedom. Once we go back to work, we really go back to work. The regular season is a breeze compared to spring training.

• • •

Before the exhibition games even start, however, there is a lot of preparation to be done. This was evident to me on the very first day I spent as manager of the team. We had planned the first workout the day before and were prepared to synchronize our drills down to the minute; each coach was given a stopwatch so that he could send the players he was working with to their next field on time. The workout was to start at 10:00 A.M. and we had a staff meeting at nine to organize our coaching responsibilities. Even as we spoke, dark skies gathered. I made some introductory remarks and the players did their stretching inside the conference room. I looked up as we took to the field and knew a breakdown was coming. Five minutes later, the weeping began before giving way to great tears that poured down in slanting bursts. Some players and staffers sprinted for the locker room, some took to the shelter of the dugouts. Writers and photographers, newsmen and cameramen captured the moment. I ended up in the locker room, wondering what to do. One thing I learned as a pitcher was to stay calm in a crisis. As I was standing there, mildly distressed and mildly amused, I found myself face-to-face with Stretch Suba, our bullpen catcher. In the aquarium of staff members, Stretch is a bottom fish. As such, he sees the field like nobody else. He arrives early, apportions balls into buckets and takes them to various fields and cages. He sets up the pitching machines, makes sure protective netting is ready, and serves as point man with the grounds crew. He was the best possible person I could have run into.

"Get everyone together and send the catchers to the batting cages to hit," he said. If this blows over, we can still throw outside."

It was certainly a humbling experience to be taking advice from the bullpen catcher within ten minutes of my first day as his superior, but that is exactly what I did. The head grounds-keeper, Rick Rausch, came in and told me that the rain should let up in half an hour and that the mounds had been covered. We could still salvage the day. The pitchers were already congregated so I decided to have a chat session. After a consultation with my pitching coach, Vern Ruhle, we launched a discussion of holding runners.

One of my goals was to get the pitchers to do their own thinking about runners. The recent trend had been to send signals from the dugout to the catcher for such things as pitching normally, quick pitching, holding the ball at the set position a long time, stepping on and then off the rubber, pitching out, and throwing to bases. I wanted to reverse that trend and reduce the signals to three: pitch normally, hold the runner, and pitch out. How they held the runner would be up to them. This turned out to be a one-sided chat. When Vern and I asked for feedback, we got none. During the momentary silence, Rausch came in and said that the rain had stopped and we could resume workouts.

There was only one problem: It looked like the rain could come pouring down again, and soon. At this juncture, I made my first unaided decision:

"We'll go straight to the last segment of the workout where the pitchers throw," I said. "If it doesn't rain, we'll do the other drills when we finish throwing." This met with general approval and we started in short order. But there was still one problem: The catchers were still hitting, and the hitting coaches, who were supposed to be in other places during this portion of the workout, were still at the cages. Somehow we muddled through and got most of the drills completed. It was a great relief to me when my bench coach, Bill Virdon, a thirteen-year managing veteran, said, "I thought it went pretty well considering. We got the work done. It was a good start." Still, I had the nagging feeling that I wasn't really in control of the team.

After I finished talking with the media, it was about 2:00 P.M. and Gerry and his assistant Matt Galante came in to talk. I have a great fondness for Matt. By 1997 he had been the third base coach and top assistant to three Houston managers. Each time a manager was replaced, Matt was a candidate for the job and each time he came up short. Quite honestly, I think his only failing was that he *is* short (5'6") and soft-spoken. He is as respected a baseball man as there is in our league, and in my opinion, which I expressed even when I was being interviewed, he should have gotten the job instead of me. During the interview it became clear that he was not going to get it even if I declined. In the world they say, "That's life." In baseball, we say, "That's baseball."

Since Matt had been preparing for this job during all the years I was broadcasting, and since he clearly had a firsthand opinion about how spring training should be run, he was full of ideas. I was sort of sad, sitting there listening to him from the boss's side of the desk, sitting in a seat he was more qualified to occupy. There was a fatherly tone that spoke silently behind his words that said, "This is how it should be done, son. This is the way I would do it. I'm okay with this. I only want to help."

His actual words of advice concerned the workout plans. He said that the demands on my time would continue to increase and that I should have the man that replaced him as third base coach, Mike Cubbage, do the detail work and assign coaching responsibilities. He said that I should just observe the workouts and tell Cubby what I wanted to cover the next day.

"The writers are going to ask you how Sean Berry threw or how Brad Ausmus hit. You need to watch these things so you can answer the questions. You also need to have an alternate plan in case it rains. You don't need to have one every day but when the forecast is bad you should be ready."

I protested sincerely that I had only attempted to plan things to inform myself, to become familiar with the mechanics of the workouts. I really had no desire to do the detail work. I was more concerned with the implementation of general concepts such as the pitchers holding runners and the bunting. I did the workout plans mostly to reacquaint myself with the process and to show the staff that I was ready to work, not just talk.

Gerry echoed Matt's thoughts about delegating and Matt reiterated them. I felt besieged and consented without further defense. I was sensitive because they didn't acknowledge my good intentions. Finally, as they got up to leave, Matt said, "I know what you were trying to do. It's like when you're in college and you take notes. Just taking notes makes you remember. And it's not a bad idea. It's good that you did it and now it's time for someone else to take it over." I cannot tell you how good that made me feel.

As it turned out, Cubby had planned the spring workouts for several managers when he was with the Mets and began doing the same thing for me the next day. I was really pleased when Matt worked closely with Cubby and me, providing good input right from the start. His willingness to help us on the field said a lot for him as a human being. I was advised to begin my managing career with a whole new coaching staff and though I wanted to keep Matt, Gerry and Tal thought his presence would be a distraction because he was popular with many of our players, most of whom would have preferred him as the new manager. Matt was not a distraction in any way, as far as I could see. He had a way of getting along with everyone. After my first year, Virdon retired and Matt came back to take Bill's place in the dugout. He had the same attitude I have now—he wanted the team to win, first and foremost.

Spring training is a working vacation for most broadcasters. It was that way when I started out in the booth. Like most teams, we only aired eight or ten of the games. Then Dick Wagner was hired as general manager and he changed our routine, requiring us to broadcast every game, ostensibly to sell tickets. I always thought this was like selling ice to Eskimos. Anyone who can listen to an exhibition game is an avid fan to begin with and most likely has tickets already.

Kissimmee is in Central Florida, relatively close to most other camps. Still, when I was broadcasting, I would put about 3,000 miles on my rental car in a month's time. Wagner made all four announcers make all of the trips, and when we weren't on TV, which was all but maybe four games, we all worked radio. Two of us broadcast the first five innings and the other two the last four. When I had the back half of the game, I had to do an interview for the postgame show. This duty required me to go down to the field in the top of the ninth inning. Many times, I worked only three innings in the booth before going to the field. Needless to say, driving three hours from Orlando to West Palm Beach and back to do a cameo appearance for an invisible audience really got my goat.

All the time I spent on the highway, I could have been digging out from underneath the avalanche of preseason publications that were dumped on me in the second week of March. It was a lot of work, but I wasn't the only one who felt overwhelmed. One spring, I interviewed some of our staff for a newspaper column.

Our broadcast director, Jamie Hildreth, compared our spring schedule to a sea cruise. "It's kind of like a luxury liner," he said. "All you see on deck are the people on vacation, but the ship would never get out of port without the guys down below in the boiler room."

One of those guys is Astros traveling secretary Barry Waters. "It's funny," Waters mused. "Every year, I'm so anxious to get down here. But after a few twelve-hour days, I'm already counting down to the end. My lunch break is fifteen minutes, eating a sandwich on the run."

Our trainer, Dave Labossiere, was too busy to talk about it. "It's long, long days in the hot Florida sun," he said. "Is that enough for you? I gotta get back to work."

Labossiere's days start at about 7:00 A.M. when the first players arrive; he finishes up just before dark when the last few guys straggle in from extra hitting or fielding practice. It's no wonder his days are long. In Kissimmee, he is responsible for the health and well-being of more than fifty players. During the season, he treats only twenty-five.

Equipment manager Dennis Liborio is caught in the same numbers game. His day starts at six, an hour before the first player arrives, and doesn't finish until the locker room is spotless and all the laundry is done and put back in each player's locker, at least three hours after the last guy leaves. If he weren't trapped in his cubbyhole, he would see the sun come up and go down while he was working. Liborio was more blunt about his feelings for baseball's season of hope. "I hate it!" he said. "All these young guys are here, and they all need me for this and that. They don't know the system like the older guys. It really makes it tough. It's like being on the road for two months, only worse."

Even Rob Matwick, the Astros' incomparable PR director, an avowed workaholic, got aggravated during the exhibition season. Matwick is ordinarily an upbeat guy, but in the spring his work backs up on him. "I really like getting down here because this is where it all starts," he said. "I love the individual competition for jobs on the team because it's different than the team-type competition of the season. But I spend so much time on the road going from one camp to another when I know I need to be in my office getting my work done for the start of the season. It's like the work of the spring competes with the preparation for opening day. Sometimes, it's frustrating."

That goes for the players too. Their days are longer, and the workouts are more arduous than during the season. All the time spent riding from stadium to stadium can flat wear you out.

Ironically, the general manager is the one guy who gets a bit of a break in March. He gets to watch the home games and make the short road trips. When there is a long trip, he can catch up on paperwork and phone calls. When Bill Wood was the Astros' GM, he told me, "This is my favorite time of the baseball year. The contract negotiating is over, and the pressure of the season has not yet begun. We spend the winter making plans in the office, and now we get to spend some time outdoors in the sun seeing how our efforts are coming together. It's really the only time the pressure eases up and the only time I get to spend out of the office. Down here, it's just watching baseball. It's my favorite part by far."

On the top deck, pastel-clad vacationers chase the butterfly dreams of their youth. Down below, Liborio stokes the boilers as Labossiere tunes the engines. Up above, Waters checks the itinerary and charts the course, while Matwick organizes the activities of the day. Up on the bow, Wood holds his right hand up to shade his eyes as he ponders the horizon.

The good ship Astros has left its port and is motoring peacefully through the harbor. Up ahead lies an unknown destiny at sea. There are many among the crew who welcome the bounding main.

• • •

The worst thing about the month of March though is that you're just idling out of the harbor. The water is calm because the games don't mean anything. Nobody really cares who wins, as we are just getting in shape and looking at some of the young players who could be with us in the near future and maybe a veteran or two who is trying to make the team as the eleventh pitcher or the fourteenth player. When I was catching fish and playing golf it was fun. But my last few years with the team were a drag.

The only guy I know who takes the exhibition games seriously is our radio broadcaster, Milo Hamilton. Milo is a one-man show. He doesn't need to read all the media guides to broadcast the game. Why talk about a player's hometown or what year he was drafted when you can talk about what you had for breakfast? Why talk about what a prospect did last year in Triple A and his chances of making the team when you can talk about the importance of winning a game? One day we were in Plant City, playing the Reds. We came to the ninth still looking for our first hit in a scoreless game. "We really need this one," he said for the handful of listeners back home. "We're already two games under and we've got the Indians tomorrow at Winter Haven." While the rest of us would just as soon see the Reds score in the bottom of the ninth so we could go home, Milo was lusting for a victory and was willing to go extra innings to get it. When it comes to passion, he's number one.

That game in Winter Haven didn't mean much to me, but a few years later, I made my managerial debut there, at Chain O' Lakes Park. That is a game I will never forget. I kept a journal that year and my entry for that day is sort of amusing to me now that I can look back with the benefit of experience:

We lost the game 9–2 as the Indians staff shut down our hitters completely. I kept the scorecard for a souvenir. I was certain that I knew enough baseball to manage, but this game was illuminating. I realized right away that it was not going to be as easy at ground level as it was in the broadcast booth. For one thing, the movement of the players to and fro and the dugout conversations interrupted my internal dialogue. I found it hard to concentrate. I was late getting signs to my third base coach, Mike Cubbage, and to our catchers. I was afraid of making a mistake on a double switch. These maneuvers seemed elementary when I was broadcasting. But when the distractions were combined with considerations about injuries, like this guy can't run and this other guy can hit but he can't play in the field, created a rather intricate web of possibilities. I did not feel particularly adroit in weaving these strands into a neat design. Oh well, they say that you are going to win 50, lose 50, and that the other 62 will decide your fate. This was not one of those that I could have changed and at least it was a start.

I told *Houston Chronicle* columnist Mickey Herskowitz that I felt inadequate and immediately thought that it was too strong a word. But I also thought that it was an honest description of my feelings. I hoped that I wouldn't have to use that word again. Maybe I wouldn't, but now I knew for sure that the job was going to be more difficult than I anticipated.

Our general manager, Gerry Hunsicker, came by my office in Kissimmee after the bus got back. He was curious as to how I felt and I told him the same thing I told Mickey. He laughed and I immediately felt better. Gerry is an intensely competitive man. But he also has a sensitive side that can be disarming. He can be hard and he can be soft. I knew I would see both sides as we went along.

The best thing about spring training from a manager's or coach's standpoint is that you have more opportunities to work with players individually. One day that first spring, pitching coach Vern Ruhle scuffed a ball while he was playing catch and he really had it sinking and sailing. He had so much fun with it that he brought it over to the mound where Darryl Kile was doing his side work between starts. After Kile got up to speed, Vern said, "Here, try this one."

The ball came out of Kile's hand dancing like Baryshnikov. Later, when the workout was over, Kile came into my office with Vern.

"Hey, what was that scuffed ball about?" he asked. "Are you trying to say that my regular stuff isn't good enough?"

I thought he was kidding but Vern wasn't so sure. He told Darryl, "We were just having some fun. You know. Watching the ball move. Sometimes it's good to see how the ball can move."

"Are you trying to say my fastball doesn't move?"

"No," I interjected. "We were just screwing around. Don't read something into it that isn't there. It was just for fun."

The conversation went on for a while, and maybe he was satisfied, but then again, maybe he wasn't. Kile could be an enigma, but he was one of the most popular guys on the team. He had an infectious smile and the attitude of a joyful servant. He was always there to lend a helping hand, always a good teammate. He lavished praise on everyone and yet was hard on himself. His death last summer left a void in the heart of every player who ever enjoyed his company. I was stunned to hear about it, like everyone else. Players flew into St. Louis from all over the country to attend his memorial service. His spirit will be sorely missed.

On this occasion, when he finally made his exit, I told Vern, "He's your project, not mine." Vern got an A+ on that project as Kile became our staff ace, winning nineteen games. Actually, Vern didn't have to work at it too much. Kile was receptive to the "go nine" attitude right from the start. Once he pitched out of late-inning trouble a few times, he became a confident pitcher. Of course, Vern is a confidence-builder. He must have been one of the few kids who listened when his parents told him that if he didn't have something nice to say, not to say it at all.

Even though it isn't critical to win games in March, nobody wants to get into the habit of losing. For this reason, it is customary to create an incentive to win. Our policy throughout my five years managing was to run a few sprints after losses and not run after wins. Most of the time we simply ran six or eight sprints in the outfield, but occasionally we ran around the bases. Running the bases was more difficult and the players hated it for two reasons: First, it was more taxing than running sprints, and second, each player could be singled out as he ran, which made it hard to goof off. Running in the outfield, the players formed a herd, which protected the weak. The herd tended to move at a gait that would never be called a sprint. But on the bases, the players ran one at a time behind each other. If you had a fast runner go first, everyone else had to keep the pace.

The base-running drill involved both sprints and turns. It started with a dash down the first base line, emphasizing running through the bag. After the first sprint, each player walked back to home plate and repeated the process. After the second sprint, everyone stayed at first base. The next phase was running from first to third with the emphasis on cutting sharply at the bag. No one could cut a bag sharper than Jeff Bagwell, and the last two years of my tenure, I had Baggy speak to the groups of runners and demonstrate the sharp turn. After rounding third, the players walked back to home plate. From there, they ran to second base as if they had hit a double. Then they stayed at second and ran home, cutting sharply around third. The next leg of the circular romp was from home to third—a triple. After rounding third, and walking home, we had them go home to third again. Another agonizing triple. At this point, a few guys were gassed, and after walking oh so slowly back to home plate, they still had to go for the inside-the-park home run.

Because the runners stayed about ten feet apart, it was necessary to keep pace so that the spacing stayed even. As you might imagine, this drill is a lot easier for fast runners, but it also is a way to test the conditioning level of all the players in a relatively short period of time. Invariably, there were players who staggered to the finish line because they were either slow and had to sprint to keep up, or they were just plain out of shape. Conversely, there were always a lot of players who could do the drill at just about full speed without much trouble. I would work this drill in at least once before the games started, when everyone was fresh. It gave me a baseline reading on the vitality of each player on the team.

When we really played poorly, we ran the bases after the game. When the word rang out, "Everyone at home plate. We're going to run the bases," there was a plaintive silence that was almost palpable. By the time the game was over, the players had been at the ballpark for about six hours. If they had been playing, they were tired from the effort, and if they had been waiting in reserve without getting into the game, they were stiff from sitting. There was no way to get around it—running the bases after the game was cruel and unusual punishment.

One problem we had with postgame running was that the players who were left over at the end were mostly young guys who came into the game after the veterans played five or six innings in, grabbed their gear, and left. These heroes were supposed to do their running on another field after they came out. But I learned that if they were left unsupervised, they would go directly to the locker room and shower up, just as I suspected.

Early in the exhibition season of 1998, we lost a lot of games. That spring, the veterans always left the scrubs with the challenge of overcoming a deficit. The guys who played early got off light, and the guys who stayed to the end had to run sprints. This wasn't so bad for the youngsters, but there were a few marginal veteran players who were hoping to get one last taste of major league competition and were, in most cases, older than the front-line players. I felt for them. Near the end of that spring, I decided to give some of the starters a day off on a road trip in exchange for playing them the whole game at home. That way, I could get them stretched out to nine innings and also give them a taste of how the other half lives. They jumped at the chance to play at home and miss a trip until they found out there was a catch.

One of those days we lost the game and ran the bases. Craig Biggio had gone the distance that day, and he had to make a few tough plays, and he also got on base a couple of times. When the game ended, he started to trudge back to the clubhouse. I called him back to home plate for running the bases, and he put his head down and muttered all the way to home plate. Afterward, we were walking back to the locker room and, under his breath, he said, "I'm not getting any younger, you know."

"I know," I said. "But there will come a day when you will do the running willingly and say, 'I feel great.' " He looked at me like I was crazy, but I knew the story beginning to end, and he was still in the middle. When players get to the end of their careers, they tend to get into better shape and try to show the staff that they're still young and ready for action.

Well, wouldn't you know, the next time we played at home, Jeff Bagwell went all the way in a humiliating defeat. Baggy is more of a go-along, get-along type of guy. He didn't like the drill, but he did it without complaint, queuing up at the end of the line. When running the final circuit, going all the way around, he slid into home plate in a cloud of dust, laughing like crazy and causing all of us to laugh with him.

And wouldn't you know, in spring of 2002, when I visited Kissimmee, Biggio, now thirty-six years young, told me that he was in great shape, that his legs felt terrific. He said he couldn't even feel the effects of a surgically repaired knee that slowed him down in 2001. Funny how it works. When you get near the end, you want to impress everyone. I know because I tried to run faster and throw harder the last few years. Age is the enemy and most guys try to prove they are winning the battle.

Spring training is just about the worst time to judge a ballplayer. The old guys are trying to look young, the young guys are trying to impress and oftentimes overdo it. The veteran, midcareer players are trying to save themselves for the season. Some guys are coming out of hibernation in the cold North. Some are already in good form because they have played winter ball. It's hard to know just what to make of what you see in March.

I found it difficult to manage situations too—especially the pitching. If I wanted to see a left-handed reliever face a left-handed hitter, I would look down the lineup three or four spots ahead of the lefty hitter and start warming up my pitcher. Then the inning would end, the other team would make changes, and my lefty would end up facing right-handed hitters. It was easier to get a look at pinch hitters, as I could alert both a left- and right-handed hitter and use the one I wanted to see when the pitcher's spot came up. Pinch hitters could be ready on a moment's notice, theoretically, but in reality, the players got restless. If they didn't anticipate being used they sometimes wandered down the foul line to shoot the breeze or went to the cages for extra hitting. Many times, early on, I called for a hitter and he was nowhere to be found. After the first year I was smarter. I emphasized the importance of being ready at all times before the first exhibition game started.

I didn't need to use any special language, however, to motivate Russ Johnson. Russ was a winner. He was always available and ready for action. In 1998, he was trying to win a job on the infield. He had always played shortstop, but we thought he was a little too slow to play the position full time. He had helped win championships in high school in Louisiana and at LSU, and then he had climbed the minor league ladder, helping more teams win championships. He was the type of player that seemed to get better in tough competition and I wanted him on the team because of his winning ways. I thought he could fit in as a utility infielder and told him that would be his role in the spring, playing second, short, and third base. "You just have to try to help the team any way you can," I said. He responded that he was ready for action—anytime, anywhere.

Russ was having a decent spring and was on a trip to Plant City. Late in the game, the team bus was disabled when it hit a wall trying to turn around in the parking lot. Afterward, we learned that we would need a new bus for the trip home and that it would have to come from Orlando, an hour and a half away. I had driven to the game and offered to take on passengers for the return trip and I called the press box in time to get more rides with members of our media contingent. I let the players decide who would ride with the broadcasters and who would stay and wait. Russ was left behind, but he was impatient—so he crawled under the bus, found the problem, and fixed it. Within ten minutes the team bus was on the way, and the bus from Orlando was canceled. Now that is a helluva utility man.

Every spring there are several pools for the NCAA basketball tournament. One is for the rank and file at $20 per team. One is for the big-time gamblers and the veteran stars that goes for $100 per team. These pools add a touch of levity in mid-March, when the days seem long, hot, and endless. Whoever draws the favored team gets most of the razzing, but even the guys who get the long shots take their share of kidding.

One spring, Luis Gonzalez came up with a plan to liven up the clubhouse even more. He put up a large photo of a big-screen television right next to the daily workout plan so that everyone would see it. Beneath it, he wrote: "Rookie of the Spring Standings. Winner gets the TV." Then he posted the spring averages of all the first-year players. All of the veteran players were in on it. Nobody would actually get a television, but the banter in the clubhouse was spirited. One guy would say, "My money is on Russ Johnson." Another would say, "Put your money where your mouth is, I'll give you four to one he doesn't get it." Johnson, of course, would be standing nearby when they made the bet. Updated averages would be posted every few days. Pretty soon, it became a source of great clubhouse chatter. In a way, it made things easier for the young guys because it gave them a goal apart from the main goal of making the team. Most of the very young guys, who were obviously not going to make it to Houston, desperately desired a big-screen TV. At the end of the spring season a winner was declared and when he got to his locker the next day, he saw a huge box. Then when he reached to open it, everybody laughed at him, for it was obvious that the box was empty.

Just about every spring a great young player emerges and threatens to make the team even though he played AA ball or lower the year before. In 1997, Richard Hidalgo was that man. He had a great spring but Gerry is generally conservative and almost never moves a player up more than one classification each year. Everyone was excited about Richard, but it was preordained that he wouldn't make the team, even if he was the only one who didn't know it. Richard was sad when we told him he was going back to Triple A but he needed to play every day. When a prospect of this caliber gets the promotion to the big leagues it is to play every day. There was no way Richard could do that for us at that time. In a way, it was a tough cut, but in another, not tough at all. We all knew that Richard would be a regular player for us at some point and a lot of us were hoping it would be sooner rather than later. I could see the tears welling in his big brown eyes, but they never spilled over. In his heart, he had to be asking, "What more do I have to do?" We tried to tell him that there just wasn't room for him on the big league roster, but I don't think he really understood. He was only twenty-one years old and I was really proud of the way he handled himself. He didn't get mad, didn't even say much.

"Your ability is in the top three of all the outfielders we have," I told him. "But right now, I couldn't play you every day. Your time will come, and it may come soon. If you keep playing the way you have been, we will make room for you." I probably shouldn't have said that. It's not my place. But I didn't see Gerry objecting. He only nodded his head.

"You can take the day off tomorrow," Gerry said. "And then report to Jim Duquette," our director of minor league operations.

Richard nodded.

"Do you have him listed for the trip to Lakeland tomorrow?" Gerry asked.

"Yes," I said.

"Do you want to make the trip?" Gerry asked.

"Yes," Richard nodded.

"You know I can't play you the whole game like I did earlier," I told him. "We have to get more innings for James Mouton and Thomas Howard now. I can probably play you two or three innings."

"Is there a Triple A game?" he asked.

"A Triple A game here in camp?" I said, "I don't know."

"Yes, there's a game here," Gerry said. "What are you getting at?"

I thought I knew. "Do you want to play nine innings in the Triple A game instead of going to Lakeland or taking a day off?" I asked.

"Yes," he nodded.

Now I was almost crying.

I never was cut until I got the ax from the Cardinals when I was thirty-one years old. I was actually relieved when I was released. It was like being let out of prison. Cardinals GM Bing Devine offered to make some calls for me to see if another team had any interest but I told him not to bother. I was tired of pitching with a sore arm and even wearier of getting my ass kicked by hitters I should have been dispatching with ease. The pain was significant, but the failure was worse. I couldn't stand pitching that way. I was 2-6 with an ERA of 4.58 in 1977. These days, that record doesn't sound so bad. It might even merit a raise.

But the thing that means the most goes beyond money, it's more to do with the ego. When you are healthy you always assume you will get back on track. But when you are hurting and the only advice you get from the doctor is to grin and bear it, it can become unbearable. It did for me.

It seemed the same way for Tommy Gregg when he was trying to make our club in the spring of 1998. Tommy was thirty-five years old at the time and his legs were gone. He had hit the ball well in exhibition games but was really hobbled toward the end. When I cut him loose, he knew it was over and I think he was satisfied. At least that's the impression I got. I had to let him go if only for my own sake because it was hurting me to watch him run sprints after a losing game.

Most of the time, the older guys can see the writing on the wall and the younger guys realize that their time will come later in the year or in seasons to come. In my case, thirteen years in the big leagues was enough. I am proud of my pitching record but I may have started too young and injured my arm by pitching too many innings too soon. In 1965, I was told that I would make the team no matter what I did in Florida because the Astros would have to expose me to a waiver claim if they sent me to the minors, but I wanted to pitch well enough to justify their decision. I did exactly that until my final start in Houston, the first game in the history of the Astrodome. It was an intersquad day game and, more important, it was the game that revealed a problem with the roof of the stadium. Fielders could not pick up the ball when it was hit into the air, losing it in the glare behind the complex structure of beams and Lucite panels.

My fastball had a little hop that day and I was inducing a lot of pop-ups and fly balls but most of them were dropping untouched. I gave up a lot of runs and for the first time worried that I would be sent to the minor leagues. Actually, I didn't mind too much because I always thought I would have to work my way up and a lot of the other young guys would be on the farm clubs. I would have more natural friends in the minors. But by that time, I had convinced myself that I could get major league hitters out. I didn't want to get cut and GM Paul Richards and manager Luman Harris were smart enough to know that most of the runs I gave up that day would not have scored under normal circumstances. I made the team.

Later on, the Astros made a mistake in a similar situation. They had traded for Curt Schilling in 1991 and he had a disappointing year going 3-5 with an ERA of 3.81. The next spring he was out of options and was not throwing very well. Moreover, he was overweight and seemed a little sluggish in workouts. I think the staff felt that he wasn't motivated enough to realize his potential. That same spring, the team had a left-handed reliever in camp by the name of Rob Murphy. Murphy was a veteran with an impressive track record but he was near the end of his career and was trying to make the team as a nonroster player. He had a lousy spring but the team needed a lefty in the bullpen so they put Schilling on waivers to clear a spot on the roster for Murphy. The Phillies claimed Schilling and the rest is history.

I remember something Earl Weaver once said about cutting an outfielder named Drungo Hazewood after the youngster had a stellar spring, hitting .583. "I never cut a guy hitting that high," said the Earl of Baltimore. "But he was making the rest of us look bad with that average." Hazewood eventually did make it to the major leagues. He went 0–5 and scored one run.

Ty Gainey did the same thing for the Astros but in a different way. He tore up the Pacific Coast League in 1985 and got called up in the middle of the season. He didn't hit much, but was still highly regarded. He had a good season playing winter ball and got another shot in 1986 but bombed out again. In '87 he did the same thing.

Still, winter ball can be a springboard to the majors, as it was for Dave Smith. Smitty had a great year in Puerto Rico in 1979 after pitching well at AA that summer. He was invited to spring training in 1980 because of winter ball. He continued pitching well, made the team, and served as a setup man for Joe Sambito as the Astros won their division for the first time ever. He eventually became the Astros' closer and still holds the club record with 199 saves. Smitty would have made it to the big leagues, anyway, but not nearly so soon.

One year a young shortstop named Leon McFadden had a Hazewood-like spring. Leon hit about .400 in March of 1969 and he also hit seven home runs. He had great speed and could cover a lot of territory on the left side of the infield, and he had a rifle arm. Leon looked like a budding superstar, and since we were decidedly inferior to the Orioles in the days of Earl Weaver, we took the bait on Leon. He opened the year as our regular shortstop. About 40 games later, he was hitting .176 with no home runs, 3 RBI, and too many errors.

One night in May of that year, I was pitching in the bottom of the ninth with a 4–3 lead on the Dodgers in Los Angeles. My family was there and so was Leon's. With runners at second and third and two outs, I got a grounder to short to end it, but not the way you might think: Leon air-mailed first base with his throw and when the ball caromed down the right field line, both runners scored. I had thrown about 150 pitches trying to win that game and instead I lost it on an error. I was really pissed, and I remember cursing all the way from the mound into the locker room. I showered quickly as I was going to my parents' house and hoping to visit a little before going to bed. I had to pass through our dugout on the way to the parking lot. Well, what do you know, there was Leon, still in uniform, sitting in the dugout with the stadium empty and the lights out. He had his head in his hands. I don't know if he was crying, but I know he was hurting. I'll never forget that scene because Leon was optioned to the minors a few days later. He was a great guy, and we were homeys (a term we used for players from our hometown or state).

When his demotion came down, I was as sad as he was. He didn't make the error carelessly and he wanted that win just like I did. As it turned out, he needed to make that play more than I needed him to make it. Leon made a cameo appearance in Houston in 1970, but that was it. He never realized his enormous potential. Neither did Michael Jordan. Baseball is a challenging sport. It isn't nearly as easy as the players in the major leagues make it look. Speed and strength are great tools, but they don't count for much unless they are sharpened.

Sharpening those skills can inspire creative thinking. Everyone is trying to get an edge on the opposition. In 1991, I was heading for a remote diamond at the Detroit Tigers' training complex in Lakeland to watch the Astros play the Tigers in an early morning B game before going back to the Joker Marchant Stadium to broadcast the big league game. Suddenly, the glint of a mirror arrested my attention. Alongside one of the outbuildings (perhaps a minor league clubhouse), I witnessed a line of pitchers delivering imaginary curves and forkballs as they watched themselves in full-length mirrors.

It reminded me of the previous spring, when Astros batters were seen taking slow-motion swings in the open air and visualizing sharp, opposite-field singles and long home runs. But the Tigers had done the Astros one better: They had mirrors.

To the uninitiated, these hurlers must have seemed vain, or at the very least, eccentric—perhaps practicing some aberrant form of tai chi. But to me, they were wistfully funny, the subjects of yet another spring training experiment. And believe me I have seen a lot of them. From the era of the ultimate baseball innovator, Branch Rickey, March has been the time to try new ideas that have been brewing in the mind over the winter.

Well, who could blame the Tigers for trying something new? I mean, didn't I read somewhere that Roger Clemens perfected his rocket launch in front of just such a mirror? The Tigers finished last in the American League in ERA in 1990; Clemens finished first. What the heck?

Still, I couldn't help smiling. It made me think of medicine balls and Exer-Genies, of leaden baseballs and bats with big fan blades on their business ends, of catchers' mitts with hot orange borders, and mannequins in the batter's box.

I joined Astros assistant general manager Bob "Bull" Watson, an old Houston teammate, behind the backstop of the field where the B game was in progress. Bull was evaluating the Astros' prospects for his boss, general manager Bill Wood.

"Did you see those guys throwing in front of mirrors?" I asked Watson.

"I saw them," he said with a grin.

"How many gimmicks have you seen at spring training?" I said, and we both thought it over.

"How about those balls hanging from wires, Bull?" I asked. "What was that about?"

Watson prefaced his answer by rolling his eyes, recalling an obscure drill from a generation ago. The drill was conducted off to the side of the stadium. It involved two posts with a wire drawn tight between them, about eight feet high. A ball was looped to the wire, hanging down about four feet off the ground.

"Well, the theory was that if you took a level swing, the ball would travel down to the other end of the wire," Bull explained. "If you hit it on the up- or the downswing, it wouldn't go anywhere," he said, as he demonstrated with his hands. "The problem is that a level swing is only part of hitting. The way it turned out, the guys who could hit the ball down the wire were not the best hitters."

The way Watson remembers it, the wire drill fouled up a few guys—like Jimmy Wynn, who had a natural home run uppercut, and Jesus Alou, who swung down on the ball like many other high-average hitters. But the wire drill didn't mess them up for long. Shortly after the season opened, Wynn and Alou reverted to their bad habits and began hitting well again.

One year, the Astros' pitching staff was met with a firm reprimand at the first team meeting of spring training. According to manager Preston Gomez, my compadres and I had blown the pennant the year before by walking too many batters.

"We were last in the league in walks," Gomez said. "This year, it will be different." He said that any pitcher who walked more than two batters in a game would be removed. That necessitated having pitchers warmed up at all times and it also caused a lot of guys, including me, to come out of the game early and fail to meet our pitch counts, thus preventing us from building the endurance we would need to be ready for the season. By calling attention to the problem he made us think about it while we were pitching. Of course it got worse instead of better and it became a self-fulfilling prophecy.

Something similar happened in my first year managing. We were in L.A. and Mike Piazza was hot. In our meeting before the game, we said, "Don't let him beat you." Our plan was to make him swing at bad pitches or take a walk. Well, we just ended up walking him six or seven times in the series, and pitching to him behind in the count almost every other time. He hit a couple of home runs and simply destroyed us. I talked with my pitching coach, Vern Ruhle, about it later. We decided that we would put a different spin on it next time. If a guy was hot we would say, "Attack him with your best stuff on the corners." This was a positive statement, while "Don't let him beat you" suggested that he would.

When I got to the mound the first day after the Gomez decree, I found strings set up along the front edge of home plate, outlining the strike zone. This was really nothing new, I had used strings in high school. Most of us could throw the ball between the strings at will. But, of course, the idea is to throw the ball just barely inside the strings—an idea reinforced by having a guy like Willie Mc-Covey standing in the batter's box.

There is something about throwing before a mirror or between the strings that made a lot of guys look good. And there was something about McCovey that made the same guys look bad. Target practice is one thing. Getting good hitters out is another.

"That wire drill was ridiculous," I told Watson. "I was never even tempted to try it."

"Well, it wasn't as bad as you guys throwing at mannequins," he said. "You just about got a few catchers killed."

He had me there.

One spring, manager Harry Walker declared the pitchers didn't know how to pitch inside. Not wanting to use live batters for plunking practice, Harry stood mannequins in the batter's box.

Problem is, the mannequins didn't know enough to get the heck out of the way and several balls caromed off the dummies and hit the catchers. Within an hour, most of the mannequins were battered beyond repair and there were rumors of an insurrection behind home plate.

"The worst thing we ever did was the Exer-Genie," Watson said. "That thing got a lot of guys hurt."

I was surprised to hear him say that because I thought the Exer-Genie was one of the few good ones. Certainly, this system of ropes and pulleys that would fit into your briefcase and build bodies nine ways was primitive by today's standards. But I actually used the thing. By hooking it to the top of a door, I could simulate my pitching motion with constant resistance. I used it a lot.

In the distant spring of Exer-Genie madness, Astros players were attached to a shoulder harness and exhorted to lean forward and run like crazy, churning against the resistance of the ropes. This was the centerpiece of the program, and I just knew it would help me if I ever had to bowl over a catcher. Of course, I never did.

Lest I sound too much the cynic, I must admit that through earnest folly, and practical science, we have, indeed, pushed the medicine ball of progress up the mountain like Sisyphus. And though we may never reach the summit, we have not allowed that ball to roll back down. Today's ballplayers are better conditioned than we were. As Yogi Berra might say, their bodies stay young older.

And even if those Tigers farmhands didn't all make it to the big leagues, at least they will be able to tell their grandchildren, "I could fire that old imaginary apple into a mirror just like Roger Clemens."

Since judging players at spring training can be difficult, it can make for some great stories. Occasionally a young kid can come out of nowhere and have a good career like I did. In the spring of 1991, Curt Schilling was just another young right-hander. In 1992, he came up with a good split and improved his slider. Within a year he was one of the best pitchers in the league.

In the end, after six long weeks in the Florida sunshine, the only thing that matters is getting your belongings on the truck that goes to the big leagues. The veterans are ready for real games and the guys on the bubble hope for an end to their suspense. When they are told to put their stuff on the truck, a great, if quiet, sigh of relief can be heard. Later on, after a few beers, they may get a little louder. But sometimes the pressure doesn't end when the truck pulls out. Most clubs like to get down to twenty-five players before leaving Florida or Arizona for the last few exhibition games else-where. Sometimes, young and rebuilding teams keep twenty-six or twenty-seven guys until the very last day before the season. It is a great feeling to see that truck loading up. It means the drudgery of spring training is over and the regular season is at hand.

Now, if I go to Florida, I can stay up on deck with the vacation-ers and the starting pitchers. I can go fishing or play golf and I don't have to make the gut-wrenching cuts. I am perfectly willing to let someone else do the hard work and make the big bucks.

CHAPTER 2

Opening Day

*You always get a special kick on opening day, no matter how many
you go through. You look forward to it like a birthday party when
you're a kid. You think something wonderful is going to happen.*

—JOE DiMaggio

MY FIRST OPENING DAY was grand. Better, I think, than any I
have seen since, and I've seen plenty. It turned out that the West
Valley League, in its inaugural season, needed two more boys to fill
out the rosters. I got to be one of them, starting my baseball career
at age seven instead of eight. Through the eyes of a child it was
all so big, so important. The energy the dads brought home from
World War Two was everywhere in evidence. Our Little League
played on one of a group of fields in the middle of a blue-collar
neighborhood. It was immaculate and it had an electric scoreboard
right from the start.

When I got to the ballpark, I saw pickup trucks decorated to
look like floats. I was on a minor league team, the 7-Uppers, and I
soon found the truck with our banner. What a feeling it was to be
in the back of our team float with all my new friends. We snaked
through the most populous neighborhoods, with a loudspeaker up
front proclaiming our debut. Up and down the street, folks were
cheering. I was bouncing with glee. This is how it all began.

I played right field when I was seven and don't remember any heroics; I'm not sure I even played in every game. When I was eight, I started pitching to my dad in the backyard. I made the majors because the Braves' coach could see that I was going to be pretty good and he wanted to have me for the next four years. When he left, so did I. I was traded to the Yankees when I was ten. Opening day was about the same from one year to the next but it was never quite as thrilling as it was when I was seven.

The Little League opener is my most vivid memory, but my first game in high school is almost as hard to forget. I was on the junior varsity and we took a bus from the suburbs of Los Angeles to a tough neighborhood in the inner city. We were, for the most part, lily-white and unaccustomed to the many shades of human color, so we got an eyeful that day. The first batter I faced was light brown, probably a Mexican. The first pitch I threw—literally the first pitch—hit him square in the jaw. I was only fifteen years old, but I could already throw hard. They carried the young man off the field and I had to pitch against both the batters and the vengeful screams of the small crowd the rest of the game. Without the constant buzz of a big crowd, the few strident voices in the stands that day stood out like cacti in the desert. Most people think a large hostile crowd is the toughest to deal with but the small hostile crowd is actually worse. I was aware of the anger throughout the game, but I finished and won. I thought they would throw at one of our batters but they didn't. If it had been up to the fans they would have. In fact, our team bus was stoned after the game and we had to hunker down in fear of broken glass. No windows were broken, but my innocence was shattered.

I made my major league debut in 1964 at old Colt Stadium, a rickety wooden structure that wasn't any better than the minor league stadium in Los Angeles where I watched the Hollywood Stars and the Los Angeles Angels in the Pacific Coast League. In September of that year, Colt Stadium occupied a small corner of what was to be the Astrodome parking lot, while the Dome itself, with all the cranes that surrounded it, issued a stark announcement of things to come. I didn't get a close look at the Dome that year, but I knew it would be open for business in 1965. What I didn't know was that I would be on the major league team for the Astros' first game. I never dreamed the steel structure I saw that September could become so magnificent in the space of six months, vaulting over Dodger Stadium and that of every other major league team, a monument unto itself.

We played a game on the last day in Florida that year, and then departed for Houston, arriving in the dark of the night. The Dome was lit up like a birthday cake when the team bus arrived. When we went inside, a bunch of guys walked out across the concourse and into the box seats to view the playing field and I was among them. My mouth fell open when I saw the field; Dodger Stadium was a bunt compared to this place. I told one of the reporters that I felt as if I had walked into the next century. It was like a huge flying saucer.

The first official preseason game in the Dome came the next day and it was played at night, when tracking fly balls was not a problem. (The exhibition game the day before had revealed that quirks in the Dome's design made catching fly balls nearly impossible during the day.) Yankees skipper Johnny Keane inserted Mickey Mantle in the leadoff spot so that he would be the first batter in Astrodome history and Mantle hit a long home run off Turk Farrell into the big ramp beyond the center field fence that served as a batter's eye, but after that Farrell settled down and pitched a good game and it was 1–1 after nine innings. We ended up beating the Bombers 2–1 in extra innings on a hit by our first base coach, Nellie Fox. Looking back, this game foreshadowed the entire history of the stadium where low-scoring games were common. In fact, when the All-Star Game was first played there in 1968, the National League won 1–0 on an unearned run!

The first regular season game, against the Phillies, was my first major league opening day. Ford Frick, the commissioner of baseball, was on hand, with the president of the U.S. Lyndon Johnson as well as National League president Warren Giles and Texas governor John Connally. Ken Smith from the Hall of Fame was also there to collect the first pitches thrown in the game with the Yankees and in the opener with the Phils.

I remember several things distinctly from that game. First,

the ceremonial opening pitch turned into opening pitches when twenty-two astronauts, standing behind the Astros dugout, threw twenty-two pitches to us players, standing just in front of the dugout. I don't recall who threw the pitch that I caught. It could have been Gus Grissom, John Young, Wally Schirra, or Alan Shepard. I don't remember them all, but they were stars in their own right. It was still a few years before Neil Armstrong would step on the moon, but these space pioneers were celebrities. It was awesome.

The other thing that stands out is the great pitching of Chris Short, who shut us out on four hits and struck out eleven batters. The Phillies won it 2–0 on a home run by Richie Allen—an opposite-field shot over the 390 foot sign in right center. I'd never seen anyone hit a ball that hard the other way. Allen used a forty-ounce bat with an extremely small handle. I got my hands on one that year and brought it back to California with me to show my buddies, including one of my friends who was on the baseball team at the University of California, Santa Barbara. I took the bat to one of his practices and said, "This is the kind of bat we use in the big leagues." They couldn't believe it. Nor could I. There was no way I could swing that bat. It would have been easier for me to divine water with it because when I held it at the knob end, the barrel immediately pointed straight to the ground.

I don't know quite how to explain the feeling I had being in the major leagues at the tender age of eighteen. In one way, I was as out of place as an altar boy in a whorehouse, but in another way, I fit right in. The pitching part was the easiest. I found that my fastball was above average and my breaking pitches were also effective. I made a lot of mistakes in the strike zone and gave up more than a few home runs but I also got away with a lot of mistakes. I knew I could handle the competition within the first month, and even though I wasn't an All-Star, I was better than half the pitchers on our staff right from the start. Once I knew that I could navigate the treacherous waters of a big league lineup, I really started to enjoy the work. As an expansion team, we were not expected to be competitive so when we won it was great, and when we lost it was not such a big deal. It was the perfect setting for a kid pitcher.

I have to admit that I was concerned about how I would be ac-

cepted by my teammates. I knew when I made the team that someone else would be cut and that made me uncomfortable. I also heard
that the umpires would make you pay your dues by calling a tight
strike zone. I didn't find either of these issues to be a problem.
When I talk to people about this now, they seem incredulous that I
could deal with these issues at the age of eighteen. I would be skeptical too, if I hadn't been there and done that.

Most of the guys on the team smoked cigarettes and consumed large quantities of beer. Back then, the Schlitz Brewing
Company was our sponsor and they gave each of us a case of beer
every home stand. At first, I gave mine to one of our older pitchers,
Jim Owens. Later, I kept the case and we drank together at the
Surrey House Motel on South Main Street just across from the
Dome. I worked out of the bullpen the first half of the year but
moved into the rotation for the last three months. The Astros had
me on a 100-pitch limit to protect my arm, which I hated because a
lot of times I was pitching well and wasn't tired when they took me
out of the game. Owens didn't like the pitch count either. He took
me under his wing, which may not have been the best place for
a young man to be, and I still remember him telling me, "Don't let
them make you into a seven-inning pitcher." Now, seven innings is
all that is expected. Greg Maddux, for example, frequently comes
out after seven innings and fewer than 100 pitches. But back then
I can remember guys accusing Milt Pappas of being a five-and-fly
guy (a guy who would come out of a game if he had the lead after
he qualified for the win by pitching five innings). Of course, Pappas
pitched 127 complete games in a seventeen-year career and forty-
three of them were shutouts. Not bad for a slacker.

I told Owens I wouldn't be making any early exits after they
took me off the pitch limit. "Don't worry about that," I said. "I'm
ready to go nine tomorrow." That may have been false bravado,
but if it was I talked myself into believing it. I still hold the Astros
record with 106 complete games. I even finished one game in my
rookie season, my last start of the year in New York. I took a perfect
game into the ninth inning at Shea Stadium and I don't know if
I was still under 100 pitches or not, but they left me in there and
I lost both the no-hitter and the game in the bottom of the ninth

when a sinking liner to left caromed off the glove of Lee May and a soft liner to second fell just off the tip of the outstretched glove of Joe Morgan, who was drawn in at second base. Both balls touched the fielders' gloves. That's how close I came to being the youngest pitcher ever to pitch a perfect game. Afterward, the writers were surprised to find me in a good mood. I don't know why they thought I would be angry, as I had just pitched the best game of my life and was going home for the winter with a solid major league season under my belt.

I learned a lot that first year. I learned how to throw a slider, which became my signature pitch, and I learned how to throw down a beer with the best of them. One night I went out for dinner and drinks with Rusty Staub. Rusty ordered a stinger (brandy and crème de menthe). So I ordered one too. Late in the evening Rusty told me to go easy on the concoction. "They'll sneak up on you," he said.

"Rusty," I said. "Don't ever esterunderate my ability to drink!"

I got my first opening day pitching assignment in the Dome in 1968 when I was twenty-one years old. I remember being posed for a picture with my opponent, Jim Bunning of the Pirates, during our workout the day before the first game. I still recall telling him, "Good luck, after tomorrow," which was a clumsy thing to say, but it proved to be prophetic.

The toughest thing for me that day was watching the clock. I tried not to look at it very often because it refused to move. Seconds seemed like minutes. I thought I would be all right if the game would just start, but at that agonizing pace, 7:30 would never come. When the game finally began, I was all right, but not great, as Maury Wills hit a looping single over short off me with two outs in the top of the ninth to give the Bucs a 4–3 lead. Bunning pitched well, as usual, but luck was on my side: With two outs and two men on base, Bob Aspromonte hit a two-run triple off Ron Kline to give me the first of my four opening day wins 5–4. I remember jumping up off the bench when the ball got by Roberto Clemente in right field. I crowned myself as the beanie on my cap hit the roof of the dugout.

I only pitched one opener on the road and that was in 1970 at Candlestick Park in San Francisco. I don't remember that game much at all, but according to the game story in the *Houston Chronicle* I got lucky again. After six innings I was down 3–2 and in the seventh, Norm Miller pinch-hit for me with two outs and two men on base. Miller hit an opposite-field homer and we hung on to win 8–5. Looking at the box score, I was amused to see that Jim Bouton pitched two thirds of an inning in the game. Bouton was a good reliever for us in 1969, the year he wrote his landmark tell-all book, *Ball Four.* In fact, he saved my twentieth win at Candlestick Park that season. This time a far less controversial reliever, Fred Gladding, picked up the save. *Ball Four* revealed some behind-the-scenes activities that enraged a few players and made him persona non grata both in the dugout and the front office, but I liked Bouton. He was a bright guy and very funny and it is no coincidence that his book is funny too. I didn't mind it because he said nice things about me, but I did think he went too far in a couple of cases. Now I guess I'm walking the same tightrope . . .

My next opener was at home against my nemesis team, the Dodgers. It's funny how that goes. I always seemed to beat the Giants. When we didn't score much, I pitched really well and when they hit me, we hit them harder. I beat the Dodgers in Los Angeles early in my career, a 3–0 victory over Sandy Koufax, but I never won another game there. It got so bad that my parents stopped going to the games though my brother, Rick, and sister, Laura, kept the vigil at the ballpark. If I ever did beat da Bums, they wanted to be there. I had better luck against the Dodgers in Houston, though. And, on opening day in 1971 I went the distance, beating Bill Singer 5–2. Singer had a great fastball, slider combination, and a spitter that made Gaylord Perry's seem like a powder puff. One thing that jumps out of the box score from this game is the crowd—or should I say the "gathering"?—only 22,421 fans came to the ballpark on opening day. The Astrodome had already lost its luster. By 1971 the local fans wanted something we never delivered—a championship. In fact, the stadium was already falling into disrepair, while Dodger

Stadium looked as fresh as ever. Rats patrolled the areas beneath the field boxes in the Dome, scrounging for peanuts and popcorn, and we would see one occasionally as we walked from our clubhouse to the dugout. Joe Pepitone, a native New Yorker, showed us how to catch them with bait hooked onto a line, just like fishing without a rod and reel. After a few years, they turned some cats loose under the box seats to eliminate the rat population. It worked pretty well, but every so often, one of the cats got loose on the field during a game.

The Dodgers and the Reds were loaded and we never even came close to winning our division while I was pitching for the team. We were always tough at home and abysmal on the road. The championships would come much later.

I got off to a great start in 1971 and made the All-Star team but could not pitch in the game because of an elbow injury. I tried it a couple of times after the break, but just couldn't pitch with it. Every time I threw, the ulna nerve in my right elbow twanged like somebody plucking an out-of-tune banjo. It felt like getting hit in the not-so-funny bone. After missing the second half of the season and nursing a sore arm for a couple of years, I got a chance to pitch on opening day again in 1975. This was my last opening game start and it was at home against the Braves and Phil Niekro. I remember this one better than the others because I felt I had something to prove. I wanted my ace designation back and I made a good start toward getting it. I pitched a complete game again, although this time there were only 14,959 paying customers. The final was 6–2, and although the score was similar, I pitched much better than I had against the Dodgers in '71. I only allowed the Braves four hits and outside of the two-run fourth, they only got two base runners. Another thing that stands out, looking back, is that I only threw ninety-three pitches and struck out eight batters. It doesn't take a genius to figure out that I was throwing a lot of strikes and that they weren't hitting them very well. For the third time in four opening day starts, I was able to pitch a complete game. I was able to go the distance right out of the gate. These days, most teams try to get their starters ready to pitch seven innings the first time out. I wasn't as protective as most managers. If our opening day starter didn't go nine, it wasn't because he wasn't ready. I tried to get my starters up to 120 pitches before the season started so that they would be able to go the distance if they were pitching well.

The 1975 season became a death march as we stumbled into the cellar early and ended up with the worst record in team history. As I prepared for my last start of the season I was 14-15 with an ERA just below 4.00. I still remember my old friend, broadcaster Bill Worrell, telling me facetiously, "Dierker, if you win this game you should get the Cy Young award." He had a point, as 15-15 would have been pretty good on a team that finished forty-three games out of first. Alas, I finished 14-16 and my ERA crept up to 4.00. That year attendance dropped to an all-time-low 858,000 fans, and Judge Hofheinz, the original owner of the team, went belly-up.

I remember my first opening day start and my last pretty well. They came at the beginning and toward the end of my career, and I guess, for that reason, they seemed more important. There was another opening day game in Cincinnati, which I didn't pitch, but did watch in disbelief. Back before television ruled baseball, the first game of the season was always in the Queen City. This honor was given to the Reds because they started their glorious history in 1869, becoming the very first professional baseball team. In 1978, everyone was looking for a pitchers' duel between Houston's J. R. Richard and the Reds' Tom Seaver, two of the best pitchers in all of baseball. But this time, the gods of the game intervened and created an interesting, if not artful, ball game. Terry Puhl hit Seaver's third pitch into the right field bleachers. Then it started raining and the game was delayed. During the delay the Zamboni machine made an error: Normally, it would vacuum up water from the AstroTurf and dump it into drains on the playing field. Sometimes it would spray water over the center field fence, where there was another drain. This time, it spewed a towering gusher of water into the r. f. bleachers, baptizing a whole section of Reds Fans. They got soaked, and then they got socked. The Astros won the game 11–9, but there were two more rain delays before it was finally finished.

The game started at one and didn't end until just after seven. An unlikely triple play on a strikeout and two tag plays killed one Reds rally and Pete Rose got hit by a ground ball as he ran between bases to spoil another. Seaver tossed up two more home run balls and gave up a total of five runs, while Richard gave up seven. And at one juncture of the game, Astros reliever Gene Pentz threw a strike while he was intentionally walking a batter. Part of the attraction of ball games is that they're unpredictable. The only thing that was certain at this game was that there would be a lot fewer fans on hand at the end of the game than there were in the beginning.

Bob Feller pitched a no-hitter on opening day. George Bell hit three home runs against Bret Saberhagen in Kansas City in another. You never even dream about that kind of start, but there is a certain energy, a type of electricity that runs through the clubhouse on opening day and it starts at least an hour before batting practice. Part of the excitement is caused by the new uniforms; throughout spring training, you wear last year's unis, and then, on opening day, the new ones appear in your locker, like manna from heaven. God, are they ever fresh! Just looking at them gives you that Christmas morning feeling that you had as a kid. You can see the other players holding them out away from their bodies, sizing them up.

This is where the problems start for the equipment manager. You see, major league players usually have major league egos and they want their uniforms to fit just so. When the uniform makers come through during spring training, taking measurements, most players give specific instructions such as "just like last year's," or "all the way down to the shoe top." Then, on opening day, it's not like last year's or it doesn't come all the way down to the shoe top. In the long hard dog days of summer, when the uniform pants have been torn and repaired a few times, the way they fit on opening day is about as important as a joke you can't remember. Who cares? But there's only one debut each year, and on that day, the players can be picky, picky, picky.

The new uniforms erase everything you have done in previous seasons. If you have been an All-Star, great—now prove that you can do it again. On the other hand, if you've been injured or under par, redemption starts now. You go from the "nothing matters" mind-set of spring training to an "every moment is important" outlook overnight.

You can feel the adrenaline during batting practice, whether you are hitting or just shagging. You pull and tug at the new uniform like a soldier preparing for inspection. You think everyone is looking at you. You look at everyone else. Yesterday, everything was flat, dull. Today it's vivid—you're floating. A little sweat brings you back down to earth. Take some ground balls on the infield or fly balls in the outfield, take a few swings of the bat, have a game of long toss. When you break a sweat, you break the spell and then introductions bring it back. After the first pitch, you settle down, riveted, ready. The whole season beckons like a siren song.

You just never know what will happen on opening day or any other during the course of the long season. As a manager, I adopted a businesslike attitude, trying to conceal my excitement. I felt that as major leaguers we should behave with professional efficiency; that we should not bounce around like I did in the back of that pickup truck. But it is almost impossible to be low-key when you're announced on opening day. Typically, the players who aren't in the lineup are introduced first. They line up from just outside first and third base, leaving enough room for the manager and the starters to line up closer to the plate. The manager is called out after the non-starters. In 1997, I was a rookie again and I was pumped. I went down the line slapping hands with all the extra players before going to my station at home plate. In the next four years, knowing that this was still just the first of 162 games, I felt like going straight to home plate to shake hands with the opposing manager. But I bowed to a stronger feeling that the players might take that as a disrespectful gesture, a lack of enthusiasm. So I jogged down to the end of the line and touched each player lightly before heading for home.

After I shook hands with the other manager, the players in the lineup were announced. Bagwell was always third. He would slap hands dispassionately, like I did. Having played virtually every day for many seasons, he didn't get all that excited over the preliminary procedures. Some of the other guys, especially the rookies, effervesced. Their feet were like feathers, like my feet in 1965.

Up in the clubhouse, the equipment manager has compiled a

list of the uniform change requests. I can imagine an employee at Uniform Central taking calls the next day from thirty teams, all with a fair number of tailoring details. Even with their exorbitant salaries, the players (and staff) are always complaining about something. Uniform issues were never big with me and they were the last of my worries on opening day 1997, when I took the lineup to home plate for the first time. It was April 1, but I wasn't fooling around. I called Mike Cubbage and asked if he wanted a ride to the ballpark that day. He did, and asked when I was planning to leave. I said about 2:00 or 2:30, hoping it wouldn't seem like I was overly anxious. He said that he might have to go separately because he and Bill Virdon were going to go over scouting reports at 1:30 and plan a players' meeting. "Fine," I said. "We'll leave at 1:00. No problem."

Over the years, I spent a lot of time sitting in locker rooms in my underwear. The underpants we wear beneath the uniform fit tight and extend down to the knees. This type of fit makes it more comfortable to wear a jockstrap and cup and also provides a slim layer of protection from the raspberries you get when you slide. I soon learned that the players and coaches of this era arrive at the ballpark even earlier than we did when I was a player. We spent a lot of time lounging around in our underwear back then and they spend even more now.

Cubby and I arrived at the Astrodome at 1:00, six hours before game time, which was too much worry time, as far as I was concerned. As an opening day pitcher, I never came out early for that very reason. As it turned out, I didn't get worried before my managerial debut. I never talked to reporters before a game I was going to pitch but talking to writers is about all I did before my first opener as manager. One of our announcers, Vince Cotroneo, came by my office and offered me a shot of some kind of liquor for good luck. It was an Italian ritual and I accepted it gladly. *Houston Chronicle* columnist Dale Roberston brought a bottle of wine for after the game. This became an annual good luck gesture. I must have done thirty or forty interviews and though the talking became tiresome, it did help move the minute hand.

During batting practice, the veterans seemed more energetic

than they had during spring training, but they seemed focused and not overly excited. The rookies, Richard Hidalgo and Tom Martin, were bouncing around like Ping-Pong balls in a lottery.

After batting practice, we had our meeting on the Braves. It didn't take long, maybe twenty minutes. We went over hitter tendencies and defensive positioning. Tom McCraw took some time to review John Smoltz with the hitters. Vern Ruhle and I talked to the pitchers. Everyone knows you can't beat the Braves with intelligence information, but following the adage that "you play the way you practice" can help and it certainly can't hurt. My philosophy is to be prepared every day, to be relentless in effort and execution. I knew we would not be able to live up to that standard on a daily basis for six months. No team can. But the closer we could get to daily preparedness, the fewer games we would give away. In baseball, you really can't have a game plan; you have to react to the circumstances of each pitch in each game. What I was looking for was not so much memorization of a plan but hitting a peak level of energy and mental acuity at game time. I was confident that our starter, Shane Reynolds, would be in that state when he threw his first pitch. He is meticulous in his regimen and never gives less than his best effort. On opening day it is more important to be settled down at game time rather than keyed up. If your pitcher is calm and collected, his attitude can settle the whole team down.

My most emotional moment came during the introductions when my coaches were announced. Bill Virdon, Jose Cruz, and Alan Ashby got thunderous ovations, as did I. The crowd got up for Vern Ruhle too, maybe not quite as much, but we were all former Astros, which was a dramatic change from the coaching staff the previous year when there were no former Astros. Mike Cubbage and Tom McCraw, who had come over from the Mets, got a polite greeting. I looked toward the seats where Judy, Ryan, and Julia were supposed to be sitting, but they weren't there yet. A lot of fans were having trouble getting into the Dome and the stadium was only half full at game time. I finally spotted Judy, in her new Hawaiian shirt, just before Shane Reynolds cut loose with ball one to Kenny Lofton. The game was on, and what a game it was.

Reynolds struck out Lofton and Mark Lemke to open the proceedings. Then Chipper Jones singled and Fred McGriff doubled.
Brad Ausmus looked over to see if I wanted to walk Ryan Klesko.
I shook my head no, and Shane retired him on a soft ground ball.
In the bottom of the frame, Biggio singled and went to third on a
hit-and-run looper by shortstop Pat Listach; I didn't give them a
sign; they just did it on their own. We took the lead on Bagwell's
chopper, but Smoltz would yield no more. The Braves tied the game
on Chipper Jones's homer in the third, right after Ausmus threw
Kenny Lofton out trying to steal. We had an offensive weapon in
Ausmus's arm: The break-even success rate for scoring runs on
stolen bases is 67 percent and Ausmus can throw out 50 percent of
the runners if the pitchers give him half a chance.

Regrettably, Jones's home run ball was thrown back onto the
field. This would have been a great show of home team support
but instead it led to a major disruption, as the team had given com-
memorative baseballs to the first 30,000 fans through the turn-
stiles. A fusillade of baseballs rained down in the outfield, delaying
play for ten minutes. Later, when Lofton robbed Luis Gonzalez of
extra bases by leaping high for a brilliant catch against the center
field fence, balls came down again. The Braves have a nationwide
fan base because you can follow them from Key West to Seattle on
Superstation WTBS. It was obvious that there were many Braves
fans in attendance on this occasion, and I suspected the second vol-
ley of baseballs to be their "in your face" reaction to the catch. A
bad situation became worse when one of the balls hit Lofton in the
leg. The behavior of the fans was deplorable but the decision to give
out the souvenirs before rather than after the game wasn't real
smart. And though home plate umpire Paul Runge didn't seem
inclined to issue any warnings, I could see the headline in tomorrow's paper: "Braves Fans Cause Forfeit." They would get the win
for their team by throwing our souvenir baseballs onto the field. It
didn't happen but it could have.

We got our second run in the third on a single by Ausmus, a
sacrifice bunt by Reynolds, a single by Biggio, and a sacrifice fly by
Listach. Smoltz was burning the corners at 93 to 96 miles per hour

throughout the game and we were lucky to get just two runs. And it is ironic, I suppose, that the two guys we obtained during the winter to improve our defense, Pat Listach and Brad Ausmus, actually generated our offense. Both of these guys had been feeble with the bat all spring. I was a little worried about Listach because we were pinning a lot of hopes on him being an effective hitter with speed at the top of the lineup. I wasn't so concerned about Ausmus's bat, as he would hit down in the lineup where offense is a bonus. In this game, they both played key roles with their bats. Listach looked better in the field than he had in Florida, but he hurt his knee on a play behind second base in the ninth. Sean Berry aggravated his groin pull and I had to put utility man Billy Spiers in the game in the sixth. Spiers ended up making a couple of great defensive plays that Berry probably wouldn't have made and saved us at least one run. He made me look like a genius but it was just dumb luck. Meanwhile, Shane kept making good pitches. In the sixth, however, he got a few balls up and his control faltered. Vern and I discussed a bridge pitcher to try and get the game to Billy Wagner. We settled on Jose Lima and got him started in the bullpen. Shane pitched out of trouble but we were still concerned. The Braves had six left-handed hitters in the lineup, so we started lefty Tom Martin alongside Lima. Shane weathered another storm in the seventh. The big pitch was right on Lofton's hands for a called strike three.

I walked over to Shane and asked him about that pitch. He said, "It was a cutter," and flashed a wide grin. The smile itself told me he had more to give. I sent him out for the eighth and started Wagner at the same time. If Shane let a runner reach base I was going to the bullpen. He did not know that and he did not allow a runner. He finished his eight innings in style as his 121st pitch of the game struck out Ryan Klesko. It was his seventh strikeout.

In the bottom of the eighth, I pinch-hit for Shane with Thomas "Tank" Howard. Tank hit a pop fly double to left, but we couldn't get him home. That brought the game to the ninth with the score still 2–1. Wagner came into the game, and Andruw Jones pinch-hit for Michael Tucker and flied out on a powerful swing. Then Javy Lopez reached first on a hot smash off Listach's glove.

The Braves pinch-ran with Tony Graffanino, but I wasn't worried about him stealing because, though he is faster than Lopez, he's not in the same league with Lofton. It wouldn't have mattered if he had stolen, however, because Wagner struck out Jeff Blauser and Mike Mordecai to put a lid on our first win.

The giveaway balls had a printed message about my four opening day starts. I saved the ball that was the last out of the game and the scorecards from our dugout and theirs. This made me 5–0 in openers, but I had no delusions of grandeur. We never won the pennant when I won on opening day as a pitcher and this win didn't assure us of anything. It only meant we would not start the year with a losing streak. Five or six losses in a row would have been disastrous for me, coming out of the booth as I did. In that sense, the first win may have been more important to me than it would have been to a veteran manager.

After the game, I was smothered by reporters, and except for a few national correspondents who were there to cover the debut of the freak show manager, the media seemed happy, almost festive. I had the bottle of wine to drink but didn't open it. With the recent get tough stance on drinking and driving we kept a dry clubhouse. I didn't get out of the locker room for at least an hour, but my daughter Ashley and her new husband, Craig, along with her Aunt Sharon and Uncle Chris waited for me all that time, which was a pleasant surprise. I was especially surprised that they all wore Hawaiian shirts, even Sharon. "This was a big sacrifice I made for you," she said. "I feel absolutely awful in this shirt." To tell the truth, she did look pretty bad. Normally she is sleek and chic. In a frumpy Hawaiian shirt she looked kind of goofy. We all joined Solly Hemus and several other friends at Carrabas, where many toasts were offered and many libations quaffed. I was still flying when I got home and I didn't get to sleep until 3:00 A.M.

In 1998, my string of opening day wins came to an end. After five straight wins we lost one, but we didn't go down easy. It took the Giants thirteen innings and four and a half hours to beat us 9–4 and our owner, Drayton McLane, was probably feeling restless by then.

He is not a patient spectator. From my vantage point in the front of the dugout, I see him in his seat one minute and gone the next. I know he likes to go up to the radio booth and visit with Milo Hamilton during the game. I suppose he thinks it will help sell more tickets and maybe he's right, but this game was good enough to sell tickets on its own—until the Giants scored five runs in the thirteenth. As it turned out, the rest of the '98 season was more than worth the price of admission. We went on to win 102 games, a team record.

In a way, it was disappointing to lose the opener. In another, it was just nice to get it over with. We didn't have any pitching left at the end and C. J. Nitkowski, new to our team from the Tigers, was in an unfamiliar role. During his career he had always been a starter and we planned to use him as a long reliever, coming into a game early and pitching a few innings when we were already behind, and also as a situational left-hander coming in to face one or two hitters. We never expected him to be in a make-or-break situation at the end of a game, but then again, we didn't expect to go thirteen innings on opening day either. As it turned out, Dusty Baker took John Johnstone out of his comfort zone too, but he finished the game and got the win. We had Johnstone in 1996 and though he had pretty good stuff, he always seemed to make a bad pitch to a good hitter with men on base. I thought we would score off him and win in the twelfth. When the Giants got giddy with Nitkowski and scored five runs, we were doomed. We did make a little noise in the bottom of the thirteenth but it was all bluster and no bite.

Judy and I had planned to have dinner with friends at Carrabas and celebrate another victory. This time it would be at a reasonable hour, as our game started at 4:00 P.M. due to an ESPN telecast. Judy and I ended up eating alone after our friends went home early because they had school-age children. I was actually glad to be alone. Sometimes you just don't feel like talking about the game, and this was one of those times.

Looking back, the opening day loss foreshadowed our defeat in the playoffs in October. Since we cannot televise locally when we are featured on national television, we have to change our game time so that we will play in prime time in as many markets as possible and maximize the TV dollars. Hence the 4:00 P.M. start on opening day. This can really get ridiculous, as it did when we faced the Padres in the postseason that October and had to start the last two games in San Diego at 4:00, in the twilight. As they say, it takes two to tango, but most of the managers I know would prefer to dance at a normal hour.

In 1999, we suffered a cruel blow before spring training even started. Our star outfielder, Moises Alou, sustained a knee injury while working out in his native Dominican Republic and it looked like he would be out for the year. It would be tough to live up to the 102 wins of the previous season, even with Alou, but the fans didn't care. As far as they knew, we were winners—had been in each of my two years at the helm. A sportswriter named Paul Needell once said that "potential is always having to say you're sorry." I hoped this wouldn't be the story of our season, and happily it wasn't.

Along the hard campaign trail, we lost almost all of our front-line players to one injury or another. In September, I had infielders Craig Biggio and Bill Spiers playing in the outfield. But the one thing we had going for us all year long was the extraordinary play of Jeff Bagwell and Craig Biggio and the near-perfect pitching of our closer, Billy Wagner. And we also had a slugger named Carl Everett, whose superb effort throughout the year helped us survive the loss of Alou.

That season was the last for the Astros in the Astrodome and it featured a nostalgic beginning as seventy astronauts lined up along the curve of the infield to watch Neil Armstrong throw out the first pitch. Armstrong was escorted to the mound by two players who participated in the first game in the Dome, Jimmy Wynn and Bob Aspromonte. How could we lose under those conditions?

Shane Reynolds struck out Sammy Sosa to end the first inning to a rousing ovation as most fans remembered the 1998 season when Slammin' Sammy hit sixty-six home runs, several of them in the Dome. Everett and Richard Hidalgo homered for us in this opener as Reynolds and Wagner squelched the Cubs to secure a 4–2 win, much to the delight of 51,668 fans, the tenth largest crowd in the history of the franchise. In the end, though, the season would be more like Apollo 13 than Apollo 11—more a case of survival than of celebration.

Now, the Dome looks like an architectural relic next to the Houston Texans' new football field. When the sun sets in the west, the Dome disappears in the shadow of Reliant Stadium. The Dome was a big draw for the first few years, but it became passé among the locals after a few years of lackluster baseball. I thought it was still one of the best ballparks in the league until the big scoreboard in centerfield was torn down to build more seats for the Oilers. Once the scoreboard came down, the Astrodome lost its personality: The scoreboard separated it from the other multi-use stadiums, but with seats going all the way around in the upper deck, the Astrodome looked about the same as Busch Stadium, Riverfront Stadium, Three Rivers Stadium, and Veterans Stadium, and having a roof wasn't enough to make it distinctive, as several other domed stadiums opened around the country. The big bowls with Astroturf became obsolete. And when we lost in the playoffs again in 1999, the Astrodome closed its doors to baseball without ever hosting a World Series.

I turned the page on a new century, a new season and a new ballpark in the year 2000. It was, as Yogi Berra once said, "like déjà vu all over again." I remembered the ultramodern Astrodome of 1965 and remembered saying that I felt as if I had just stepped into the next century. Now, ironically, I really did take that step, as the Astrodome, old and decrepit, was replaced by a new ballpark that was designed to look old.

Enron Field turned out to be a beautiful ballpark and it was christened, like the Astrodome, with an exhibition game against the Yankees. The retractable roof of the new stadium cost $30 million; thirty-five years earlier, the entire Astrodome was built for $33 million. On both occasions, the opening exhibition game was sold out. When the Dome opened, Lyndon Johnson and Texas Governor John Connally were there. Another Texas icon, Nolan Ryan, was on hand for the Enron opener. On both occasions, the nature of the first ball game was a harbinger of things to come.

Think about it: In the first game at the Dome, little Nellie Fox, an old-timer, won the game for the Astros with a little single. In the Enron opener, Daryle Ward hit the telling blow, capping a four-run explosion in the eighth as the Astros won 6–5. Ward, a youngster, and a big one at 6'2" and 250 pounds, won the first game at Enron Field with a long home run. The first game in the Dome was a 2–1 win in eleven innings.

Sitting in the Yankees dugout for the exhibition was Houstonian Roger Clemens. The Rocket said he was just happy for the city and he said that he hoped the new ballpark would revitalize downtown Houston like Camden Yards had Baltimore and Jacobs Field had Cleveland. "It's a special stadium and it's going to be awesome," he said. "There are a lot of things to look at."

Another Houstonian, Yankees second baseman Chuck Knoblauch, said that the three and a half hours he spent at the ballpark was the longest time he had spent downtown in his life.

After the exhibition games with the Yankees, the Astros headed for Pittsburgh to open the season while construction workers went back to put the finishing touches on Enron Field. I was already feeling ambivalent about our new ballpark: It was beautiful, no doubt. But it seemed to be a hitter's park and that bothered me. After watching batting practice for a couple of days, everyone was talking about the Crawford Boxes, the 12–15 rows of seats above the scoreboard in straight away left field. You could practically drop-kick a ball out of the park in that direction. The right field seats weren't quite so easy to reach, but they were close. I usually take the approach that the conditions of the game don't matter because the conditions are the same for both teams. But I knew how Coors Field ravaged the Rockies' pitching staff and I could only hope that the same thing didn't happen to us at Enron.

A lot of attention was given to the steep hill in deep center field. Our team president, Tal Smith, worked more closely with the architects than anyone else on our team and Tal cut his baseball teeth in Cincinnati, where old Crosley Field had a similar embankment in left field. At Enron the fence, and thus the hill, was about seventy feet deeper than in Cincinnati. Our flagpole was actually in play, out there on the center field incline. I wasn't worried about an outfielder getting hurt by running into the pole. If a ball was hit that far, the fielder wouldn't be able to get all the way back there in time to collide with the pole. I was worried, however, about our defensive coverage in center. There was so much ground to cover and our center fielder, Richard Hidalgo, was at least a step slower than most center fielders.

Three Rivers Stadium looked antiquated next to the glory of Enron, and Pittsburgh itself was even more uninviting on April 4. It was just plain cold. Opening day was postponed due to the freezing weather and when we took the field on April 5, shooting for a fourth straight division championship, it was only a little warmer. I raised a few eyebrows by choosing Shane to start the opener because Jose Lima had won twenty-one games the year before and looked to be the logical choice. But Jose was high-strung and I was afraid he would have trouble controlling his emotions. Shane had pitched four openers for us and had been through the nerve-wracking experience of the endless wait before. This time, when he took the mound against the Pirates, it was a longer wait and I have to admit I was concerned about it. Shane is a creature of habit. Any little change in routine irritates him, especially on the day he pitches. Several times, after starting well in a game, he was forced to wait during a rain delay and each time he came back out as if he had never pitched before in his life. Now, I feared he would be thrown out of whack by the change in his routine, but this time he came through like a champ. Reynolds, Doug Henry, and Billy Wagner braved temperatures that dropped into the thirties by the end of the game. Richard Hidalgo's grand slam was enough to ensure a 5–2 victory.

We ended up winning two of three with the Pirates and were eagerly anticipating more success against the bottom-feeding Phillies at home. I have been around long enough to know that three games in April don't mean all that much. I have also learned the hard way, both as a pitcher and as a manager, that the quality of the opponent doesn't always dictate the results of any individual game. But the team was riding high and I was flush with confidence when we got back to the stadium in Houston, and I could tell immediately that the construction had been proceeding apace. In the parking garage our cars were flocked like Christmas trees with a layer of dust. "Boy, oh boy," I muttered as I walked to my car. "Look at all this dust." Chris Holt, a second-year pitcher who had accomplished very little in his professional career, was within hearing range and I didn't know it. "Yeah," he said. "You'd think they would have cleaned our cars up for us while we were gone." I'll never forget him saying that, for it speaks so eloquently to the dreamworld of the modern major league ballplayer. One year you are in the minor leagues, hoping to get your uniform laundered once in a while, and then suddenly you are such a great man that you assume people will wash your car without being asked. I was thinking about the new stadium, the new century, the challenge of winning another championship. He was worried about his car.

The next night the stars came out, celestial and otherwise. Down low, behind home plate in the Diamond Level Seats, Drayton hosted such luminaries as former president George Bush, his son, then governor George W., George's mother, Barbara, and Nolan Ryan. Most of the capacity crowd of 41,583 arrived on time, but the U.S. Army Golden Knights, scheduled to drop out of an airplane and sky-dive onto the field to deliver Old Glory for the National Anthem, were late. And so the Enron Field era started not with a hit but with an error. Unfortunately, our dramatic win over the Yankees in the exhibition opener didn't presage the events of the regular season. On our official opening day, we lost 4–1 to a young Phillies left-hander, Randy Wolf, one of those pitchers (and there are quite a few of them) who don't throw real hard, but get everyone out with fastballs. It is exasperating to get shut down by this type of pitcher. When we lost to lefty Chris Short in 1965, it was understandable because he was just plain nasty. That night you couldn't really say Wolf had wicked stuff, but he sure was effective. Octavio Dotel pitched well in losing, just as Bob Bruce had done in 1965: Dotel gave up home runs to Scott Rolen and Ron Gant;

Bruce gave up a home run to Richie Allen. Richard Hidalgo hit one for us, but we lost the Crawford Box home run derby 2–1, starting a disturbing trend that would plague us throughout the year.

In the first season of the Dome, we were still feeling the effects of expansion and had never won a thing; the year before we finished ninth in a ten-team league and would finish ninth again with a record of 65-97. In the year 2000, we were coming off a 97-win, division championship year. But that didn't help us in the year 2000 as we struggled throughout the first half of the season and had to finish with a rush to get out of the cellar.

After the horror show of the 2000 season, it was important to get off to a good start in 2001, especially at home. I cannot name a single team that has played .500 ball or less at home and won a championship. Our fans were less optimistic than I was about our prospects, as only 36,526 of them showed up for the opener with the Brewers. I couldn't believe we drew an opening day crowd that was smaller than our average crowd the year before. Enron Field lost its appeal quickly, just like the Astrodome. As it turned out, the 6,000 fans that came dressed as empty seats missed a rousing performance by the home team. Moises Alou had to be scratched from the lineup due to a calf muscle injury and Daryle Ward replaced him—and then some. The young slugger hit a grand slam and drove in six runs as we pounded the Brewers 11–3. Craig Biggio, coming off knee surgery, went 5-5 and Scott Elarton, after making airline and hotel reservations for his parents, his sister, and his grandmother, was relieved at having something so simple to do as to win a ball game. Billy Wagner, also coming off surgery and perhaps the most important player in our scheme to return to prominence, pitched a perfect ninth inning. I was relieved to get an easy win, as it seemed like every win the year before was excruciating. Never in my thirty-seven years had I been so anxious for redemption. This was a great start.

CHAPTER 3

Pitching

You pay all that money to great big fellas with a lot of muscles and
straight stomachs who go up there and start swinging. And they
give them a little of this and a little of that and swindle 'em.

—CASEY STENGEL

AS USUAL, CASEY SAID something that's confusing but also makes a lot of sense. Yogi does the same thing. Is there something in the water at Yankee Stadium?

I found another way of saying the same thing in a poem by Robert Francis:

Not to, yet still, still to communicate
Making the batter understand too late.

To credit a pitcher with swindling a batter, or confusing him, you have to assume the pitcher has the ability to make one thing look like another. The best pitchers, like the best magicians, deal in illusions. They make fast pitches appear to be slow and vice versa. They make balls look like strikes and strikes look like balls. And, in the vernacular, they have balls. They're not afraid of losing because they believe they're going to win. For this reason, they are almost totally unpredictable.

The first thing a scout looks for when he is evaluating a pitcher is arm strength. How hard can this guy throw the ball? That used to be a subjective judgment. The scout could see if a guy was throwing extremely hard or not hard at all, but he couldn't differentiate among the great majority of pitchers that throw about the same speed. Now they can—all they have to do is point the radar gun at the pitcher and they'll get a reading in miles per hour. This is a useful tool but it's only a place to start. If the pitcher were a wood sculptor, his velocity would be the saw: This is where he would start to make an impression, and as he whittled down the work with chisels and knives, the form would take on a life of its own. Then, when he sanded and polished and applied colors, a work of art would emerge. For too many baseball scouts, the radar gun is the beginning and the end. For me, the fine strokes, the carving and polishing, are more important. These are the tools that require command of the material; they are the implements that allow a finesse pitcher to fool a hitter. They are swindling tools—they make the hitter understand too late.

My son's high school coach is consumed with velocity readings. He is probably attuned to the radar gun because the professional and college scouts at the games all use it and talk about mph all the time; one of the boys said that if you can't throw 85 mph, you can't pitch for him. I found that especially amusing as I watched Jamie Moyer shut the Astros out last year without ever throwing a pitch harder than 83 mph. For me, the important thing is runs allowed. I don't care how hard a pitcher throws if he can get the hitters out. But in high school, the coach doesn't have the luxury of watching a kid throw thirty or forty innings to get a feel for his ability. He almost has to go with arm strength.

As with most things, there is a point at which overarching talent obviates the need for artistry. For example, relief pitchers like Billy Wagner, Rob Nen, and a few others can sometimes pitch the ninth inning without throwing anything but fastballs. In the 1997 playoffs, John Smoltz worked the first three innings in the Astrodome, dispatching us three up and three down, three times with nothing but fastballs. It's no secret that pitchers with great fastballs sometimes get away with pitches down the middle, pitches that would make Tom Glavine cringe. But Smoltz wasn't throwing the ball down the middle. He was "painting" the black edge of the plate almost every time. When a guy is throwing 95 mph, his other pitches don't have to be great because the hitter has to start the bat early to hit the fastball. It is that way now and has always been that way. Consider this interview with former big leaguer Rube Bressler from the seminal baseball book, *The Glory of Their Times* by Lawrence Ritter:

> "Of course, there are two kinds of pitchers, power pitchers—like Dazzy [Vance], Walter Johnson, Lefty Grove, Bob Feller—and manipulators—like Eddie Plank, Herb Pennock, Grover Cleveland Alexander, Eppa Rixey. The power pitchers are the toughest all the way through, for the simple reason that you're always hitting at terrific stuff. They overpower you. They can make a mistake and get away with it.
>
> "But the manipulators, oh brother, Rixey got behind a hitter deliberately, so he could throw him the change of pace. I roomed with Rixey six years at Cincinnati. (I only roomed with the best—Bender, Rixey, Vance. If I couldn't hit, at least I'd find out why.)
>
> " 'How dumb can the hitters in this league get?' Rixey used to say to me. 'I've been doing this for fifteen years. When they're batting with the count two balls and no strikes, or three and one, they're always looking for the fastball. And they never get it. They get the change of pace every time—and they're always just as surprised to see it as they were the last time.' "

Of course, the best way to pitch is with the great fastball, good control, and a few other good pitches: In that '97 playoff game, Smoltz started throwing breaking balls and change-ups the second time through the order—it was almost like he was toying with us, proving he could get us out with all fastballs or with his other pitches. It worked well for Smoltz that day but not so well for former All-Star pitcher Sam McDowell one day when he was facing the White Sox. Sudden Sam had three great pitches (fastball, slider, and curveball), and one mediocre pitch, the change-up.

One day in 1963, when McDowell was with the Indians, he told White Sox slugger Dave Nicholson that he was going to strike him out four times the next day with four different pitches. I know because Nicholson was traded to the Astros in 1966 and he told me the story. The first three times McDowell fanned him with his three best pitches. That wasn't as difficult as it might seem, as Nicholson struck out more than any other major league player that year. The fourth time Dave came up, he immediately fell behind in the count. "I looked for a change-up because of what he told me the day before," he said. "If he had thrown me the other pitches I couldn't have hit them anyway." Sure enough, McDowell threw the change-up and Nicholson hit a game-winning home run.

Smoltz can throw just about as hard as Wagner, Nen, McDowell, anyone. Most of the time, he mixes his pitches as the Braves' closer. The most effective relief pitcher of all time, Dennis Eckersley, was also a former starter who used a variety of pitches. He used the good fastball on the corner as a pedestal for his art. Even Wagner and Nen have to mix it up once in a while, as there are a few hitters in the major leagues who can get around on a 100 mph pitch when they know it's coming. If you can throw in the upper 90s, you can get away with a few mistakes. But if you hit the corners at the same velocity, you can get away with a hanging curveball most of the time. The key is the location of the fastball. If the hitter knows you can blow the corners off the plate, he is almost out before he ever steps in.

As with most artistic endeavors, there are many ways to create a masterpiece. But for simplicity's sake, consider just two and you will be able to rate almost every major league pitcher: 1) base runners per inning, and 2) opponent's slugging average. If you know how many chances a pitcher typically gives his opponent and how many extra base hits he allows, you can rate him without looking at his won-loss record or ERA. Getting on base, whether by walk, hit, or error, is half of the formula for scoring; getting runners home is the other half. If the most important attributes of offense are getting on base and getting extra-base hits, the most important attributes of pitching are the opposite.

Tom Glavine prevents runs by limiting extra-base hitting. He walks a lot of batters, but he seldom throws the ball down the middle and his pitches generally have downward movement. He doesn't give up many home runs and he induces a lot of double plays. Greg Maddux and Curt Schilling, on the other hand, do it the other way: They give up more home runs, but they seldom walk a batter. When you total it up, it comes out about the same in terms of runs allowed. It is a lot more fun to watch Maddux and Schilling because they keep the game moving, forcing the batter to swing, but the bottom line for the fans is the score. I don't think Braves fans quibbled about the way Glavine did it; they just liked the result—wins (although they probably aren't thrilled by his results now that he's signed with the hated Mets).

Pitching coach Leo Mazzone of the Braves believes in throwing off the mound exclusively. He doesn't like his pitchers to play catch in the outfield even though pitchers on most other teams play catch every day. Instead, Leo has them throw off the mound every day, even if it's only at half speed and even if it's only for five minutes. I think this approach is a bit extreme, but it makes a good point. Pitchers do a lot of flat ground throwing to get a feel for spinning the ball; this can be useful, but it doesn't simulate what they do in the game. The only place you can really perfect your mechanics is on the mound. Perhaps Mazzone gets too much credit and perhaps his pitchers deserve more: As I recall, Greg Maddux was a pretty good pitcher before he signed with Atlanta; and strong-armed closer Mark Wohlers had to go to another team to conquer the Steve Blass scattershot syndrome. However, Leo's logic still holds: You must throw a lot, especially off the mound, to be totally prepared. I don't know if the Braves have been the preeminent pitching team for the last decade because they throw so much on the side, but it is hard to argue with their results.

One benefit of throwing less than full speed off the mound is that it reinforces the importance of controlling a pitch over the importance of throwing it hard. If you keep practicing your delivery, both from the windup and the stretch, you will get to a point where you don't have to think about your body's mechanics and you will build arm strength. If you are always throwing at a target, the target becomes unnecessary because the pitch has already been perfected in the mind. That's why Maddux and Glavine are Zen archers.

My control wasn't as good as theirs, and I didn't throw on the side as much as they do. I did throw all my pitches when I played catch in the outfield and I did play long toss a lot between starts. If I had it to do over again, I would still play long toss, but I would practice my pitches off the mound to improve my control instead of throwing them off flat ground in the outfield.

In one of our pitchers meetings, pitching coach Burt Hooton asked our pitchers to guess the width of a catcher's mitt. They seemed to agree that it was eight or nine inches wide. "Well," he said, "if the mitt is eight inches wide and the plate is seventeen inches wide, what does that tell you?" He got only blank stares from our pitchers but I knew what he was getting at. "If you think you're a major league pitcher, you ought to be able to hit the mitt most of the time," he said. "If you miss the pocket of the mitt by four inches one way it is a decent strike. If you miss by four inches the other way, it is close enough that a hitter might swing at it or an umpire might call it a strike. This is all I am suggesting, that you should be able to hit the mitt. If you can't you should be up on the mound practicing as much as possible."

Later, I told Burt that I used to get mad when I warmed up on the side if I couldn't hit my spots. One of our pitchers, Shane Reynolds, did the same thing. Not surprisingly, Shane was one of our better pitchers. Every time you throw a pitch warming up you can pretty well imagine what the result would be if you were pitching in a game. I tried to block out all thinking about the game until I was actually warming up. For the last five minutes of my warm-ups I imagined pitching to the other team's lineup. If it was the Reds and Pete Rose was leading off, I would try to get him on a four-seam fastball up and in. If I missed over the plate, I would credit him with a single and pitch to an imaginary Ken Griffey from the stretch. If I got the double play ball, I would go back to the windup. I would practice this way, mixing my pitches and locations, all the way through the batting order. When I got out to the mound, I would make my eight warm-up pitches count. I would find the strike zone with my fastball and then start shooting for the corners. I didn't just throw the ball in there.

When I speak of hitting spots I am not concerned so much with the mitt as with the strike zone. If you take the rectangle that is formed by the zone and superimpose a diamond on top of it, you will get four small triangles at the corners and a large diamond in the middle.

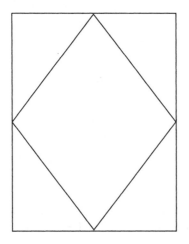

The idea is to keep the ball out of the diamond and in one of those triangles. Most pitchers will find it easier to hit one or two of those spots than the others. Those locations will become his bread and butter—something he can count on—say, a sinker low and away or a curveball at the knees. For me, the bread-and-butter pitches varied slightly from one game to the next. Most of the time it was a sinker-slider combination—low pitches with downward movement. On some occasions, when I was throwing a little harder, I could get my four-seam power fastball by the hitters up and in. One of the keys for a starting pitcher is to identify the bread-and-butter pitches early in the game. By keeping the ball out of the big diamond, you will keep it in the ballpark. At least 90 percent of all home runs are hit off pitches in that diamond. That's the danger zone and unless you're behind in the count to a weak hitter it is better to miss the little triangles for a ball than to hit the big diamond for an extra-base hit. Just ask Tom Glavine.

Every major league pitcher will tell you that the location of a pitch is more important than its movement and velocity, but movement and velocity are important too. Movement is a matter of spin—it can be (and should be) practiced on *every* ball you throw after your arm is loose—even when playing catch. Velocity is mostly God-given; it can be improved a little by throwing a lot to gain arm strength and by having a good delivery, but placing great emphasis on velocity is a trap. Whenever I go to one of my son's games, I hear fathers talking about this kid or that kid throwing 90 miles per hour. I hear them talking about strength training designed to help pitchers' velocity. I may ask them why Roy Oswalt, a skinny pitcher who weighs 165 pounds and doesn't lift weights, throws a lot harder than Scott Elarton, who is 6'7", and weighs 260 pounds and lifts all the time. Throwing to a target is the most important thing a pitcher can do, and just throwing a lot will build more velocity than a whole gymful of weights.

One method of building arm strength without throwing the ball involves the use of surgical tubing. The tubing is attached to a hook on the wall or to the top of a door, and the pitcher stands far enough away from where the tubing is attached to create resistance. Then he assumes the pitching position with his chest facing home plate and replicates the throwing motion, strengthening the appropriate muscles. I believe this exercise is far more beneficial than a bench press routine. It won't create the handsome pectoral muscles that look so good at the beach. But it may save a few runs and get another win or two.

Another thing that's important, and sometimes overlooked, is leg strength. Once again, this is no quick fix or automatic velocity builder; more than anything, strong legs allow a pitcher to throw a lot of pitches without getting tired and losing velocity. A running program can build leg strength and also stamina. Once in a while a National League pitcher will have to score from first on a double and then go straight to the mound because the next hitter makes an out on the first pitch. If the pitcher gets into trouble and has a taxing inning, the only way he can survive it is by being in good shape. I also believe in the type of leg strength that can be developed by doing thrusts and squats. It is obvious that Nolan Ryan has big, strong legs; Billy Wagner does too. Some people think that their velocity comes from their legs, and to some extent it may be true, but Oswalt and Pedro Martinez throw hard as well, and they have skinny legs.

I think velocity comes mostly from the wrist action of the throwing motion, which cannot be taught. I have watched both Wagner and Ryan play catch: Even when they don't use their legs, the ball jumps out of their hands. I also believe that this is true of most hard throwers. It's like foot speed—you can learn to run faster by improving your stride and the strength of your legs, but unless you are born with a gift, you probably won't win any races. Speed is a gift from God, but you can make full use of the gift by practicing.

You can maximize whatever throwing gift you have by paying attention to hitters. If a guy is standing way off the plate, I would assume he has trouble with the inside pitch until he proved otherwise. If he was close to the plate, he probably didn't like the outside pitch. If he was way up in the box, he usually had trouble with the breaking ball. If he stood erect and held the bat high, he was most likely a low-ball hitter. You can make some general assumptions simply by observing the hitter's stance, but you see even more as you pitch to him. If he swings at your best inside fastball and hits it hard but pulls it foul, you don't want to throw the same fastball out over the plate because he might hit it hard and fair. Who cares if he hits it hard foul? Not me—I would continue to pitch the guy hard inside to keep him in the macho mind-set; then I would mix in slow pitches and breaking balls away and swindle him.

You never really know what a hitter will do until you face him. I learned this lesson firsthand early in my career when I faced Reds first baseman Lee May. Lee was a big, strong power hitter who later became my teammate with the Astros. Our scouting report on him was to throw him breaking balls away and fastballs inside. This is a standard approach to all hitters but especially to home run hitters and our plan worked pretty well against Lee, except when I was pitching. It seemed like every time I threw him a fastball inside he hit a double or a home run, but he didn't hit the breaking balls. One day I decided not to throw him any fastballs at all and I held him hitless. If I ever threw him another fastball after that it was only a show pitch (a pitch thrown out of the strike zone on purpose to make the hitter think he will get the same pitch in the zone). Our other starters were able to jam Lee, but I couldn't. When I threw him a strike, it was going to be a breaking ball or an off-speed pitch away. What I'm saying is that there are two scouting reports on each hitter: the one you get from a scout and the one you develop on your own.

The first time I faced Hank Aaron he hit an inside fastball for a home run into the left field bleachers at County Stadium in Milwaukee. Our general manager at that time was Paul Richards, a former catcher who had some good ideas about pitching. He told me that my fastball was fast enough and had enough movement that I should throw it over the middle of the plate early in the count. "It'll probably move to the corner anyway," he said, "and once you get ahead in the count, you can throw for the corner." This was great advice and it helped me succeed as a young pitcher. But there were some hitters, Aaron among them, who could hit a fast pitch with movement when it was over the big part of the plate. During the first few years of our many confrontations, Aaron hit more homers off me than he did later on. As my control improved, I quit throwing him fastballs on the inner half—I kept the heater away and threw breaking balls. He made the adjustment and continued to get his hits, but he didn't hurt me near as much.

Aaron was not only a talented hitter; he was smart. When I was young, he figured he would get a fastball inside if he just waited for it and he was right. After I proved that I could keep the fastball away, he didn't wait for the pitch inside so much. I had to prove I could keep it away before I could get the ball in on his hands.

A lot of pitchers keep a book on the hitters they face (with laptop computers it's really pretty easy to do), but I didn't go for the scientific approach. I wasn't facing Pavlov's dogs; I was facing men with brains and free will. Sure I stayed with a simple plan for some batters, but the better hitters make adjustments. One time I was facing the Reds in the Astrodome and I struck Bernie Carbo out with a 3-2 slider down and in. Later in the game, I threw the same pitch with the same count and he hit it into the upper deck. The lesson here is to avoid a predictable pattern. Perhaps the hitters looked for Eppa Rixey's fastball when it was 2-0 or 3-1, but they had the count in their favor and if they didn't swing and make an out, they still had a chance to get a good swing at him. With two strikes in the count, a hitter doesn't have that luxury. He has to be ready for anything, fast, slow, or breaking, which is why you can often get a fastball by him with two strikes that he would hit early in the count. Sometimes I instinctively felt that I should change my pattern before he changed his. I should have done this with Carbo.

I remember one meeting we had just after changing managers. The new manager called for a pregame meeting with my catcher, the pitching coach, and me. He opened the proceedings by asking, "Okay, how are we going to pitch these guys?"

"I don't know," I said.

"No, really," he said. "Let's start with the leadoff hitter."

"I don't know how I'm going to pitch him because I'm not sure how I'm going to feel yet. If I have a good fastball, I'll challenge him. If I don't, but feel good about my curveball, I may throw him curves. We haven't faced these guys in two months. What if a guy who was crowding the plate has changed his stance and is off the plate. Should I pitch him the same way as before?"

We talked for a few more minutes and I finally said I would try to pitch to the scouting report but would have to go with my instincts too, depending on the circumstances. Since I didn't know what the circumstances would be, it would be impossible to plan my attack ahead of time. This didn't make the manager feel very comfortable, but since I was a veteran and was having a good year, we left it at that. Knowing a hitter's weakness helps a lot; assumptions you might make by looking at his stance are sometimes availing as well, but there are also some simple strategies that have stood the test of time.

I was sitting next to Tom Seaver at the Baseball Writers dinner in New York in 1999 and he told me a story that reveals how simple it can be—if you have good control. The story goes something like this:

"My first two games with the White Sox were a disaster. We had meetings before those games and our plan of attack on the hitters was intricate. We would try to throw a hitter certain pitches with nobody on base and other pitches with men on. We would try to throw certain pitches ahead in the count and other pitches behind. It was so complex I could hardly remember it all. So I asked [manager] Tony [LaRussa] if I could conduct the pitchers meeting the next time I pitched and he said yes. When we had the meeting I said, 'Well, here's how I'm going to pitch these guys. I'm going to pitch them hard inside and soft away. I'm going to go hard upstairs and soft down. And I'm going to throw them hard stuff ahead in the count and soft behind. I'm going to throw every damned one of them the same way. End of meeting.' Luckily for me, I pitched a good game and won."

I usually had a general plan in mind before I stepped onto the mound. That plan frequently changed as the game progressed. When I took the mound on July 9, 1976, I was determined to mix my pitches and locations and to forget about trying to throw the ball by the hitters. This was near the end of my career and I felt that I had been overthrowing, trying to prove I could still throw hard and had made too many mistakes going for velocity over location. In the early stages of the game, the plan worked well; but when I got to the seventh inning with a no-hitter in progress, I started feeling the adrenaline kick and noticed that my fastball was sailing and that I was able to throw it by the hitters. At that point, I abandoned my original strategy and started throwing fastball after fastball. I didn't throw anything but fastballs in the last two innings and I got the no-hitter. The last time I had one going in the ninth was in 1969, and I lost that one on a slider that was chopped into the hole at short for an infield hit. This time, I had a 6–0 lead and I was determined to get strikeouts, pop-ups, or fly balls. I didn't want to chance losing the no-hit bid on an infield hit again. But even my revised plan wasn't foolproof: I struck out Pepe Mangual for the first out in the ninth, then immediately fell behind Jim Lyttle 2-0. I came back with three straight fastballs to strike him out, which brought Mike Jorgensen to the plate. Mike was a good fastball hitter and he had hit me pretty well over the years. Still, I made up my mind to go with my bread and butter, which, at the time, was the fastball. The first pitch moved up and in on him, and he not only got around on it, he also got on top of it, pulling it on the ground to our first baseman, Bob Watson.

That last out came more on luck than design, but it does serve to illustrate a point that we made time and again with our pitchers when I was managing: Attack the hitter's weakness, but when in doubt, go with your own strength. It also shows how important it is to monitor your pitches as you go along and to emphasize the ones that are working well. In the postgame interview, I told announcer Loel Passe that I didn't throw an off-speed pitch after the fourth inning, which is exactly the opposite of the strategy that I was determined to employ at the beginning of the game.

In the minor leagues it is hard to get a scouting report on a player because you don't face him many times. If you stay in the majors for a few years, though, you start facing the same guys over and over again. A lot of times, the hitter's approach to the pitcher is based upon the pitcher's reputation: When I was managing the Astros, I told our guys to wait on a fat pitch from Greg Maddux, and they looked at me as if I were a lunatic. But I had seen Maddux on TV enough to know that he throws a lot of pitches up and out over the plate. He gets away with a lot of these pitches because the hitters are surprised to see them, and aren't ready to swing. After four or five winning seasons with very few walks, Maddux became known as a control pitcher. As a result, he developed a reputation. When hitters step into the box against him, they never even think about getting a walk. They are aggressive and it plays right into Maddux's hand. His control is excellent. Most of his pitches are on or near the corners. He throws a lot of pitches that look like they're going to be out of the strike zone and then break into the zone at the last second, and he throws a lot of pitches that look like they are going to be strikes but then break out of the zone. The hitters tend to swing at the balls and take the strikes and it must frustrate them when Maddux throws a pitch down the middle and they just watch it go by for a strike. Even after I told guys to look for the mistakes, they never really did it. I don't think they believed he would throw a fat pitch until they understood—too late. Our catcher, Brad Ausmus, who is one of the most intelligent players in the league, couldn't hit Maddux at all. Brad was trying to figure Maddux out and got swindled every time.

I had a couple of years where I pitched well enough to get help from the hitters. When they think you're capable of throwing a nasty pitch, they want to hit the first pitch they think they can handle. They don't want to get two strikes in the count because they don't want to strike out. They often did just what I wanted them to do: swing at a pitch on the corner and make an out. If they think you're wild, though, they will do the opposite: wait for a pitch down the middle and knock the tar out of it. After watching several thousand games on television I have come to the conclusion that hitters should wait for a pitch down the middle all the time, against every pitcher. If the guy is good enough to keep the ball on the corners throughout the game, you're not going to hit him hard anyway. I can't tell you how many times I have seen hitters take a fastball right down the middle off Maddux and then get mad at themselves. They weren't expecting a mistake and so they failed to take advantage of it.

What a great feeling it is to throw a fat pitch to a good hitter and have him take it for a strike; I could not have done this against Aaron early in my career, but I might have gotten away with it later on. It all depends on what the batter is looking for when he steps into the batter's box. If he's any good, he will be sitting on a certain pitch or location. Good pitchers get lucky because the hitters aren't always prepared for a fastball down the middle. They're looking for anything but a mistake!

Since the location of a pitch is the most important of the many variables, the ability to throw the ball where you want it to go is the primary concern. It is much easier to do this if you can repeat your delivery time and again. That's why Mazzone wants the Braves starters to work from the mound so much between starts. What I would call the standard, or "Spalding Guide," delivery is a good place to start, but most big league pitchers throw with some deviation from the standard. Tom Seaver was known for a delivery he called "drop and drive," because he dropped his weight onto his push-off leg so severely that his right knee scraped the ground. Using his strong legs to improve the thrust he generated toward the plate, Seaver started a relentless journey to Cooperstown in 1967. Another Hall of Fame pitcher, Don Sutton, said that Seaver could drop and drive all he wanted. "I prefer," said Sutton, "to tilt and topple," and that is exactly the way his pitching motion looked. When Seaver was with the Reds, one of their young pitchers, Frank Pastore, practiced his delivery so much that the only way you could differentiate between his and Seaver's was to look at their faces. (And, of course, their results.) In 2001 the Braves had a young left-hander named Damian Moss who is a Glavine look-alike. I guess they decided he wouldn't measure up because they traded him to the Giants. I don't recommend copying another pitcher. I think you have to start with your natural throwing motion— the way you would throw the ball if you were playing catch or throwing to one of the bases. Once you know what your arm angle should be, you work to incorporate it into a delivery that has the coordination and tempo to produce good control. Find your own way, not somebody else's.

Just after I signed with the Colt 45's, our general manager, Paul Richards, came down to the Rookie League in Cocoa, Florida, to watch me pitch. He told me that the fastball and curveball that I had taught myself as a youngster were good enough for the major leagues. "But," he said, "you are going to have to develop a change-up to get the best big league hitters out." He suggested I try the slip pitch that he had taught Bob Bruce and several other pitchers with the Colt 45's. The method was to take your fastball grip and then push the ball back in your hand, removing the fingertip pressure and holding the ball mostly with the base of the fingers and the thumb. Then you would take your hand and rotate it clockwise so that your fingers would be on the outside of the ball. Since there was nothing on top of the ball, it would slip out when you released it—hence the "slip" pitch. I tried it and it really slipped—it slipped out everywhere, high and low, in and out. I could get the "fast arm, slow pitch" result he was looking for, but I couldn't throw it for a strike. Paul just laughed. "Keep working on it," he said. "I'll be back in a month or so to see how you're doing."

I practiced the slip pitch for about a week and perhaps I would have mastered it if I had stayed with it. Though I was certain that it was not the pitch for me, I was just as certain that I needed a change-up. I have big hands—even in high school, I fooled around with a forkball, spreading my index and middle finger to reduce the spin on the ball. I started experimenting on a variation, using a loose forkball grip and the straight change concept of pulling the pitch down instead of extending my arm forward and throwing it out. I soon came up with a pitch that had loose slider spin, just like the slip pitch. When Richards came back and asked to see my slip pitch, I hid the ball in my glove and threw the slow forkball I had taught myself. "That's it!" he exclaimed. "You've got it."

Most good pitchers are, to a large degree, self-taught. The coach can teach, but only the student can learn. When I coach young pitchers, I tell them that what I say isn't gospel. It is only a starting point in the process of learning to pitch.

When Richards showed me how to throw a slider I picked it up immediately. He told me to throw it like a football, with spiral spin. I found it easy to do and marveled at the way it moved and how hard I could throw it. As the years went by, I found out that I would get more downward movement by gripping the ball tighter with the tip of my index finger.

I had a good slider but Larry Andersen had the best slider I have ever seen. He was a relief pitcher and I watched him work during the height of his career with the Astros. I would estimate that 90 percent of the pitches he threw were sliders—he could throw it up, down, in, out. He almost had to throw it when he was behind in the count because he had better control with his slider than he did with his fastball. When I asked Larry how he threw his slider he said that he gripped it tightly with his middle finger and crimped his hand toward his head and threw it as hard as he could. Since then, I have asked a lot of pitchers who have good sliders how they threw them. All but one, Mike Jackson, said they gripped it more tightly with their middle finger. What it boils down to is that there are as many ways to hold the ball and throw various pitches as there are hands and arms.

Sometimes it seems like the universe is aligned against you when you're on the mound. The umpire misses a call on a 3-2 pitch and you walk a batter. The next guy gets a checked-swing hit. You try to force the runner at third on a bunt and he beats the throw. Now there are bases loaded with nobody out and you haven't even done anything wrong yet. One of the best pieces of advice in a situation like this is to tell the pitcher that no matter how much trouble he is in, he can get out of it with one good pitch. In this case, the pitch produces a double play and you get the next guy out, limiting the other team to one run.

Speaking of great escapes, I got a lesson early in my career from our second baseman, Joe Morgan. I was pitching in San Diego with a short lead and the game was in the late stages. There was a man on first with nobody out. The batter hit a ground ball to Joe— a perfect double play ball—and Joe kicked it. The next batter hit a ground ball to Joe—a perfect double play ball—and Joe kicked that one too. Now I had the bases loaded with nobody out when I should have been back in the dugout. After the second boot, Joe came walking to the mound. I was pissed and really didn't want to talk to him, but I listened and he said something I have never forgotten and have told numerous young pitchers.

"I'm sure glad you're pitching," he said. "Because you're the one guy who can get us out of this."

The one guy. Us! I can't tell you how good that made me feel. I pitched out of it allowing only one run, and we won the game. And I can't tell you how good that made *him* feel.

Another lesson I learned in the first few years was to forget about how I threw warming up. One time Tom Griffin asked me how I felt as I came into the dugout in St. Louis. I just rolled my eyes—my arm was sore and I didn't have squat. Once the game started, I had to bear down and I started hitting spots and throwing harder. The hitters brought something out of me that I couldn't simulate in my warm-ups, and I ended up pitching a shutout that day. Another day in New York, Griffin looked awful warming up. Our bullpen coach, Buddy Hancken, came running into the dugout ahead of Griffin. "You better get someone warmed up quick," he advised our manager, Harry Walker, "Griffin doesn't have a thing." It turned out that Griff pitched a shutout himself that day and struck out thirteen batters.

That was back when I was writing songs and we were singing on the bus. I penned this one to the tune of "If You Knew Susie:"

> *If you know Buddy, like he knows everybody*
> *Oh, boy, is he ever bright*
> *He said of Griffin*
> *His arm will stiffen*
> *He won't get anybody out tonight*
> *His arm is hurting that I can see*
> *He's not too fast, he'll never last*
> *Don't you agree*
> *That I'm not blind*
> *Yes I'm a mastermind*
> *Oh, boy what a coach*

Another thing to remember is that a good session in the bullpen doesn't ensure a well-pitched game. One year I was going to pitch the second game of the season in Cincinnati and a rookie named Doug Konieczny was going to pitch game 3. "If I can just get through the first inning," he told me, "I'll be all right."

"Don't worry about that," I said. "It's not going to happen. I've been in this league for eight years and I've never been knocked out in the first inning." Well, guess what? It didn't happen to him but it happened to me. And I felt as good in the bullpen that day as I ever had in my life.

There were a few times during my career where we were playing just to complete the schedule. We were out of the race and so was our opponent. There was no crowd to speak of and I didn't feel like I was up for the game. After getting hard lessons a few times in this type of situation, I vowed not to let it happen again. The next time I felt that way was in San Diego. As I was walking to the bullpen to warm up, I knew my heart and soul weren't with me. Instead of wading into the game uninspired, I kicked myself in the ankle. No kidding; I actually kicked myself hard enough to make it hurt. The wake-up call seemed to help. Pain provided the incentive I needed to pitch a good game.

With the modern trend toward using setup men and closers, the importance of pitching a complete game has diminished. Still, when you're a starting pitcher, you have to concentrate for at least two hours if you are going to succeed. Shortly after the 1996 season, I was talking to Darryl Kile and he asked me what he could do over the winter to improve for the next season. I told him to play golf.

"No, really," he said.

"Play golf," I reiterated.

"Seriously, what does playing golf have to do with pitching?"

"Everything," I said. "First you need power off the tee. That's your fastball. Then you need accuracy to hit the green. That's your control. Then you need finesse for chip shots and putts. That's your off-speed and breaking pitches. Then you need mental toughness. I'm talking about maintaining your concentration over the course of nine innings. Or, in golf, eighteen holes. You can't let one bad hole or bad inning beat you. You have to put the mistake pitches and bad breaks behind you. What if your perfect approach shot hits a sprinkler head and kicks sideways into a trap? Do you maintain composure, or do you flub your trap shot?"

"My wife is going to like this," he said with a grin. " 'I have to play golf again, honey,' Dierk's orders."

"Hey, I'm serious," I said. "And I'm talking about real golf. By the rules. No mulligans or mad balls. Establish a handicap and try to get it down throughout the winter. Then you will be ready for spring training."

"And divorced," he quipped.

"Ask her if she wants you to pitch like a Hall of Famer like Tom Seaver, Jim Palmer, or Don Sutton. Ask her if she wants you to pitch like Greg Maddux, Tom Glavine, or John Smoltz. All these guys are great golfers. Do you think it's a coincidence? Think of how much money you will make. Flynn'll [Darryl's wife] be driving you to the golf course and won't come back to pick you up until you have played eighteen and hit a couple buckets of balls."

I don't know how much golf DK played that winter. But he did win nineteen games in 1997 and started the first game of the play-offs for us against Maddux.

When Don Drysdale set a major league record by pitching fifty-eight straight innings of shutout baseball, he remarked on how he couldn't believe hitters were so stupid. They kept falling for his tricks, just like they did for Seaver's when he went hard in, slow away; hard ahead, slow behind; hard up, and slow down. Pitching for zeros instead of strikeouts can actually be easier than pitching with passion—sometimes it's not so much getting the guy out as letting him get himself out. Seaver was near the end of his career when he held his strategic meeting with the White Sox and it's likely that he didn't know all of the simple truths he espoused in that meeting when he began his career with the Mets. Most pitchers come up throwing hard and snapping off breaking balls that can be knee-buckling when thrown properly; as they age they lose a little arm speed and have to come up with some new tricks. I came up a power pitcher and after a few bouts with tendinitis, learned to use power when I had it and to survive most of the time when I didn't. To survive without a flash-dazzling fastball, a pitcher must learn the nuances of changing speeds and creating subtle movement on his fastball. Above all, he must have good enough control to keep the ball out of the danger zone without walking too many hitters.

Sometimes it's prudent to walk one hitter in favor of pitching to the next, especially with two outs and a home run hitter at the plate. The last few years I pitched, I was behind in the count a lot—especially to good left-handed hitters. I wasn't wild, just careful. When I fell behind I tried to take a little speed off my sinker and throw it low and away, the idea being that when the hitter becomes more aggressive, looking for hard stuff, I become less aggressive by taking a little speed off and thowing what we called a "dead fish fastball." If the hitter tried to jack it out of the yard, he usually pulled it on the ground for an out or perhaps a single. Like Rixey, I tried to prey on the hitters' long-ball lust.

One of the best hitters I had to face at the end of my career was Ted Simmons of the Cardinals. I still remember a game in the Astrodome when I got him out the first time on a cut fastball, moving in on his hands. The next time I started with the same pitch twice; both were inside and he took both ball one and ball two. The third pitch was the dead fish and I threw it exactly where I wanted to, expecting him to hit a ground ball to second base. Instead he waited back and hit the ball precisely the way he should have— a sharp ground ball through the left side of the infield. If I had been a showboat I would have tipped my cap to him. I got a chance to tell him what a fine piece of hitting I considered it to be the following year when I was traded to St. Louis.

Pitching carefully can also conserve energy. I doubt Tom Glavine throws full speed more than 15 or 20 percent of the time. He often throws harder at the end of a game than in the beginning. These days, most starting pitchers go all out all the time and they reach 100 pitches in the sixth inning, already getting tired. Since they rely on power pitching, they become ineffective when they run out of gas. That's why you don't see many complete games.

Glavine is known for nibbling at the corners and refusing to throw a fat pitch even if it means walking a batter. It may be smart to pitch around one hitter to get to the next guy, but it's something else entirely to pitch around everyone. The difference is that the former approach is strategic, and the latter is defensive.

During our first year at Enron Field [now Minute Maid Park], I thought most of our pitchers became defensive. Our starters would hit the 100-pitch mark in the fifth inning. They were afraid of everyone and their body language stated it loud and clear. I was known as a manager that went longer with starters than most and I think we finished last in relief appearances in all three of my seasons managing in the Astrodome. But as the first season at Enron unfolded, I went to the bullpen a lot. It seemed like the pitchers felt vulnerable to the home run ball all the time. If I could get one good inning out of a reliever, I occasionally went to another pitcher in the next inning, even when I didn't have to. If you stand out there waiting for the ax to fall it will, and our pitchers acted as if the guillotine would fall at any moment.

Every time someone suggested that we didn't have enough ground ball pitchers, I said that what we needed was more good pitchers. Scott Elarton was our best starter that season and he was a fly ball pitcher. What he did that most of the other pitchers did not do, was pitch aggressively. What kills you at Enron Field and Coors Field is not the home runs but the walks that precede them. In the past two seasons, Astros pitchers have been much more aggressive in the strike zone at home. One thing that helped was bringing up guys like Wade Miller and Roy Oswalt who never experienced the luxury of the Astrodome and weren't afraid to throw strikes. Whether you are pitching in a National Park or a Little League Park, you have to attack the hitter aggressively often enough to let him know you aren't afraid. If the wind is blowing out at Wrigley, there will still be a winning and losing pitcher. The other guy has to deal with the same conditions you do, so you'd best get out there and get after it.

I must say that there are more good hitters in the game now than I can ever remember, especially power hitters. It used to be that you would get a break at the end of the order facing hitters, usually catchers and middle infielders, who couldn't hurt you with the long ball. That is not true anymore. Nowadays, with weight training, smaller ballparks, and lighter bats, even the hitters at the end of the order are dangerous. There is precious little wiggle room in most modern lineups.

Good pitchers like Glavine, Maddux, Schilling, Johnson, and Clemens can pitch well when they're tired; their good control allows them to succeed without going full bore. Most pitchers don't have good enough control to pitch this way, and they would get mad at themselves if they gave up a hit throwing less than full speed. Generally speaking, the hits they give up are in the big diamond, not the small triangles. If they threw less than full speed with good control, however, they would be able to pitch deeper into the game. This is what we encouraged our pitchers to do and when we played in the Astrodome they were usually able to do it. Once we moved to the bandbox downtown, they seemed to lose their confidence. Although the circumstances vary from one ballpark to another, the name of the game is still winning: You can survive and win in a small park just as you can in a big one, but you must have good enough control to throw your breaking ball or change-up over the plate when you are behind the hitter and be able to hit the corners with your best fastball at will. At one point, we had our pitchers chart every pitch they threw so that they would be able to see the results, right or wrong. I talked to many of them about being aggressive. "I'd much rather pitch here than at Dodger Stadium," I said. "At least you can count on your team scoring runs." I didn't mind winning 8–6 at Wrigley with the wind blowing out. I much preferred it to losing 2–1 in Los Angeles.

The emergence of the setup man and the multiyear contract have cut into the workload of many starting pitchers who could, given the chance, pitch more complete games. When I was pitching, I hated to hand the ball to any pitcher other than the closer. Most of the time, our middle relievers weren't very good: Back then, all the best pitching prospects were used as starters. Young pitchers were never groomed to be relievers like they are these days. More often than not now, the long men in the bullpens and the setup relief pitchers are young guys with good arms. Nowadays, you frequently see a young pitcher with a great arm in the eighth inning and another one in the ninth. There seem to be fewer good starting pitchers now than when I played and more good relievers. Most managers prefer to go to the bullpen in the eighth and ninth inning now. This seems to help the relief pitchers stay sharp and it lightens the starters' workload. Finally, when you have a guy signed to a five-year guaranteed contract, you don't want to blow his arm out throwing 150 or more pitches in a game. I pitched into extra innings several times during my career and Juan Marichal and Warren Spahn once dueled for sixteen innings before Willie Mays finally hit a home run to give the Giants a 1–0 win. Do you think these two Hall of Fame pitchers were expending energy to the max on every pitch in that game? Think again. They were pitching for results, not for radar gun readings. They were pitching intelligently, not passionately.

During the Big Red Machine days of the 1970s, Sparky Anderson employed the bullpen extensively. He had better relief pitchers than starters and his strategy was not only sound, it set an example that became the norm; Whitey Herzog did the same thing with his bullpen in St. Louis. Throwing legions of pitchers at the enemy has become a standard practice now, and managers will probably operate this way for years to come. Still, knowing when to pull a pitcher is a tricky proposition. When I was in the booth I could usually tell when a guy was at the end of the line by watching his control on the television monitor. As a manager you can't see if a pitcher is hitting corners. You can use pitch speed information that is posted on the scoreboard to determine when a guy is losing velocity, but the most important thing, control, is much more difficult to evaluate. When we got near the end of a game, I usually asked the catcher if the pitcher still had command of the strike zone. It was hard for me to accept the practice of using pitchers just for a fresh arm and I seldom took pitchers out of the game when they were effective, especially in the Dome—sometimes I let a relief pitcher bat so he could keep pitching. I know from experience that some days you have good stuff and control, and some days you don't. I hated to take a chance on a guy having an off day when I already had a guy on the mound who was throwing well.

Once in Cincinnati, I just about left Roy Oswalt in too long. He had come into a game in Cincinnati in the seventh inning, trying to protect a short lead. Roy was a rookie at the time and he was near the bottom of our pecking order. He wasn't our setup man, but he was making a good case for himself, stringing up zeros with apparent ease. In this game, he hit 98 mph on the radar gun and had good control. He overpowered the Reds in the seventh and eighth innings. I let him hit in the eighth and when he went out for the ninth, I had Billy Wagner start throwing. Roy got into trouble immediately and I went out to see how he was feeling. He was still throwing hard and he wanted to stay in. The Reds had the tying and winning runs on base with two outs, and when Sean Casey came up I finally called on Wagner to get the last out, which he did. One disadvantage of using a closer is that no one else on the team ever pitches in the ninth with a short lead. When your closer is overworked or injured, someone else has to do the job and they usually have trouble. Oddly enough, when Wagner was injured in 1998 and 2000, our bullpen had a good save ratio. But when he was in the bullpen, it seemed like every pitcher, starter or reliever, who worked the ninth inning was looking over his shoulder.

Everyone agrees that you win with good pitching. But good pitching isn't just having Maddux and Smoltz or Schilling and Johnson. Good pitching is a collective effort that involves the whole staff. In my day, that meant nine or ten guys. Now, with greater emphasis on the bullpen, it means eleven or twelve. It is critical to establish your pitching early in the season and to find roles for the pitchers. When I started managing, I told our relief pitchers that their role was trying to help us win games. I was prepared to use anyone, except for Wagner, in any inning up to the ninth, but I soon found out that the guys were uncomfortable unless they knew when they would likely be used. I tried to designate a long man, who came into a game early, if necessary, and pitched three to five innings, and I tried to use the other guys in a consistent way, some pitching mostly in the seventh and some in the eighth. When you get some positive momentum going pitchers assume their roles and it can be contagious. One pitcher feeds off the others, and sometimes picks up one of his mates by pitching out of trouble and not allowing inherited runners to score. But when the momentum starts going awry, the glue that holds the staff together disintegrates and you can almost hear each domino as it hits the floor.

The point is, it's a team game. I've talked about the teamwork within a pitching staff, but there must be teamwork between the pitchers and the players too. On the good teams, hitters and pitchers put their differences aside and work together. Sometimes they even become friends. If an opposing pitcher hits one of your players on purpose, and you know it is intentional, you have to hit one of theirs, even though you might get kicked out of the game. A lot of times I tried to discourage this when I was managing because I wasn't certain the initial hit was intentional and I wanted to keep my pitcher in the game. But, as a pitcher, you still have to win the respect of your teammates and retaliating is one way to do it. Another way is to pitch out of trouble that they have created such as the situation I encountered in San Diego with Joe Morgan.

Some pitchers thrive on the emotional edge, like Don Drysdale, Bob Gibson, and my former teammate, Don Wilson. In another way, the Mad Hungarian, Al Hrabosky, did the same thing. By creating anger in the opposing team, these pitchers brought themselves up to a higher level. I think it is important to learn to operate on this level because it will seek you out from time to time whether you want it or not. I preferred the "let sleeping dogs lie" approach.

It was almost impossible to take that approach when the Astros played the Mets in 1968. In just the fourth game of the season that year, Tommie Agee took Joe Morgan out on a slide, breaking up a double play, and we thought he was out of line—out of the baseline, and overly violent about it. Joe ended up having knee surgery and missed the entire year. After that there was an undercurrent of animosity whenever we played them. Part of it was the Agee slide; I think part of it was the natural rivalry of the two expansion clubs. Later that year, in a game in the Astrodome, Doug Rader hit a sure double down the third base line. As he approached second base, he hesitated and then when he saw the left fielder lobbing the ball in, kicked into high gear and sped toward third. The throw got there a little late and Doug hit third baseman Kevin Collins with an elbow to the jaw as he hit the bag with a pop-up slide. The Mets thought it was an intentional act and they were outraged. After some jawing back and forth, our manager, Harry Walker, ran out to third base and started arguing with the umpire and ended up yelling at Mets third base coach Joe Pignatano. Piggy shoved Walker and when Harry came back at him the benches emptied. In the ensuing brawl, Don Cardwell blindsided Rader with a haymaker and the whole pile came right down on top of him. When it was over, Doug looked like he had been in a prizefight. After that, Tom Seaver hit Norm Miller with a pitch and I hit Cleon Jones. Jones got his revenge in the eighth when he doubled in two runs, knocking me out of the game. We hung on to win 4–3 and I was happy to get the win but I did not enjoy the atmosphere at all.

When I came down from the booth, I was surprised to find so much civility in the dugout. When I was playing, it was not uncommon for players to scream at each other from the dugout. I know the Mets were screaming that day, and we were too. When I looked back at the game story in the *Houston Chronicle*, there was a sequence of photos of Rader's slide; as he was coming up off the bag he was looking down and his elbow was about an inch from Collins's face. I'm sure he came in hard on purpose, but I doubt he could have delivered the blow with such stunning accuracy without looking. Collins was out cold for a few minutes and ended up with a broken jaw. Roy Campanella once said that you have to be a man to play major league baseball, but you have to have a little boy in you too. I liked the boy part much better.

When you take the mound, you must be prepared physically, mentally, and emotionally. If you are, there is no better place on the planet. But if you are unprepared, the mound can be as lonely as a prison cell. The only way to learn how to pitch is by doing it. Working off the mound is good practice, but when you have to face a power hitter and there's a base stealer on first base, you have a situation that's impossible to practice on the side. It is also to impossible to practice pitching with the specter of a brawl errupting if you happen to hit a batter with a pitch.

I am often asked to coach youngsters in our neighborhood, and I'm not sure that they want to put in the time it takes to be an ace. Pitching is like real estate: It always boils down to the same thing— location, location, location. I have asked countless major league pitchers to rank the importance of three variables—pitch location, pitch movement, and pitch velocity—and every single one of them has placed location above movement and speed. So how do we obtain good location? Practice, practice, practice. This is where I lose most of my students. They come to me with decent pitching mechanics, looking for a secret formula, an easy fix, and they leave with instructions to throw every day. I advise them to have a baseball and glove with them while they are watching television and to practice switching from a fastball grip to a curveball or a change-up grip easily, without looking at the ball. If you want to be a good pitcher, you have to become one with the ball. If you really want to excel, you will perfect your delivery to the point where you can throw strikes with your eyes closed. If you don't believe me, get a mental image of Tom Seaver and Fernando Valenzuela: Seaver looked down during his delivery and did not pick up the catcher until he was about to release the pitch; Valenzuela did the opposite, looking up during his delivery. Watch the pitchers in any major league game and you will see that many of the good ones don't stare at the catcher's mitt throughout their pitching motion. They know where they're going to throw the ball because they have practiced so much that they have a mental image of the ball in flight before they release it. The best golfers, bowlers, billiards players, and jump shooters do the same thing.

Last summer, I watched my son, Ryan, play ball for his high school team and I was appalled to learn that his coach called every pitch for every pitcher. Then I learned that all the other coaches were doing the same thing. I don't know how long this has been going on but if it has been standard procedure for any length of time, it could explain the lack of good pitching in the major leagues today. If you want to steer the ship, you have to be at the helm. After Billy Wagner had elbow surgery during the 2000 season, we used Octavio Dotel as our closer. Dotel gave up game-winning home runs in two straight games and, after the second one, he was really distraught. He asked if he could speak with me and with Burt Hooton. We met with him in my office for nearly half an hour. He said that he felt indecisive on the mound and didn't trust our catchers to call the right pitch. He wanted us to call pitches for him.

"How can I call pitches for you?" I asked. "I can't even see where the batter is standing in the batter's box. I don't know how you feel. Whether you think you can get your breaking balls over for strikes or you think you have a good fastball."

Burt told him much the same thing. Still, Octavio felt like he was throwing the wrong pitches and blowing the game for the whole team. I finally closed the meeting by telling him he was going to have to learn to call his own pitches if he wanted to learn to be the best pitcher he was capable of being. We never called a pitch for him and he got out of his slump. With his lively fastball, he was bound to succeed most of the time. In this instance, he just needed to be patient, but that's a difficult task for a young pitcher.

It may also be difficult to concentrate on where you're going if you are riding shotgun in a car to a destination across town and there are many turns involved. If your driver says, "I can't make it tomorrow," you will feel lost: Sure, you were in the car, but you weren't watching every turn. It's the same way with a pitcher. If he always throws what his coach wants him to throw, he will learn slowly, but if he charts the course and steers the car, he will learn a lot faster. It's really a shame that coaches in youth leagues call pitches. They are only retarding their pitchers' progress. What makes it laughable is that most of the coaches were not pitchers. Tell me this: How does a coach, from his position on the bench, know when his pitcher feels like he can get his curveball over the plate?

In spring training, I used our intersquad games to force our pitchers to think for themselves. I told them that the sign would be "two" for a curveball on every pitch. "If you want to throw a different pitch, add to the two by wiping your shirt with your glove. Each time you wipe, the sign goes up one so that if you wipe your shirt twice it will be 'four' for a change-up. If you want to subtract, wipe your leg. One wipe makes it 'one' for a fastball, and so forth." Using this method I was able to get the pitchers to call their own games, but when the real exhibition games started, they all went right back to shaking off signs with their heads. A lot of them simply threw whatever the catcher called for. If you have good stuff and good control, this can work just fine—good stuff on the corners will get hitters out even if they know what pitch is coming. When I was at my best, I felt strongly that one pitch or another was appropriate for a specific situation. Sure, I wiped to a different pitch and then had my chosen pitch hit over the fence many times, but at least I was in charge of my own destiny and the team was getting the best I could offer, both mentally and physically. All the successful starting pitchers I have known have called their own games.

The modern approach has changed the pitcher's viewpoint. He doesn't have to think as much. Doug Drabek won the Cy Young Award when he was with the Pirates, and when he came over to the Astros, I asked him how he liked getting signs from the bench concerning the holding of runners. "I like it," he said. "That way, all

I have to think about is my pitch." Doug was one of the best pitchers in the league at the time, but I think he would have been even better if he had been in the driver's seat. When I was managing, I think we were the only team in the major leagues that didn't have a five-point system for holding runners (hold the ball, step off, throw to first, slide step, pitch out). I had just two signs: Hold the runner, and pitch out. As with the five-point plan, I gave the sign to the catcher, he gave it to the pitcher. I wanted the pitcher to know when it was a base-stealing situation and to learn how to deal with it on his own. A pitcher should know when a runner is likely to try for a steal. But just in case, I reminded him by yelling at him and pointing to the runner. Then it was his responsibility to hold the runner. He could do it by using a slide step, holding the ball at the set position for a couple of beats, stepping off, or quick pitching. Most of our guys didn't work the base runners all that much; they focused their mental and physical efforts on the batter, which was exactly what I wanted them to do.

Anyone who has been a baseball fan very long has heard the assertion that pitching is anywhere from 70 to 90 percent of the game. When you think about it, it seems a breach of logic. It is patently obvious that half the game is the runs you score and the other half is the runs you allow. Pitching, however, is the most important component of runs allowed. So if it's, say, 90 percent of defense and fielding is the other 10 percent, pitching is only 45 percent of the entire game. So why would anyone with half a brain say that pitching is more than half the game?

In the early 1990s, the Detroit Tigers finished near the top of the American League in runs scored every year and never finished higher than third in the standings. That team looked more like a herd of elephants than a pride of tigers. It would have won the league title in weight lifting, but was too slow to cover ground on defense, which made a shaky pitching staff look totally incompetent. Conversely, the 1906 Chicago White Sox team finished last in the American League in team batting average and first in the standings. That year they defeated the Cubs in the World Series despite the fact that the Cubs won 116 games, the most wins ever by any team in a single season. This early vintage Cubs team led the National League in both hitting and pitching, and over the long haul they would have beaten the Sox, but in an individual series any team with great pitching can overcome a team with better hitting.

With Greg Maddux, Tom Glavine, and John Smoltz leading the way, the Braves were the best pitching team in the National League for the last decade. It is no coincidence that they have gone to the playoffs every year, despite the fact that their offense has been less consistent—good in some years, just average in others. Having observed these Braves from the broadcast booth and the dugout I can tell you that they are a confident team. Just about every single day, they think they can win with only a few runs, even when they are facing Randy Johnson or Curt Schilling. They know they can win because they have the deep-seated belief that their own pitcher, whoever that may be, can shut the other team down. Even if they were facing Cy Young in his prime, they would think they were going to win before the game even started. This is why pitching is more than half of the game; it isn't logical—it's psychological. The Braves know that if they make the defensive plays, they won't have to score many runs to win.

On a poor pitching team, the position players run out onto the field in the first inning every day thinking they will have to score a lot of runs to win. Over the course of the long season, a team with poor pitching feels the heavy load every day. Sure, they will get some well-pitched games and they will out-hit their opponent occasionally. But the burden will still grow heavier day by day, week by week until it becomes unbearable. No matter what we do in life, we do it better if we expect to succeed. Confidence is everything and there is no way to fake it. Even if you have Knute Rockne delivering a pregame pep talk, you will not be confident unless you really feel it deep down inside. Hitting brings excitement to the game; pitching and fielding bring confidence and wins.

CHAPTER 4

Managing

Of the basic managerial gifts—passion, character, brains and
wisdom—the least valuable, at least as a guiding virtue, is
intelligence. In baseball, as in the rest of life, brains make a
good servant but a poor master.

—THOMAS BOSWELL

FORMER PITCHER JOHN CURTIS once said that the manager
has become a wishbone between the players and the owners. And if
the players and owners are unable to crack the bone, the fans and
the media are sure to step in and apply the necessary pressure. I
have noticed that the president of the United States, shouldering
the burden of so many problems, goes gray and wrinkled at an
alarming rate. I don't know how my time in the dugout and in the
spotlight affected my appearance, but I know I aged more than five
years during my tenure at the helm with the Astros. The gray hair
at the temples came as it would have anyway and the wrinkles were
inevitable too, but the turmoil inside grew like a fungus. It came on
slow, so that I hardly noticed it. It increased as I realized how many
things I couldn't control. I gained twenty pounds, and as the burden
grew, both literally and figuratively, my frustration increased.

When I started out, I really thought I could make a difference. And, in a small way, perhaps I did. But I didn't even come
close to winning the players over to my way of thinking. I tried to

encourage a lot of subtle changes in the way the game is tradi- tionally played and I failed: Our runners didn't get good jumps on the hit-and-run play; we never bunted with runners on first and third; most of our pitchers never developed the kind of control that would allow us to crowd our defense to one side of the field or the other; we even had trouble getting most of them to call their own game. My goal was to form a team that had nine cap- tains on the field, all thinking together and playing a smart brand of baseball, and although it was somewhat comforting to see that the teams we played had the same problems, it was still frustrat- ing. I learned that many players don't have the most important tool—focused intelligence—and that it is impossible to teach it.

I think it was Gene Mauch who said that the worst day of his managing career was the day he realized that the players didn't care as much about winning as he did. I never got to that point because we had a lot of players who brought the devotion of a saint to the ballpark every day, a group that included all of our stars. But caring about it doesn't make you play better unless you can find better ways to accomplish that goal. I encouraged indepen- dent thinking and made some specific suggestions, but our players played the game the way they always had. And as the years un- folded, I found myself becoming more conventional. I was going in their direction when it should have been the other way around.

My predecessor, Terry Collins, was a stormy petrel. His strate- gic ideas were more conventional than mine, but he still felt frus- tration when his vision of the team went awry. I internalized my regrets while he expressed his loud and clear. When things went wrong during the course of a ball game, say a pitcher failed to get a bunt down, Terry screeched like an owl. He had plenty of passion, but he may have been short of wisdom. The players heard his in- vective too many times. I would venture a guess that when that pitcher was trying to get a bunt down, that pitcher could already imagine the as yet unspoken outrage of his manager. This type of pressure might motivate some guys, but it would almost certainly inhibit others; I have played for screamers and it is no fun. I knew I would not go that route.

It just so happens that Ryan, my eighteen-year-old son, is

playing for this type of coach now. I had a fiery coach in high school too and a few managers who were screamers in the big leagues. One day, after a particularly poor performance, my high school coach held a team meeting before practice. He called us every name in the book, and in so doing, used two of his favorite expressions: "You can lead a horse to water but you can't make him drink" and "You can't make chicken salad out of chicken shit." I had pitched that game and was the prime culprit in the loss, but when our coach got to the "chicken salad" part I started to laugh and, not wanting to get caught, lowered my head and muffled the sound. I suppose my body was jiggling a bit in the process and my coach said, "You ought to hang your head, Dierker." I guess he thought I was crying.

Another time, I was playing for Harry "The Hat" Walker, another passionate manager. Sometimes Harry got so mad when we played poorly that he gathered the team in the clubhouse after the game and lambasted us before he allowed the writers to come in. If you do this sort of thing three or four times during the course of the season it can be effective, because during the 162-game campaign a team can lose its edge and sort of go through the motions from time to time. If this is the case, a scolding might have value. But a manager who erupts on a weekly basis loses his audience. I remember one time when Harry was really ticked: He used every epithet in the English language and then, right at the end, he said we looked like "Tom Thumb going downhill on a scooter." I still laugh when I recall that tirade. It was like being beaned by a Nerf ball.

After a while, most managers get a reputation for being a player's manager or a management tool. I think I was the former, although I'm not sure the players felt that way. There were a few times when I was urged to get tough with the guys and I hardly ever did. It's easier to face the heat from upstairs once in a while than to face it in the clubhouse on a daily basis. I was never criticized in the media for being too lenient although they probably would have blasted me if they ever picked up on it. My feeling was (and is) that you win or lose because of the quality of your players and the effort they give. If you don't have the horses, you can't lead them to water, and if you have too much chicken shit, you can't make a salad. I only had two or three postgame tirades in my five years. I guess I was lucky to inherit great players who also played with great desire. Rarely did we lose a game to laziness.

Even if you have enough talent you can screw it up by creating a noxious atmosphere in the clubhouse. All you have to do to lose control is scream a few times about something a player fails to do. Everyone knows failure is baseball's middle name: It's not that easy to get a bunt down and even the best hitters fail to get runners home from third base with less than two outs. As a matter of fact, I still recall the first two innings of a game I pitched against the Cardinals in the Astrodome. Lou Brock tripled for openers and I stranded him on third. Tim McCarver tripled to lead off the second and I stranded him too. I wonder what Cardinals manager Red Shoendienst was saying right about then. Knowing Red, I doubt he said much. Terry Collins would have blown a gasket.

Getting an approval rating from the players can be difficult, even if you give them everything and take nothing. As Mark Twain once said, "If you take a hungry dog and feed it, it will not bite you. The same cannot be said of man." There are biting dogs on both the management's and the players' side of the fence, and tiptoeing between them requires perfect balance. I probably lost a little in the area of acceptance by being too lenient, and it took me a year or so to realize that I couldn't make everyone like me. That took some of the fun out of it. It was kind of like being a parent: You want to provide tough love, but tough love is an oxymoron, and as such it is difficult to achieve. The players actually do want some discipline, but only when it is warranted. But who decides when it is warranted? They do, of course. To be tough enough to merit respect, a manager almost needs to have a sixth sense. He has to be able to discern when to lay down the law, when to levy a fine, and when to look the other way.

Consider infield practice as an example. It used to be a given that the team would practice defense after batting practice by "taking infield." In this drill a coach or manager hits fly balls and grounders to each outfielder so he can practice catching the ball and throwing it to the bases. After the outfielders finish, the coach hits grounders to the infielders and they practice catching them and throwing to first and to second to simulate a double play. When I was playing everyone had to come out for infield and if they couldn't participate for one reason or another (and there were all kinds of reasons), it was deemed that they were unfit for the game. Sometimes the regular players grumbled, but, for the most part, nobody minded taking infield all that much. One day, about three or four days in to my rookie season as manager, Craig Biggio asked me if we were taking infield that day and I said yes. The next day, Derek Bell asked me about it. I immediately went into the coaches' room and asked them if they knew why the players kept asking me about infield. A couple of them just laughed.

"These guys don't like to take infield anymore," Cubby told me. "The Braves hardly ever take it and since they win all the time, the players on all the other teams want out of it too."

I asked Cubby what he thought was appropriate and he said we could take it a couple of times a week, and skip it before day games. The coaches, to a man, believed that the infielders took enough ground balls and throwing during batting practice. They felt that the only thing that was important about the drill was the outfielders throwing to bases, which they did not do during batting practice. During my last year, we never took infield, but we did have the outfielders come out early a couple of times each home stand so they could practice their throwing.

In the early stages of the 2000 season, we played more like chumps than champs. I held a meeting and told the players that if we couldn't hit, we could at least play better defense. To emphasize this aspect of the game and create an incentive plan, I said that every time we lost a game we would take infield the next day. We were playing so poorly that nobody complained, but when we continued to lose and take infield, they started bitching. One day Biggio told me I was going to be fined in kangaroo court for not being on the field for infield that day. He didn't know that I only missed it because I was in a meeting with Gerry Hunsicker. "Fine," I said. "Next time I'll get Dennis [our equipment manager] to meet with Gerry." Bidge obviously didn't think that was funny because the next day he came out for infield with his shirttails hanging loose, which is a violation of a league rule. Gerry saw him and he wanted to do something about it. "We are already on thin ice in terms of losing the winning attitude that has taken us three years to build," I said. "What do you think we should do?"

Gerry outlined the possible actions. First, we could fine him $500 for breaking a rule, which would be like poking him in the ribs. Since he was making many millions of dollars, it wouldn't hurt, but it would probably piss him off. Second, we could fine him a larger amount, say $5,000, to get his attention and make it hurt a little bit. If we fined him any amount over $500 we would likely face a grievance claim by the players association—a major hassle. The other thing we could do was bench him. That didn't make any sense at all because we were struggling to win and he was one of our best players. After reviewing the options, we did nothing. I'm sure Bidge knew that he had won a victory over authority even though we did not discuss it. This was not a good thing for us at all, and looking back, I believe we should have fined him $500 just to let him know we were watching. He wouldn't have liked it, but the whole team might have needed it.

Matt Galante was the coach who hit infield for us and he came to me a few days after this incident and told me that the players felt that taking infield after losing felt like punishment. I said, "Well, that's what it is."

"I know," he said. "But I'm not sure it's the right way to handle the problem."

"What do you suggest?" I asked.

He said that taking it a couple of times a week was enough in terms of preparation and so we went with that. In this case, acting like a players' manager was probably the right way to go. After all, the players didn't want to lose, and after a couple of weeks of this "no-infield" incentive, we were no closer to solving our problem.

Another area where I caved in to the players was travel. I let them drive their cars to exhibition games in Florida even though most teams required all players to take the bus. Our upper management felt that we should make them ride the bus, both to encourage togetherness and to protect against the possibility of them getting into an accident and exposing the team to a lawsuit. I didn't think the lawsuit angle stood up because only a few players take the bus during the season. It made sense to let them drive their cars because most of them were living fifteen or twenty miles west of our headquarters and for any trip west of our complex, they would have to double back, both coming and going. I was living out west myself and when we went that direction, I drove. When we went east or south, I rode the bus.

While I wanted to foster togetherness, I also wanted to discourage dependence. I wanted them to take responsibility for their actions. As a father, I want my children to be able to think for themselves; if I do everything for them they'll never learn to act independently. I told the players before the very first workout my first year that if they wanted to be puppets, they were on the wrong team. I would expect them to know where to station themselves defensively and I expected a pitcher to know how and when to hold a runner. All of them had been on teams where a coach positioned them from the dugout and the manager controlled the running game by giving signs to the catcher, who would in turn relay them to the pitcher. I was determined not to do that. I wanted players who could think, who understood game situations and could anticipate the actions they needed to take.

I told them they could drive to exhibition games if they got permission the day before. I also told them that if they drove to a road game they had to be at the ballpark before the bus arrived or we would all take the bus from that day forward. During my five years, all the players who drove arrived on time. Some were a bit behind the bus, but they were there in time to change and stretch without exception. However, the second year, some of the guys started traveling separately without asking permission, even when we went east or south. At that point, I drew the line—everyone had to ride the bus on those trips. On long trips, we even hired a second bus to leave early after the front-line players came out of the game. Still, by the fourth year, everyone was driving on western trips, even the minor league players who were only in camp because they were on the forty-man major league roster and we had to invite them. They had no chance of making the twenty-five-man team and since they lived near the ballpark, they had no reason not to take the bus. By my fourth year, it seemed like the only players on the bus were the Latinos. I decided that this was unacceptable and made the young guys ride the bus. I tightened the reins after the fourth year and imposed a rule that you had to have five years service in the major leagues to earn the privilege of driving your own car (with permission) and that only applied to western trips. I think this was a good compromise between discipline and common sense.

My lack of managerial experience made off-the-field decisions difficult. It wasn't a problem managing the game but it was impossible to instinctively know what to do in some other situations. Experience is worth a lot when it comes to issues such as infield practice and transportation. If a player's wife is about to give birth or has given birth to a child while we are on the road, the player is allowed to go home for a couple of days. The same rule applies if an immediate family member dies. But what about if an uncle dies? One of our relief pitchers, Brian Williams, asked me about that one day in Cincinnati. "My dad left when I was too young to know him," Brian said. "My uncle was like a dad to me." My inclination was to let him go to his uncle's funeral, even though we were worn thin in the bullpen at the time. I asked Gerry first and he agreed. I asked Brian to return as soon as possible. As it turned out, he decided not to go.

One more thing about the bus trips in spring training: They are worthless in terms of togetherness. I can't explain why, but the players always sleep on the bus during the day and stay awake at night. I did it too. Perhaps we would stay awake if we won a big game, but after a loss, the bus is like a narcolepsy ward. When I was playing, we all slept on the same bus. Now there are two buses, one for players and one for staff. I could sleep just as well on either one of them although I have a hard time sleeping on an airplane. Some guys can sleep anywhere—even on the training table before a game.

One of the funniest bus scenes I can remember came after the first game of the playoffs in 1997. Darryl Kile pitched a marvelous game that day in Atlanta, but lost to Greg Maddux 2–1.

After the game, owner Drayton McLane stepped onto the team bus and asked, "Does everyone have an assigned seat?" I always sat in the first row, so I said, "This is your seat right here," and slid over to the window seat so he could sit down. "So, why did we lose that game today?" he asked as the bus pulled away from the stadium.

"It was just one of those things," I said. "The bloop double that landed on the foul line was the difference. Sometimes they get a break like that, sometimes we do. This time, it went against . . ." I looked over and he was nodding off. About that time, the bus came to a red light and stopped. This brought him out of the spell.

"So, what are you going to tell the team tomorrow?" he asked.

"Not much," I said. "We'll have our individual meetings with regard to defensive positioning and how we're going to pitch each hitter. I may talk to some of the guys about being patient with Glavine and taking the walk if he nibbles at the corners . . ." Same thing. He nodded off.

When the bus started up again, he asked me if I thought Mike Hampton would pitch a good game the next day.

"I don't know," I said. "He's had a great second half, but he is high-strung. If he can keep his wits about him, he should be fine, but I . . ." Same thing. At least he wasn't snoring.

There was a lot of traffic and it took us fifteen minutes to traverse the three miles between Turner Field and our hotel. Whenever I started talking, he fell asleep. Whenever the bus stopped he woke up and asked me another question. If he had just slept the whole way, I would have too. Later, I was talking with Gene Pemberton, one of Drayton's longtime associates, and I told him about that bus ride.

Gene smiled, but was not surprised. "You know he does that in meetings sometimes and, at first, if you don't know him, you tend to stop talking. That's when you find out he isn't really asleep. I bet he could tell you everything you said to him that day."

Gene was probably right. As the years went on, I noticed that Drayton's mind seemed to wander in meetings from time to time, but whenever he chimed in, he was right on the subject. Like a lot of successful men, Drayton would rather lose sleep than lose a deal. Perhaps he has taught himself to recharge the battery with the engine running.

Fortunately we did not have a rule against sleeping on the bus, but we did have some rules that were hard to enforce. The most difficult one concerned children. A lot of guys liked to bring their kids to the ballpark with them, but the ball club didn't want to be responsible if they got hurt. The rule stated that children must stay in the dugout or in the box seats behind the dugout once batting practice started. One of my coaches, Jose "Cheo" Cruz, liked to bring his son, Enrique, to the ballpark. Enrique shagged in the outfield during batting practice, which seemed all right to me because he was nineteen years old and played baseball at Rice University. He wasn't likely to get hurt out there. But Biggio's boys were much younger, and when he brought them to the ballpark, they ran around like banshees and could easily have been struck by a ball and injured. Gerry reminded me that if I let Enrique shag, it would be hard to make Connor and Cavan stay in the dugout. Jose was indignant because Enrique could take care of himself and the players didn't mind having him out there, but I told Cheo his son had to stay off the field anyway. He was mad at first, but he got over it. Enrique didn't stay in the dugout, however. He went upstairs and hit in the batting cage, which was better for him anyway.

All these things influence the mood of the team and, in turn, its performance. Nothing is more important than team chemistry. I still recall former Houston Oilers coach Bum Phillips saying, "The minute you think your system will win for you, you're ready to lose. It is not the system, it's the players' efforts and nothing else." This is what I believed and what was most important to me. The one thing that comforted me even when we failed was the intensity of our effort—we always played hard. Still, nothing I could do to create a good atmosphere was as important as winning. During our four championship years, our chemistry wavered between good and great. In the quagmire of the 2000 season, backbiting was pervasive. A lot of guys didn't like each other and by the end of the year, nobody liked our rookie catcher Mitch Meluskey, and nobody liked me. I was frequently asked if I thought I was going to be fired, and after a while, that made me irritable. I told the writers that I knew what the players were saying behind my back because I was a player on a lot of losing teams and I remembered what I was saying back then. If I could have gotten Leo Durocher fired I would have done it in a heartbeat.

Leo was a manipulator. He was pretty good at it but at that stage of his career he was getting old and couldn't remember what he had told various players and he was frequently caught lying. When Leo was young he was smart as a whip, he had a passion for victory, and he was a good strategist on the bench. But he lacked character. He played favorites, which made some guys like him and some hate him. In my opinion, he was unprofessional.

One time, while I was on the disabled list, I threw a simulated game and performed well, without any pain. I was ready to be activated so Leo called me into his office and told me he would put me back on the list just as soon as he could get rid of outfielder Bob Gallagher. He ripped Gallagher up one side and down the other. I didn't know if he knew that Bob was my roommate and one of my best friends on the team; maybe he said those things for precisely that reason. He didn't have to tell me what he thought of Gallagher. All he had to do was to tell me I was going to be activated. I didn't relay Leo's feelings to Bob, as it would have served no useful purpose. A few days later, we went to San Francisco and Bob's dad met him at the airport. Leo just happened to be nearby and Bob took the opportunity to introduce Leo to his father. He mentioned that his dad had grown up in Boston and was there when Leo sprang from Beantown to the big leagues. The two Gallaghers were beaming and I was right there to witness the exchange. Leo told Bob's father that he had raised a fine son and that he was thinking about using Bob as his regular right fielder. "You should be proud of Bob," he said. "He's a fine young man and a helluva ballplayer." I thought I was going to vomit.

I'll never forget that scene. As much as any other single event, it taught me the importance of honesty. I was determined to be honest, right from the start. I felt that Bill Virdon was the best manager I had ever played for because his honesty and his character were unassailable. He didn't pass out too many bouquets but he didn't scream when we failed either. Honesty is a good thing but honesty can hurt; Bill could be brutally honest. A player would go to him and ask why he wasn't playing. "Because you're not good enough," Bill would say. I was hoping to be honest but also tactful. I guess I oversimplified; it took me a few years to learn that honesty can be premature and turn out to be a bad policy.

In 1997, my rookie year, the first guy I cut was Mike Gardiner. Mike was a thirty-one-year-old right-hander who had some big league experience. In 1996 he had pitched for the Triple A Tidewater Mets, and had a sensational year. His problem in our camp was that the numbers were against him. After he signed we made a trade with Detroit that brought us three pitching prospects and then we picked up another pitcher in the rule 5 draft. Later, we signed free agents Russ Springer and Tommy Greene. All of these guys threw harder than Gardiner. That didn't necessarily mean they could pitch better but there is certainly greater margin for error when you have a lively fastball.

The other number that doomed Mike was our scarcity of position players. After three or four guys got injured we didn't have enough bodies to play the three B games on our schedule. If we had played these games, Mike would have pitched at least three times. As it was, he pitched only once, coming in in the middle of a wildfire inning. He got burned in that frame, but settled down and got 'em out one, two, three in the next. This guy was a starter at the Triple A level the previous season and he went something like 14-2. It was not fair to judge him on just two innings of work. We were, however, aware of what it would take for him to succeed in the major leagues because we had seen him throw in an intersquad game and on the side. I thought he was a little short of stuff and my pitching coach, Vern Ruhle, did too. We couldn't see him getting any more chances to pitch in major league camp with our starters pitching more innings each time out. In minor league camp, he could get ready for the season. If he performed well, there was a chance we might need him, but that's not what he wanted to hear. At the beginning of camp, I told him he would get a taste of the action but he barely got a sniff. I was being truthful when I told him he would get a chance to compete, but it ended up sounding like a lie.

Mike was dedicated, sincere, and professional, but he was a victim of circumstance. As he unburdened himself, talking about a whole career of similar frustrations, all Vern and I could do was listen and agree.

"This is horseshit," he said.

We nodded our heads. I had the distinct feeling that blue language did not often pass his lips.

But he was right. Horseshit! What could we say?

Just after I was hired in 1996, I saw Donne Wall working out at the Dome. I told him he would make the team. He was only a rookie the year before and had mixed success, but I liked what I saw and was certain he could help us. Gerry was never a big Donne Wall fan, mostly for understandable reasons: Donne didn't throw hard and didn't have a good breaking ball. He had to hit corners with his fastball and use his excellent change-up to be effective. In 1996, he was able to do just that most of the time. One time, he beat Greg Maddux 1–0 in a ten-inning game.

In the spring of '97, Donne stunk. He couldn't get anybody out. At the end of camp when we had to make the final cuts, most of the coaches and Gerry thought Donne was the odd man out. Vern and I still thought he would come around, but we were outnumbered. We ended up sending Donne to Triple A New Orleans. Luckily, he was a pro about it. He admitted he was pitching poorly and only asked that we wouldn't lose track of him in the minors and would call him back up if he pitched well.

I couldn't promise that because if everyone in Houston pitched well, there would be no room for him on the team. "You know how it is," I said. "I can't promise you anything, but I know you can pitch and it is likely that someone will either get hurt or fail. Just pitch the way we know you can and you will probably be back in the big leagues." Well, he made it back, but he did not pitch well for us in '97. We traded him to San Diego and they put him in the bullpen where he found his niche. He never became an All-Star, didn't even maintain a winning record as he had in the minors, but he did yeoman's work for several years.

I thought I had finally learned not to forecast what a player's role would be. Experience taught me that I could tell a lie even while I was sure I was telling the truth. But I still made the same mistake halfway through the 2000 season, when Roger Cedeno got hurt. I replaced Roger with Lance Berkman in the outfield. Lance was a promising rookie but Cedeno was a proven veteran and we had traded Mike Hampton to get him. I told Roger he would be back in there as soon as he was able. Well, during the month or so of Roger's rehab, Lance caught fire. He was hitting for a good average, driving in lots of runs, and playing better outfield than we thought possible. When Roger got well, I started playing him and Lance wondered what he had done wrong. I told him that he had made a favorable impression and would continue to get playing time, but not every day.

Roger was rusty and didn't do too well at first. I started playing Lance and Roger got mad. He said that he couldn't get back in the flow of things if I didn't play him. But this was not spring training. Lance was a better player at that point and I wanted to see more of him with an eye toward the next season. I told Roger the truth at the time of his injury but it became a lie when the circumstances changed. Roger came into my office, very upset, and accused me of lying. Once again, I was speechless.

That situation was only one of many distractions in the 2000 season. Before we lost Cedeno to injury, we lost Moises Alou to a calf muscle pull. Afterward, we lost Billy Wagner to elbow surgery, and Biggio to knee surgery. Mitch Meluskey and Matt Meiske got into a fistfight. Tim Bogar wasn't hitting his weight and a couple of my coaches had serious health problems in their families. Worst of all was the bullpen—our relief pitchers blew more leads than they preserved.

I thought my honesty, integrity, and easygoing attitude would enhance the chemistry of the team, but my strategies frequently undermined the atmosphere I was trying to create. When I failed to make the obvious move, even when I was sure I was making the correct one, I sensed a stirring of the ranks. Some of my best-laid plans blew up in my face and the chemistry of the team deteriorated. The only thing that saved us was, ironically, the injuries. Every time a veteran got hurt, we called up a youngster and the young players weren't distressed about the sad certainty of our fate. They were thrilled to be in the major leagues and they really played well. I think our position in the standings made it easier for them to relax. Jeff Bagwell, Moises Alou, and Richard Hidalgo all finished in a flurry of home runs and RBIs. Despite the noxious atmosphere that pervaded the clubhouse, we continued to play with great energy. We lost a lot of games but we never quit trying to win them, and Gerry and I were on the same page all year long. He never blamed me, and, in fact, he encouraged me to forget about the talk of being fired. "I don't know where they get this information," he said. "I have never talked to Drayton about dismissing you. If I did, I would tell you." I believed him because he was always forthright with me and I knew he didn't like to let things stew. He preferred to take action sooner rather than later.

Toward the end of the season, Drayton announced that I would be coming back to manage the team the next year. I was relieved but also apprehensive. I wanted a chance to redeem myself, just like the players. But I was so weary of being assailed from within and without that for the first time in my life I didn't enjoy the off-season.

The best thing about the job was actually managing the game. I have gone up against some worthy skippers, such as Jim Leyland, Dusty Baker, Bobby Cox, Bruce Bochy, and Tony LaRussa. In 2000, Bobby Valentine was clearly the top manager in the league. The Mets had good pitching, but beyond that, Bobby had to juggle position players in and out of the lineup all year long, in what became a strategic masterpiece. I was amazed that he could make it all the way to the Word Series and give the Yankees a tough battle with the team he had.

• • •

Having been a pitcher, I looked at offense as defense in reverse. I used statistics to make decisions knowing that, over the six-month season, the samples would get big enough to make a difference. The most important statistics in terms of evaluating a hitter are his on-base average and his slugging percentage. Using OBS (on base average plus slugging average) I could get a good fix on a player's offensive ability. Foot speed and base-running ability are not included in this calculation and must be considered as minor factors one way or the other. In addition to knowing a hitter's offensive potential, I factored in what he had done in the past against a particular pitcher, and whether he was on a streak or in a slump. Then, I could get a *feel* for the odds of him succeeding in a specific game.

Still, my strategic philosophy often clashed with my instincts. For example, there were numerous times in 1997 and 2001 when I knew we would have a better chance to score if I used a pinch hitter for our fine catcher, Brad Ausmus. Brad was not a great hitter but he was one of our team leaders and he relished the chance to come through in the clutch. Most of the time, I let Brad hit, even in late-inning situations, because I thought a key hit here and there would boost his confidence and improve the whole team. I also wanted the rest of the players to know that I wasn't going to give up on him just because he was in a slump. If I were constantly moving guys around, in and out of the lineup, up and down in the batting order, based only on statistics, I would appear to lack confidence in my players. Brad's primary value was his fielding. His work with the pitchers had a major impact on the team. And wouldn't you know it, he clinched the division championship for us in 1997 with a game-winning home run against the Cubs.

Sometimes I did the same type of thing with a starting pitcher. Let's say, for example, that my starting pitcher came up to bat in the sixth inning and we had a runner on second and two outs, down 4–3. If the pitcher had not thrown very many pitches and was pitching better in the fourth and fifth innings, I might leave him in because I could save the bullpen and probably hold the other team down. We would likely have better chances to score in the coming innings. The statistical advantage of pinch-hitting for the pitcher is usually about 10 percent. The typical pinch hitter is a .250 hitter and the typical pitcher about .150. The player would get five hits every twenty at bats and the pitcher three. Our chances of scoring weren't that good either way, so I would base my decision primarily on stopping the other team the rest of the game over trying to score the tying run with two outs. However, if the pitcher were leading off the sixth inning, or if I thought he would have trouble holding the line in the next inning, I would pinch-hit for him.

Generally speaking, I liked to let the power hitters hit and we had a lot of them. We didn't use many trick plays and we didn't bunt or hit-and-run very often. The last two years, at Enron Field, we didn't put runners in motion too often, primarily because of our personnel, but also because our hit-and-run type players at the top of the lineup didn't run as aggressively as I wanted them to.

Sometimes the players played the game the way they thought they should play it instead of the way I wanted them to play it. It bothered me a little but not that much. Fact is, I had trouble convincing my own coaches that the hit-and-run play should involve more risk for the runner and put more pressure on the defense. Tradition dictates that the runner on the play is not trying to steal, but merely running with the pitch and watching to see what happens with the batter. In our modern heyday of home runs and strikeouts it is really risky to depend on the hitter to make contact, especially if he is a slugger. A few times, we even hit into double plays when the hit-and-run was on. The runners started late and didn't run full speed; the infielders didn't have to give up their defensive positions immediately so they were still in position to field a ground ball. On a sharply hit ball, they could still get the out at second base. Several times we got solid singles to center and right and our runner still wasn't able to make it to third because he got a bad jump. If the runner breaks hard and runs full speed, these things shouldn't happen. If your base runner is fast enough to steal second on an off-target throw, fine. If not, there is a great risk he will be hung out to dry. Still, the thought that has been pounded into players' heads from high school on up is that you *do not get picked off* when the hit-and-run is on. I felt, and still feel, that there is a greater risk of being thrown out at second if the batter does not make contact or misses the sign than there is of getting picked off first base.

I had a vision of a team that could manufacture runs and put pressure on the other team by doing a lot of running. The first few years we did exactly that, but by my last couple of seasons we were not a fast team anymore. I didn't have the type of players to play the running game. And I remembered something a coach once said to the effect that if you ask players to do something they're not capable of doing they will not question their ability—they will question yours.

Was it a big issue? Definitely not. In 1997, when we were a fast team, it appeared that we were playing hit-and-run all the time. What we actually were doing was stealing and hitting. Most of the time, I like my base runners trying to steal because it puts pressure on the pitcher when he thinks a runner might go. But I like power hitting even more than stealing. Sometimes the two go together when a pitcher rushes his delivery and makes a mistake over the middle of the plate. I did not require the hitter to take a pitch when a runner was in motion. Hitters are only going to see a few pitches each game that are really fat, extra-base-hit type pitches. I wanted them to swing at those pitches. That was my favorite hit-and-run play—the accidental one.

When we moved from the Astrodome and AstroTurf to Enron Field and infield dirt, Bagwell and Biggio were not able to steal as often. We also moved from a home run hitter's hell, the Astrodome, to a bandbox of a ballpark downtown. I'd have been a fool to hit-and-run much and my successor, Jimy Williams, evidently felt the same way. It really bugged me when a runner loped off first base and got thrown out by a mile because the pitcher threw an un-hittable pitch.

Some people, and even some of our players, thought we were unimaginative, but we ended up with one of the top offensive teams, year after year. We didn't sacrifice much with our regular players. Our opponents didn't bunt much either. I know a lot of older fans like the hit-and-run and bunt plays, but these strategies really don't make sense these days. When one run was all we needed late in the game, or when the pitcher was hitting, I used the sacrifice bunt. Early in the game, I encouraged our speed players to bunt for a hit. It's not that I don't like playing little ball. I know it is hard to beat the best pitchers with home runs, but the real odds of scoring a run from first with no outs are exactly the same as scoring from second with one out—40 percent. In other words, with the average hitter at bat, you would have to be 100 percent successful with the bunt to break even. Who wants those odds?

But everything is situational. Play for one run, or play for the big inning? First of all, what inning? What hitters are due up? Egghead fans generally prefer the big-inning theory, which states that fully half the time, the team that wins the game scores more runs in one inning than the losing team scores in nine. I first heard this when I was broadcasting and I didn't believe it. I checked it against my scorecard for an entire season and found it to be true. What's more, I found that when the Astros won, they scored as many runs in one inning as the other team did in the whole game 70 percent of the time. There just aren't many games where a few one-run innings are enough these days. Some managers bunt in the first inning because they know that the team that scores first wins something like 70 percent of the time, but the team that scores first can also score four runs in the first and, if they do, the rally probably doesn't include a sacrifice bunt.

So put me with the eggheads if you will and perhaps you will find a chink in my armor. But, first of all, put me among those who feel that stopping the other team is more important than anything you can do to score runs yourself. The teams with the lowest ERAs almost always go to the playoffs. During the deciding game of the divisional playoffs last year between the Giants and the Braves, it was stated that the three teams with the lowest ERAs in the National League were the Braves, the Giants, and the Cardinals. At that time, the Cardinals had already won their series with the Diamondbacks, the team that many people thought had the best pitching. The teams that score the most runs don't always make it: Give me good pitching and fielding and I'll take my chances with an average offensive team.

Strategy comes into play on defense too. When do you change pitchers? When do you order an intentional walk? I believe most of our guys thought we should issue more intentional passes, especially with first base open and the pitcher on deck. I knew that scoring the run from second with two outs was unlikely, whether the eighth hitter was at bat or the pitcher. The vast majority of the time it worked out that way but on the few occasions when we got burned by the eighth hitter, I sensed a collective anger among our veteran players. At first I tried to reason with them, but I found it almost impossible to convince the players that their gut feeling was wrong. I finally ended up walking a few more guys but never used that strategy as much as most managers. Perhaps that's because most managers are former position players.

With the eighth-place hitter up there, I knew that the odds of the other team scoring were slight and I also knew that we could gain a significant defensive advantage in the next inning when our opponent had to start the inning with the pitcher batting. The odds told me that the likely outcome would be the eighth hitter ending the inning by making an out. I know, when I was pitching, I didn't want to walk a .230 hitter and I loved starting an inning with the pitcher. After all, the guy is hitting eighth for a reason. He is usually in the lineup for his defense.

Most of the managers I went up against let our eighth hitter hit. When they walked Ausmus, I was happy. That way, either we would score by the pitcher getting a hit and bringing Biggio to the plate with runners aboard, or we would start the next inning with Biggio leading off. Once again, my philosophy was to play for the big inning on offense and to try to avoid letting the other team put up a crooked number.

One of the reasons I led off with Bidge is that he is a mid-range power hitter—a good RBI man. When I was pitching against the Reds, I knew Pete Rose came after the pitcher and when I was up against the Cardinals I was aware of Lou Brock. Conversely, when I faced the Braves, it was Felix Millan and the Dodgers, Maury Wills. I knew Rose and Brock could hurt me themselves and I also knew that our outfielders would play shallow against Wills and Millan making it difficult for them to score a runner from second even if they got a hit. Wills and Millan were one-dimensional—they were get-on-base-and-score guys, not RBI men, but when you have an

RBI man hitting leadoff, it forces the pitcher to throw strikes to the eighth hitter. And believe me, the eighth hitter appreciates that because pitchers don't throw him many fat pitches with the pitcher on deck. He hardly ever sees a good pitch to hit with a man in scoring position, but he has a much better chance to drive in the run if the leadoff man is a dangerous hitter.

I suppose I could dream up all kinds of hypothetical situations and espouse my managerial theories, but the best way to sum up my tactical view is to present a chart that I referred to several times during each season so that I could maintain my general knowledge of probabilities. Here it is:

RUN SCORING PROBABILITY

Chance of Scoring (Based on all scoring in the major leagues in 1999)

Outs	Bases Empty	1st	2nd	3rd	1st and 2nd	1st and 3rd	2nd and 3rd	Full
0	.29	.42	.61	.83	.64	.84	.86	.88
1	.17	.27	.40	.66	.42	.65	.65	.67
2	.07	.12	.22	.25	.22	.27	.24	.30

Total Run Potential

Outs	Bases Empty	1st	2nd	3rd	1st and 2nd	1st and 3rd	2nd and 3rd	Full
0	.52	.89	1.14	1.38	1.51	1.82	1.91	2.36
1	.28	.54	.67	.99	.94	1.16	1.29	1.58
2	.11	.22	.32	.37	.43	.48	.54	.73

To use this table, you have to rate your batter. Is he better than the average hitter? If so, you should probably let him hit instead of having him bunt. If he is a weak hitter, like a pitcher, or if he is an extremely fast runner, by all means bunt if you have a good hitter coming up next. If the league average for on base percentage plus slugging (OPS) is .750, all you have to know is whether your hitter is significantly better or worse than the average .750. If a hitter goes over the .1000 mark, he is exceptionally good. So good, in fact, that his average at bat is better than an intentional walk (.1000 on base added to .000 slugging), so, statistically, it would be better to walk him every time he comes up. This was evident with Barry Bonds in 2001 and even more in 2002. Each year there are a handful of batters that surpass .1000. Even these hitters make a lot of outs and in many instances it is better to try for one of those outs than to put the guy on base. Conversely, if you walk the eighth hitter, you make him a .1000 player for that at bat when he is ordinarily .700 at best.

I believed in doing everything in my power to avoid letting the other team have a big inning. As a result, my teams were almost always last in intentional walks. In this way, I think it helped me to see things from a pitcher's perspective. I know how it feels when you have a man or two men in scoring position with first base open. You can pitch carefully and often entice the batter to swing at a marginal pitch because he is hungry for the RBI. If you pitch carefully and walk the guy, they still might not score, but if you walk the guy, intentionally or not, then you have to throw strikes to the next guy. That may not be so bad with two outs, but with one out, you're playing with fire. Most hitters hit for a higher average with the bases loaded because the pitcher is compromised by the specter of a run-scoring walk and would rather take his chances with a pitch down the middle if he gets behind in the count. This is also true, to a lesser extent, with a man on second.

Most managers don't know how it feels out there, but I think they would appreciate my way of thinking if they were aware that the average frequency of a double play is 10 percent in all force-out situations. I knew this from my days as a broadcaster because I used a book published by the Elias Sports Bureau. Among the stats on every pitcher in the majors the previous season was a grade on inducing double plays. The very best at that time was Greg Maddux, who got one twin killing in every five chances. On the other end of the spectrum, strikeout pitchers like Nolan Ryan induced one in twenty. If you walk a batter to get a double play, you're drawing to an inside straight.

• • •

Many times during my five years in the front of the dugout, I trusted my instincts instead of conventional wisdom or logic. Last year, on July 15, the Astros were leading the Pirates 5–4 in the top of the ninth with two outs and a man on second base. Billy Wagner was on the hill and he was throwing well. Most of his fastballs were 98 and 99 mph. The Pirates' batter was Aramis Ramirez and he was having an off year after a great season in 2001. During that season, he single-handedly won a game for the Pirates at Enron Field, hitting three home runs. I was watching last year's game on television and I had a feeling that Billy should either pitch around Ramirez or intentionally walk him. Conventional wisdom dictates that you do not walk the guy who represents the winning run. But with two outs, I would have been tempted to break that rule. At the very least, I would have gone to the mound to talk to Billy about it. I watched as Jimy Williams squirmed. I knew how he felt. I don't know if Brad Ausmus had a signal from the dugout to pitch carefully to Ramirez (tempt him to swing at a bad pitch) or not, but Billy went right after him. He got ahead in the count and then made a mistake with the fastball and Ramirez hit it out of the park to give the Bucs the lead. The next hitter was the pitcher and Lloyd McClendon pinch-hit with Chad Hermanson, who made the last out. I don't know who he would have used for a pinch hitter if Jimy had intentionally walked Ramirez, but suffice it to say, there was no one on the bench with Ramirez's power.

In the bottom of the inning, the Astros got a runner to third base with two outs and Lance Berkman, who was leading the league in RBIs, was the hitter. McClendon didn't hesitate. He ordered the free pass. Jeff Bagwell came up with a chance to win it but Mike Williams retired him by deflecting a smash up the middle to his shortstop for a 1-6-3 putout. Jimy Williams was in the American League when Ramirez hit his three home runs at Enron. I'm sure he had the stats but he didn't have the memory and obviously didn't have the sense of foreboding that I felt watching the game. He played it by the book and lost. McClendon took a bigger risk because Bagwell is a far better hitter than anyone the Pirates could have used to pinch-hit.

After Billy Wagner had elbow surgery early in the 2000 season, I tried a number of closers, finally settling on Octavio Dotel. Dotel has a lively fastball and an unusual delivery. He is really hard to hit. The only problem we had with him was that he got wild occasionally. We also had Joe Slusarski on the team that year and he was an old veteran with an average arm and good control. One night, we had a one-run lead and Marc Valdes was pitching in the bottom of the eighth at home. When the inning started, I had Dotel throwing. Valdes walked a batter and the next batter bunted for a hit. I got Slusarski up at that point and sent Burt Hooton to the mound to stall for time. I foresaw a situation where the next batter reached base and we couldn't afford even one walk, which is exactly what happened. When I went to the mound everyone was expecting Dotel to come into the game, but I signaled for Slusarski instead. Slu came through like a champ; he saved the game—and saved me the agony of trying to explain why I had used him instead of Dotel. This is another example of making an unconventional move. When it works, you're a genius; when it doesn't, you're a bum. If you make the conventional move and it doesn't work, it's the player's fault.

If there were a book of conventional wisdom and it always worked, there would be no art to managing. One time, in the year 2000, Buck Showalter walked Barry Bonds with the bases loaded. Talk about going against the grain. That was the ultimate, but it worked and the Diamondbacks won the game.

The gut-feel aspect of managing brings to mind something Jimmy Leyland said when he was managing the Pirates and was booed for a decision that backfired. "I respect the fans," Leyland said. "Without them we would have no game. They pay our salaries. And I appreciate it. But I can't manage for the fans. If I did, I would soon become one."

Every time you lose a game, someone fails. Most of the time it isn't one guy but a whole herd of goats. Oftentimes the manager is among them. In this sense, managing a team is not any easier than playing. Failure is lurking over your shoulder and in your shadow. Sometimes your strategies make sense but the team doesn't execute them properly. Sometimes you just screw things up yourself.

One time, in my rookie year, I brought Wagner in to pitch in the eighth inning in Miami, intending to let him finish the game. The pitcher's spot was coming up third in the top of the ninth and I should have double-switched but I simply forgot. By the time I got to the mound I knew I had made a mistake, but it was too late to change. Knowing that just about everyone was aware of what had happened, I confessed immediately. "I screwed up, guys," I said, as I reentered the dugout. "I should have doubled Billy into the game. Pick me up." They did and we won, but not before Billy scared the hell out of me. He hit a swinging bunt and took off down the line like a rabbit. I feared a pulled hamstring. Thank God it didn't happen.

I suppose I could have come up with a plausible excuse for playing it the way I did, but why? I told the guys in the beginning that we were all going to make mistakes and that we would have to overcome them. After that, I asked Bill Virdon to remind me whenever a double switch might be possible. I did the same with Mike Cubbage and Matt Galante. I don't recall making that mistake again and I expected the players to learn quickly, too, especially with regard to mental mistakes: Learn from them, don't repeat them.

I guess the most vexing player I had was Jose Lima. Jose is a pretty bright guy. He learned English quickly and mixes easily into any crowd. But Jose has more adrenaline than common sense. We kept telling him to pitch low for outs and high for effect. We told him to keep the high fastballs in tight on the hands. But he kept leaving the ball up and out over the plate and set a club record for home runs allowed in 2000. We also told him to throw to first occasionally and to vary the rhythm of his delivery times to home plate to control the running game. Still, he never varied his timing and what made it worse was that he leaned toward home before lifting his left leg, which made it easy to steal on him—even for slow runners. When we told him these things, he always nodded as if he understood perfectly. One day I called him into my office with Burt Hooton. I told Burt in advance that I wanted Jose to do the talking. "Let's see if he can remember what we have been telling him," I said.

"So, you're pitching tomorrow," I said. "What is your approach?"

"I'm going to pitch low for outs and keep my fastball in on the hands," he said.

"What about base runners?"

"I have to vary my time to home plate and throw over more often. I can't lean like this" (he demonstrated) "because they can get a good jump."

After he left, I asked Burt if he thought Jose would put those pointers into practice the next day.

"Oh, sure," he said, with a chuckle.

It wasn't so funny the next night. Once the adrenaline kicked in, the brain shut down. The first two innings were a carousel of home runs and stolen bases.

The most frustrating part of managing is knowing what a player has to do to succeed and being unable to coach him into it. There were times when I wished I could have gone out there myself. I'm sure Burt felt the same way and I know Jose Cruz would have relished a clutch hitting assignment if he still had the sharp eyes and quick bat.

I have already discussed the most obvious challenges every manager has to meet—the mood of the team and the strategy of the game. But these are only part of the picture. Perhaps the most consuming of the collateral issues is the media. If I was amused that players weren't taking infield every day, I was floored by the intensity of the media coverage. When I was playing, there was a beat writer or two covering each team and several more writers in New York. Sports talk radio was in its infancy and the local TV guys rarely came to the ballpark. My, how times have changed.

Whenever there is competition, there is intensity, even in the media. Each major league city has several all-sports radio stations now, and they are out at the ballpark, competing for the scoop. Some of them get to the ballpark as early as four hours before the game. It has become fashionable for the local television sports anchors to come out for live interviews too. On the other hand, the number of beat writers has increased only slightly. Most papers use two writers to cover the home team these days, but it still doesn't double the coverage because both guys have time off during the year. Also, with electronic coverage increasing, many newspapers have folded. Most of the baseball writers who lost jobs in the print industry have moved to Internet providers and are still working the games.

I could have done interviews, if I chose to, every minute from my arrival at the ballpark at 2:30 until just before game time. I knew what it was like around the batting cage from my experience as a broadcaster, but I didn't know that reporters started showing up in the locker room in the middle of the afternoon and sometimes after batting practice as well. After a month or so of my first season, I mentioned that I was spending more time on the air as the manager than I did as the broadcaster, and I was not being facetious.

It didn't take me long to realize that I could not accommodate everyone one-on-one. I had to stipulate a time when I would be available and do one long media session for about twenty reporters each day. I still did one-on-one with the big networks and our own beat writers: They needed to provide more in-depth coverage and they asked better questions. Most of the others didn't mind doing their interviews en masse. In fact, a lot of them could not have done an interview on their own. They seldom asked a question, favoring the piggyback approach—let someone who knows what to ask do the questioning and jockey for a position with your microphone. Get the sound bite and take it back to the station. A lot of these guys and girls didn't know the first thing about baseball and probably would have been challenged to name ten players on the home team. I felt no obligation whatsoever to go out of my way for them.

I didn't feel like helping fill time for sports talk show hosts either, especially if they were doing shows from cities in the American League or in smaller cities like Portland, Oregon, where there's no major league team at all. The problem is that all these people have to do to reach you is buy a publication called the *Red Book* in the American League or the *Green Book* in the National League, which are available in most bookstores at the start of the season. In these books they can look up the name and the phone number of every hotel in the league. Most of the star players go by aliases when they're on the road. They know how to call each other and give the code names to their family and friends. I asked Gerry if I could do the same because the manager gets just as much attention as the star players when it comes to reporters. Gerry told me that it was my job to promote the team by doing interviews, whereas it was not the players' responsibility. I ended up letting the phone ring and using the voice mail most of the time. When I was expecting a call from Gerry or one of the coaches, I picked up the phone. Sometimes a reporter from a city like Las Vegas got through to me this way. Funny how that would happen just as I was going out the door. Sometimes I was just plain rude when they asked me when I would be back. I would estimate that I got about one call per day from a sports talk show when we were on the road. Some of them got my unlisted home number too. It can really become intrusive. What gets me now is that they're still calling.

The gaping maw of the American sports fan is insatiable. The juicier the subject, the greater the appetite. Toward the end of the 2000 season, the media mantra in Houston was "Will Dierker get fired?" How would you feel if you had to answer a question like that three or four times a day? I thought my skin was thick enough to repel the most penetrating questions. I learned that I was wrong. When we were on the road, I spent a lot of time in used bookstores where nobody could get through to me. I also found refuge in the work—one day at a time. Try to win this game; then try to win the next. Don't look forward and, for sanity's sake, don't look back. Still, it began to get to me. Several times I challenged reporters to come up with an original question. They looked at me as if I were speaking in tongues.

I thought the interviews would be the easiest part of the job for me because I had worked in the media and was comfortable doing an interview. I was also sympathetic to reporters because I know it isn't always easy to get an interview. When I was working in radio, I was responsible for the "star of the game" show. At least half the time, the guy who was the star blew me off. Sometimes, the guy would go on TV if it was a national game. Local radio was not worthy of his time.

In 1964 I made my professional baseball debut playing in the Rookie League, but because the Colt 45's were an expansion team, it wasn't long before I was promoted to the majors. (COURTESY HOUSTON ASTROS)

Hall-of-Famer Jim Bunning and me hanging out at the Astrodome. Notice the panels in the ceiling, which, as we discovered during the first day game played in the dome, made catching fly balls nearly impossible. (COURTESY HOUSTON ASTROS)

On my eighteenth birthday, in 1965, I took the hill at Colt Stadium for my first big league game and, in the first inning, struck out the great Willie Mays. (COURTESY HOUSTON ASTROS)

The very stylish Astros broadcast team of 1981: Gene Elston, Dewayne Staats, and yours truly. (COURTESY HOUSTON ASTROS)

One of the great joys of spring training in Florida was enjoying a few cold ones at the Big Bamboo, maybe the only bar in the world that a former big-leaguer has written a song about. (COURTESY OF THE AUTHOR)

Shaking hands with Atlanta manager Bobby Cox before a playoff game at the Astrodome against the Braves, our all-too-frequent playoff nemesis. (COURTESY HOUSTON ASTROS)

I was never much for jawing with umpires, but sometimes it just comes with the territory. That's me restraining Scott Elarton and arguing his case after he was wrongly ejected for throwing at Kansas City's Rey Sanchez. For the effort, I was eventually tossed as well. (REED HOFFMAN / AP/WIDE WORLD)

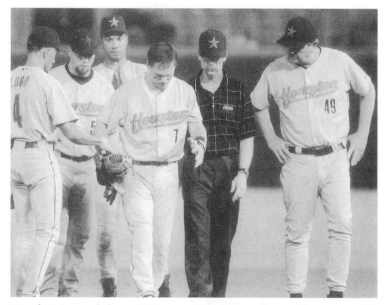

Murphy's Law ruled our 2000 season: Everything that could go wrong, did go wrong. Here, Julio Lugo, Jeff Bagwell, Moises Alou, Assistant Trainer Rex Jones, and I watch as Craig Biggio limps off the field after blowing out his left knee. Craig was lost for the season. (AMY E. COHEN / AP/WIDE WORLD)

The team gathers to pray in front of our dugout after I suffered a grand mal seizure in the second inning of a game against San Diego on June 13, 1999. Ironically, the thing I'm best known for, I remember nothing about. (COURTESY HOUSTON ASTROS)

After I had missed a month and a half of the season, my first game back after suffering the seizure, on July 24, was cause for celebration. Some of the best moments from that day: throwing out the first pitch to Dr. Rob Parrish (top), who performed life-saving brain surgery on me after the seizure; sharing a laugh with bench coach Matt Galante (center); and saluting our fans after the game for their prayers and support. (TOP: BILL BAPTIST / AP/WIDE WORLD; CENTER: PAT SULLIVAN / AP/WIDE WORLD; BOTTOM: COURTESY HOUSTON ASTROS)

After we lost to Atlanta in the 2001 Divisional Series, the Astros and I decided to go our separate ways. Although we won four National League Central division crowns in five years, we never made it past the first round of the playoffs. (Pat Sullivan / AP/Wide World)

After I had been involved with the franchise in some capacity for nearly forty years, the Astros retired my number in May 2002. I wonder what Milo Hamilton thought as I took a victory lap in this vintage "Woodie." (Courtesy Houston Astros)

More from the retirement of my number: The guys look on from the dugout (top) as I bid the crowd "Aloha" (above), then hand the ball to my son, Ryan (left), for one of the ceremonial first pitches. (COURTESY HOUSTON ASTROS)

My place in the sun . . . (COURTESY HOUSTON ASTROS)

During the 2000 year when we stunk up the joint, I kept getting questions like, "How frustrating is it when you get the runner
on third with no outs and still don't score?" "How frustrating is it
when you lose by one run all the time?" "How frustrating is it
when the bullpen gives up the lead time and again?" One day I said,
"What do you want me to do, rate frustrating on a scale of 1 to 10?
I can't quantify frustrating, can you?" As aggravating as the 2000
season was for me, it was just as bad for most of our players. Since
we had won our division three years in a row, we all felt we would
be a contending team again. We were so far behind by the All-Star
break that we couldn't see the playoffs with a telescope. That's
when the backbiting and second-guessing bounced around our
clubhouse like a pinball. Managing that situation wasn't difficult—
it was impossible.

The 2000 season was the worst of my tenure, but my media
problems started in the playoffs in 1999. We had a great year but
lost in the first round of playoffs for the third straight season. I had
won the Manager of the Year award in '98 but, considering the circumstances, I thought I did a better job in '99. Moises Alou injured
his knee right before spring training, had surgery, and was out for
the season. We lost just about every player we had to injuries, lost
me for a month with a seizure and brain surgery, and still won
ninety-seven games, just one more than the Reds. It was a great
race. Thank goodness we didn't lose Bagwell, Biggio, and Wagner.
They were solid all year long.

We split the first two games of the divisional series in Atlanta
that year and came home thinking we would finally get over the
hump. In Game 3, we were tied 3–3 going into the top of the
eleventh. Jay Powell walked two batters in that frame and they
were on second and third with two outs when Brian Jordan came to
the plate. Andruw Jones was on deck and was not as good a contact
hitter as Jordan. Since Andruw seldom walks, I could have issued
the intentional pass to Jordan without too much risk of walking in
the lead run, but I was still worried that Jay would walk Jones or
give him a fastball down the middle to hit. I went to the mound and
told Jay to pitch around Jordan, trying not to give him anything
good to hit and not to worry about walking him. Our spray chart

indicated that Jordan had not hit a single ground ball down the first base line all year. Consequently, we had Jeff Bagwell playing way off the line. Naturally, Jordan reached out and hit a pitch that was about six inches wide right down that line. We lost the game and went down 2–1 in the series facing elimination the next day. It was the toughest loss I suffered in my five years at the helm.

Afterward I went to the interview room with steam coming out of my ears. One reporter asked me if I considered walking Jordan. The way the question was phrased is what got me: If he had just said, "Why didn't you walk Jordan in the eleventh?" I would have answered him. But he didn't, and though I don't know if he was suggesting that I hadn't considered it or was just trying to set me off, he succeeded in the latter. It was my first media blowup. I could have said that I considered it and decided against it for the reason I just stated. Instead, I took the question as an insult, and so I said sarcastically, "No, I never thought of that. It must have slipped my mind."

The day after the Brian Jordan hit, we had Shane Reynolds on the mound and we were facing elimination. Shane pitched well but the Braves chinked him to death. Bloopers, choppers—you name it—they attacked him like a horde of Lilliputians. The last batter he faced hit the ball up the middle, and Shane deflected it. The ball rolled toward third, and he didn't go after it. His body language told me that he had about given up. I've been in that position myself and it is really deflating.

After the game, I was asked why I hooked him so fast. Actually, it wasn't that fast, but it was fast for me. I said that when Shane didn't go after the ball, he seemed to have had enough. The media talked to him, and he objected strongly. He said he wanted to keep pitching, and I knew how he felt. One time, when I was pitching in San Diego, I got a visit from our manager, Preston Gomez. He said, "Larry, you're not concentrating." I said, "How do you know?"

I should have left Shane in the game, as it turned out. But I couldn't read his mind. In saying he looked finished, I insulted and embarrassed him. I called him at home the next week to apologize.

I got great satisfaction out of the next round of playoffs when the Braves advanced to meet the Mets. Perhaps I was the only one who noticed the irony in the way the Braves got into the World Series. Bobby Valentine faced the exact situation I did in the last game of the series. Jordan was at bat and Jones was on deck. With runners on second and third, Bobby ordered an intentional walk to Jordan. I might have done the same in his shoes because Kenny Rogers was on the mound and he has better control than Jay Powell. But this time Rogers was wild. He walked Jones and the Braves won the series. What I'm saying is that there is no right or wrong way ahead of time, only afterward. Or as Tommy Lasorda once said, "A second guesser is a guy who doesn't have a first guess and needs two guesses to get one right."

We moved to Enron Field in 2000 and with all the excitement of a new ballpark, I really thought we would finally win it all. Instead, we wallowed in or near last place for the first half of the season. It was miserable. We were worse at home than on the road and the most demoralizing aspect of our failure was that we lost our abiding strength, Billy Wagner, early in the season. Billy was throwing just about as hard as ever but he kept blowing saves. I couldn't figure it out—I would call to the bullpen to get him warmed up and about three minutes later they would call back and tell me that he was ready. I never could have guessed that he had an arm problem but, as it happened, he had to have scar tissue removed from his elbow. We had to shut him down for the season, and the next year he returned to form.

In one game at Enron, he gave up a home run to Ken Griffey Jr., and we lost the game—it was a body blow. Afterward, I was asked if I knew what was wrong with Billy. I said that I didn't know. "He's throwing just as hard, but he's not getting the clean swing and miss this year. It seems like they can foul it off most of the time and obviously they are hitting it square more often too. I don't know how to explain it."

One of the writers went directly to Billy and said, "Dierker said that you've lost your fastball." Billy replied that if I didn't like it I could go out there and try it myself. It was a heat-of-the-moment type of thing. I talked to Billy the next day, and after sleeping on it, he felt better. I told him that it was an old trick with the writers to pit one guy against another by relaying quotes. "The next time they tell you something that doesn't sound right, come to me and ask me what I said before you talk to them," I advised.

In 2001, we won the division again, but I wasn't the same guy who took the reins in 1997. I was skeptical, cynical, jaundiced— definitely not the fun-loving, aloha-shirt-wearing skipper anymore. Early in the season, we lost eight straight games and the "Fire Dierker" mantra came over the media again. Then, late in the year, after we had built a comfortable lead in our division with just a week left to go in the season, I went off on the fans, using the worst spokesman possible, the media. The Giants were in Houston for a three-game series and all we had to do to clinch the Wild Card was to win one game. Our final three games were in St. Louis and the Cardinals were playing great baseball, especially at home. I did not want to go to St. Louis needing even one win to get into the playoffs.

When the Giants got to Houston, Barry Bonds had sixty-nine home runs and needed just one more to tie the all-time single season record. We packed the house for all three games. The first two were disappointing for everybody—Bonds did not hit a home run, but he walked a lot and we lost. In the third game, the Giants opened a big lead. With one out in the seventh inning, Rich Aurilia hit a ball down the left field line and hustled to stretch it into a double. With first base open, I walked Bonds. This was a move made more of anger than intelligence. It may have been the only time in my five years that I walked a batter with only one out in an inning. At the time, I was seething. They were so far ahead there was no reason for Aurelia to attempt reaching second base. If they want to rub it in, I thought, I'll play that game too. Bonds trotted to first and the fans booed. Jeff Kent hit into a double play to end the inning— lucky me. I put a young left-hander, Wilfredo Rodriguez, in to pitch the last inning. Rodriguez gave Bonds the pitch he was waiting for and he hit a long home run to tie Mark McGwire for the single season record at 70.

Bonds was excited, the Giants were excited, the fans were excited. I was fried. It was the fans that set me off. They kept booing when we failed to throw strikes and give Barry a fair chance. In some cases, we didn't want to throw him strikes; in others we were trying to get him out, but didn't throw him strikes. The pitchers could have been afraid, or too careful, or they could have just been wild. In several cases, it looked like the home plate umpire was squeezing them when they did make good pitches. I resented the implication that we were pitching him differently than we did in San Francisco when we swept them the week before. I was especially angered by the assertion that I was walking Bonds. Sure we intentionally walked him a few times, but I did not order most of the walks and I didn't throw a single pitch. I really felt betrayed when our own fans booed us and cheered for him as they did after he finally tied the record. It's one thing to recognize an extraordinary accomplishment. A tip of the cap is enough for me. It's another to rub your own team in the dirt with repeated hosannas to the enemy. Our fans kept cheering until he came out for a third curtain call. In the media session after the game I said that anyone who reacted that way couldn't really be an Astros fan. I don't know if I ever really got over that. I know those fans hadn't given their lives to the team for thirty-six years . . . but I had. I learned later that a lot of fans felt the same way I did, but that's not what I heard at the ballpark.

The next day, I got roasted in the newspaper and on the talk shows. I also learned that some of our players didn't agree with me. I overheard Biggio saying that the fans were "awesome."

After the debacle in Houston, I was really proud of what we did in St. Louis. We won the first game to clinch a playoff spot. Then we won the last one to win the division. Six days later, we were in the playoffs and we lost the first game at home. We had a 3–2 lead after seven innings but the bullpen, which was an abiding strength for us in the second half, lost the lead, and eventually lost the game. Todd Fedewa was there to usher me to the media room afterward, and he could tell I was boiling. "Do you want to take a few minutes to cool off?" he asked diplomatically.

"A few minutes isn't going to change anything," I said. "Let's get it over with."

Little did I know, I was about to get it over with for good.

Tim Melton from Channel 13 asked me why I used Mike Jackson instead of Octavio Dotel in the eighth inning and I bristled. "Because Mike has been better lately," I said. "Check the record."

One of the writers checked it and put it in the paper—it was pretty ugly. Both of them were ineffective after the September 11 hiatus. Dotel had been practically unhittable in the second half but was having severe control problems after the layoff, and his velocity was down. His unusual delivery just wasn't in sync. I could almost always count on Billy Wagner in the ninth and I could almost always count on Jackson too. When Billy went down early in the year, Jacks was our closer, and he went four for four in the save department. Dotel was as good as Wagner between the All-Star Game and September 11. Throughout most of the year, we could almost always count on the win if we had the lead in the eighth inning.

I went with Jackson because he was the veteran. He could throw strikes and generally forced the hitter to swing. He got hit a few times that way, but he didn't walk many batters. Dotel was the opposite, a young hard-throwing kid with no fear. He could be overpowering, but he was prone to control lapses. He could walk two or three batters in the same inning, and that's what I was afraid of with the pressure of the playoffs. I also knew that the Braves were one of the few teams that Dotel had trouble with. I guess I should have explained it that way. With a second guess I would have chosen Dotel. As it was, they hit Jackson, but they didn't hit him hard.

After that humiliating defeat, we went down without much of a fight. The burden of playoff failure had become an unbearable load. In our four failed attempts in October, we never really hit. I am frankly nonplussed to figure out why. Sure, the pitchers are generally better in the playoffs than the standard rank and file of the regular season, but there were times in all of our championship years where we hit good pitchers, even when they were throwing well. I know fourteen games is a small sample, but 2-12 is just not acceptable. In that way, I concurred with Gerry when he said that I had probably run my course. It hurt a lot: I had spent thirty-six years with the team, never coming close to the World Series as a player, but having a chance almost every year as a manager. I had another year on my contract and was ready to serve, but I know it would have been hard to create the right atmosphere.

Just writing about the experience of my last season informs me that I had had enough. Would I do it again after resting for a year or two? At first I thought not, but as time went by, I started equivocating. The lure of competition is hard to resist and I couldn't resist it the first time. But the first time I was innocent. I didn't really know what I was getting myself into. I thought I could bring some fresh air to the situation and help the team become more fun-loving and efficient at the same time. I didn't know what the pressure would be like. Now I know. Would I have done it differently if I could? No, I wouldn't trade those division championships for anything and I am proud of what we accomplished. I would, however, be smarter if I did it again. Experience is the best teacher, but she is a hard grader because she gives the test first and the lesson later.

At the time, I was concerned that if we won in the playoffs and advanced to the World Series I would have to consider a contract extension. Talk about ambivalence. I would have been hard to turn the money down. And I probably couldn't have done it. But I was really growing weary of the race. If I did manage again, I would try to follow the advice Art Howe gave me right after I got the Astros job. "Never," he said, "manage in the same city where you live."

After observing the Astros in 2002 from the comfort of my living room, I know it worked out for the best. Money is like a legal drug. You can become addicted, enslaved. And, all the while, people will think how lucky you are. In a way, I accomplished my goal. We were a winning team in all but one of my five years and I departed with my character, wisdom, and intelligence intact. I never had the fiery kind of passion that everyone can see. I certainly cared deeply but it is my nature to keep my feelings inside. I was aware of my tendency to analyze everything and think outside the box. And I knew I couldn't always beat the opposing manager on the field even if I could beat him on an IQ test. In a perfect world, a baseball manager would equally balance passion, character, brains, and wisdom. And no one would ever grow gray and wrinkled because no one would ever lose a game. But we don't live in that kind of world and the one I inhabit now is a lot more relaxing. I didn't know the weight of the burden I was carrying until it was lifted. Getting fired after winning a division championship was, in a way, a blessing. It is simply impossible to be all things to all people—especially in your hometown. I got a lot smarter after Jimy Williams started managing the Astros just like Joe Torre got a lot smarter when he went from the Cardinals to the Yankees. At least I went out on top. Most managers have to lose a lot more than I did to get fired.

CHAPTER 5

Broadcasting

Last night I neglected to mention something that bears repeating.

—RON FAIRLY, FORMER OUTFIELDER AND BROADCASTER

ON AUGUST 5, 1921, the Pirates and Phillies played a routine afternoon game at Forbes Field in Pittsburgh, and KDKA made history. Most Pirates fans checked the box score the next morning, but some of them already knew the details of the game, thanks to the reporting of Harold Arlin, a twenty-eight-year-old electrical engineer. Arlin worked for Westinghouse, the parent company of KDKA, the station that pioneered radio broadcasting. The station hit the airwaves on November 2, 1920, and a little less than a year later, the Pirates formed a relationship with KDKA that survives to this day. Looking back, it is hard to imagine how the executives of the station and the Pirates took so long to discover the natural affinity of the two businesses.

"That first microphone," Arlin recalled later, "resembled a tomato can with a felt lining. We called it a mushophone." Harold Arlin was KDKA's first full-time broadcaster, making him the world's first recognizable radio voice. After five years as a full-time announcer in Pittsburgh, Arlin returned to Mansfield, Ohio, to work in industrial relations for Westinghouse. At the time of his retirement from broadcasting, he was internationally famous. One British newspaper called him the best known voice in Europe.

In 1972, Arlin was invited back to the Pirates' broadcast booth by announcer Bob Prince. The Pirates were playing the Padres that day, and the Padres sent a right-hander to the mound by the name of Steve Arlin. This was not a coincidence, it was a plan: Steve pitched while his grandfather Harold called the game with Prince. Steve Arlin later heard a tape of his granddad and he remembered the old-timer having a good strong voice. "The thing that he remembered most," Steve said when I talked to him a few years later, "was that they gave him a certificate for a pair of shoes for appearing on the broadcast. He was really proud of those shoes. He forgot about me winning the game, but he wore those shoes all the time."

Harold Arlin died in Mansfield, Ohio, in 1986. And, yes, he did get more than notoriety and a pair of shoes out of his time with Westinghouse Broadcasting. Perhaps the finest high school football stadium in the country is located right there in Mansfield and it was named after the man who made baseball come to life: Harold Arlin.

It wasn't long after Arlin's first broadcast that radio became the rage in America. Most folks could afford to buy one and it was the perfect medium for baseball. Newspaper accounts of ball games played before the advent of radio contained a lot of flowery language; the writers of that day could embellish the game because there was no way to dispute what they wrote. When radio burst onto the scene, the writers had to do a little more than slip the final score into stories full of clever phrases and high drama. Radio trumped the newspapers when it came to news. Once the games went out on the airwaves, most fans knew who won the game and most of the particulars before they got their morning paper. Consequently, baseball reporting changed, as writers had to start including quotes from the principals so that the fans could read something in the morning that they hadn't already heard the night before.

Back then, Ring Lardner was among the most creative of sports journalists. The effect radio had on him is evident in one of his game stories from the 1926 World Series:

"The Washington Senators and the New York Giants must have played a doubleheader this afternoon—the game I saw and the game [broadcaster] Graham McNamee announced." Lardner was listening to a radio in the press box, but there were no transistor radios at the time. If you listened to the game, you could not possibly see it unless your house overlooked the stadium. Generally speaking, if the radio broadcaster took creative liberties with his account of the action, who would know the difference? Although television had long since been on the baseball scene when I first started doing radio games with Milo Hamilton, I remember him describing a routine fly ball to right center like it was the greatest catch of all time. "There's a drive out into right center field . . . Cruz is after it . . . He's racing into the gap. . . . Will he get there? Yes, he got it! Holy Toledo! What a catch by Jose Cruz!" After the final flourish, he looked over to me and winked.

Many people feel that baseball is still a radio game and that television has intruded upon it. I think there is a greater sense of drama when you can't see what is going on. And, of course, the drama reported is often greater than the drama that actually occurs.

On August 27, 1939, almost twenty years after Arlin's first radio broadcast, Red Barber slid up to the microphone and said, "This is Red Barber speaking, and let me say hello to you all." With those unassuming words, the history of major league baseball on television began. The *New York Times* report of the game said, "Major League Baseball made its television debut as the Dodgers and Reds battled through two games at Ebbets Field before the two prying electrical eyes of station W2XBS in the Empire State Building. . . . Television set owners as far away as fifty miles viewed the action and heard the roar of the crowd. . . . At times it was possible to catch a fleeting glimpse of the ball as it sped from the pitcher's hand toward home plate."

Two cameras, one in the second deck behind home plate, and one near the visiting dugout down the third base line, covered this game. NBC had televised a game between Princeton and Columbia earlier in the year; now they were in the big leagues and the landscape of the game started changing.

The game itself has not changed much over the years. The

145

rules and strategies are still the same as they were when Arlin started broadcasting for the Pirates. But it is hard to imagine how baseball looked sixty years ago. Most fans have seen the baggy uniforms in film clips of Babe Ruth or in still photographs. But when the Dodgers and Reds played the first televised game in 1939 there were no black or Latino players; there were no modern stadiums, no indoor stadiums, no AstroTurf. Now there's a big television at the ballpark—it's known as Diamond Vision, and there are smaller TVs on the concourses and at the concession stands so that fans can move around the stadium without ever losing track of the game.

The art of televising baseball has changed a lot more than the game. Old-timers tell me it still sounds the same on radio, though they complain that it takes a lot longer to play. And why does it take longer to play? Television and money. When I started broadcasting in 1979 we had sixty-second commercial breaks. If you didn't wrap after the half-inning quickly, you could miss the first few pitches of the next one. Now, the breaks are from 120 to 150 seconds, which gives the players plenty of time to get ready for the next half-inning, and with two or three video replay machines in the truck, the half-inning often ends with a replay, which means that the telecast may still miss the first few pitches after coming back from commercial. One time, I told our director that we were going to miss a first pitch home run if we kept replaying the last out before going to commercial break. He didn't seem to mind.

"Don't worry about it," he said. "If we miss a home run, we can always replay it."

"Yeah, but I thought the 'live action' was the reason for the telecast."

"It is. And I hope we don't miss anything important. But we paid a lot for these replay machines, and when we have a good replay, we have to use it."

I didn't want to pursue this discussion, because I knew that within its logic there was a chasm that more than a few old-time radio broadcasters could not cross. Is it live? Or is it Memorex? In TV, most everyone knows the difference. But not everyone agrees about which is best.

Now that the length of the commercials dictates the time between innings, players jog in from the field and stroll back out at a lazy pace. Some players even stay in the dugout for a while after the end of an inning and wander out to the field after a minute or so has elapsed since it doesn't take that long to warm up. I hadn't thought about how this looked from the stands until I went to a college football game last year. When the game stopped and the players and officials were just standing on the gridiron, I asked my friend what was going on. "It's a commercial time-out," he said.

It seems ironic that as the pace of modern life quickens, the pace of modern sports goes slack. In the days of my youth, the coaches would yell, "Hustle in, hustle out," between innings. Now, my son's team has a football-type huddle before they bat and before they take the field. Unwittingly, we are programming our children to play the game like the big leaguers and since there is a time limit at many youth tournaments, the kids don't get to play as many innings and get the full value of the competition because they waste too much time between innings. It seems as if the umpires are in cahoots with them. The home plate ump often wanders down the first base line to visit with the base umpire between innings. All this because of television; no wonder the average game now takes three hours instead of two. There is simply too much dead time.

In televised sporting events, the Golden Rule is scrupulously followed: He who has the gold makes the rules. Since baseball has more games than any other sport, it tends to lead the advance of the gold standard. Do you remember when all the World Series games were played during the afternoon? If you do, you are an old-timer, like me. I bet you prefer radio to television anyway, and you bemoan the fact that you never know when the game is going to start. A nationally televised game on the West Coast will likely start in the twilight at 5:30 or 6:00 P.M. so that it doesn't come on too late for East Coast viewers. Games on the East Coast often start at 8:00 P.M. Now the World Series and most playoff games are televised in prime time only. There are no day games during the week when most adult consumers are at work.

Sponsors pay more money for prime-time exposure. The networks need all the money they can generate to pay Major League

Baseball's exorbitant rights fees. Because the broadcast companies provide such a large slice of the revenue pie, they have a lot of leverage. They usually pay more for the rights than they can hope to recover, and bargain for more control over the coverage to maximize earnings and cut losses. When I started in broadcasting, cable TV was in its infancy and rights fees were more closely tied to projected revenue. The expense of televising a game was far smaller than it is today—it seems like the technology improves every year and the number of cameras, graphics generators, and videotape machines multiplies.

I like a good replay as much as anyone, but I hate to miss live action. My preference is to see the game as it happens. To me, that's the whole purpose of television—the beauty of the pictures and the immediacy of the live event. Replaying a leadoff homer that got lost in a commercial is like cleaning up a mess that you didn't have to make to begin with. I really get perturbed when I watch a basketball game and they stay on the "hero shot" of the player who has just scored as he jogs back down the court while one of his teammates steals the inbounds pass. It doesn't happen often, but it doesn't have to happen at all. I would save the hero shots for free throw and time-out situations. Similarly, in baseball, I would use the replay sparingly so as not to lose the rhythm of the game. Using television to make players more heroic only costs money in the long run. Broadcasting companies squeal about rights fees, but they're the ones who are driving the cost up. The players simply play the game.

It is ironic, I think, that the networks are in the same boat with the owners and the players are steering it. Staring losses in the face, owners cut expenses; office workers, scouts, and development people get fired; there's a freeze on salaries; when one person is let go another isn't hired to replace him, and the responsibility of the fired employee is heaped on the already full plate of another worker who is lucky to still have a job. Teams put more signage up in the stadium to create more revenue; they leverage one broadcast station against the other and finally one of them overpays to get the games because it's an "image" buy. When they find they have spent too much, they start cutting staff, and trying to increase revenue by scheduling commercial announcements during the progress of an inning. They slip these ads in while the game is being played so that if you want to watch the action, you have to watch the commercial.

Some people in the industry think the broadcast companies are losing more than the owners, while the players' salaries ratchet up year after year. Finally, last year, most telecasts had fewer cameras and tape machines than the year before. The people who have been so thrilled by the new technology have been trumped by the bean counters: Those extra cameras and video machines are expensive.

My first director, Joe O'Rourke, was a throwback. He had been directing games since the 1950s and had seen the proliferation of technology firsthand. Still, he wasn't impressed. "It's like *Donkey Kong,*" he said on more than one occasion. "If they want a game show, they should invent one. If they want a ball game, show the ball game. Don't put all that crap up on the screen. If I want to read, I'll get a good book."

I couldn't agree more. I find myself yelling to the invisible director, "Get that shit off the screen!" when I am watching a game.

My son, Ryan, thinks I've lost a few marbles. "Don't worry about it, Dad," he says. "You don't have to look at it if you don't want to."

He's accustomed to graphs and charts. He can look at them or through them. After several hundred hours of Nintendo, he can see a lot of things on the screen at the same time without being distracted. He is just eighteen years old, and he gets bored easily. He flips back and forth between stations during commercials. Impatience is his middle name.

"Don't you think the pictures would look better without all the writing on top of them?" I ask.

"Not really," he says. "If something good happens, they'll replay it without the writing."

We were watching the first Houston Texans football game last September, when the Cowboys asked the referees to review video on a fumble. Up on the screen went the query, "Do you think the call will be overturned? Log on to *www.somethingorother.com* and cast your vote." That surprised even Ryan. "How are they going to get people to log on and vote before the ref looks at the replay?" he asked.

"They would have to be logged on already," I answered. "But how many people would want to watch a game that way?"

I got my answer directly—they had over 10,000 votes before the referee finished reviewing the play.

Perhaps the broadcast is attuned to the lifestyle of the young and restless. In baseball, I think catering to the young crowd is a big mistake. Baseball marketers are afraid that the game is dying because they don't get good ratings in the eighteen-to-twenty-five-year-old segment, of which my son is a part. When they try too hard to lure this audience with a lot of gimmicks they turn their true customers off. They worry that the game is too slow and that with all the standing around kids will get bored. This is probably true: so what? If you think back to the days when you were eighteen to twenty-five, you will likely remember more sowing of wild oats than sitting still. Baseball is not so appealing to a young man who is bursting with testosterone. When he gets married and has a son, what do you know? He starts going to the ball game again. As long as youth baseball flourishes, baseball has a future. It's a lot like religion—if you are raised in the faith, and then stray, you will likely come back. I don't think anyone has considered rewriting the Bible because the adolescents in the flock have started sniffing around and gotten away from the shepherd.

The game has been diced, chopped, and packaged to make the images appear rapidly. I think the networks are trying to use their technology to create the illusion that the pace of the game is fast and furious. I doubt we will ever again see a broadcast where the game is the main thing and the broadcast rides the ebb and flow of the action.

Doing television is more challenging than doing radio because the director has control over what the announcer talks about. In radio broadcasting, the play-by-play man has control of the format: He can decide when to read a promotional announcement or give out-of-town scores; he can focus on the game when the action is hot and heavy and tell stories and give scores when the game drags. In TV, however, the format is set in advance and in order to get all the announcements in and maximize revenue, the announcer sometimes has to allude to a sponsored chart or graph when he should be talking about the situation and the strategy. As a broadcaster, up in the booth, I was often eager to talk about the game, but had to bite my tongue because we were doing other business.

The primary business of covering baseball is difficult for a director. He has to call the camera shots at split-second pace as the ball travels around the park. Then he has to hope his cameramen can find some interesting crowd shots to help fill the time between pitches.

One thing, though, is certain. There can no longer be any doubt that umpires miss a lot of calls—television catches them constantly—and that is the beauty of pictures. Showing the umpire missing a tag play by looking at it frame by frame from several angles is really interesting, and it shows how difficult it is to play and umpire the game. Generally speaking, TV makes the game seem easier to play than it is. The outfielders are a lot faster than they look; hitting looks almost simple to the point where you wonder why a guy would ever swing at a breaking ball in the dirt or fail to connect with a fastball down the middle. But there are times when the replays capture the artistry of the sport as no radio announcer ever could.

First it was "Take me out to the ballgame," or read about it the next day. Then it was attend, listen, or read. Now it is attend, listen, watch, read. Finally, the voracious maw of the tube is providing reading material too, and as a bonus, you can log on. That, as Yogi might say, is progress in reverse.

My philosophy, as an announcer, is perfectly simple: I try to have a good time, which is easy when the game is halfway competitive. I figure that if I'm enjoying myself, the guy back home is having fun too. I ride the game like a boogie board, splashing around in the surf, waiting for the perfect wave. I seldom feel the need to hurry and only occasionally feel that I'm drifting in the doldrums.

I try not to second-guess the manager, preferring, when possible, to first-guess him. The way I like to handle it is to say that the manager has options X, Y, and Z; I'll give the plusses and minuses of each option and then, if I have time, I'll say, "This is what I would do because . . ."

If you do this for any length of time, fans will realize that the manager is sometimes right and sometimes wrong, just like the announcer and the fan back home or at the stadium. If we could see the future, we could make the right calls every time. But we cannot.

My doctor once told me that the best physicians are the best guessers; the same can be said for managers. The risk of a bad guess in the field of medicine could mean life or death or some dramatic consequence in between. Too many bad guesses in the dugout won't kill anyone, but you'd never know it listening to fans. At least the doctors have a little privacy. They also have malpractice insurance. I'm not sure a manager's job is insurable.

Broadcast jobs are generally more secure—especially if you work for the team and not the station. When you work for the team you're expected to promote the club, which is easy to do if you're a fan. That was my position throughout my time with the Astros. I always hoped the team would win and I always gave the opposing team credit. In fact, I tried to make the enemy seem as formidable as I knew they were. A lot of fans don't know much about the other teams; they think their own players are the best and can't understand why they don't win more often. If you build the other guy up, it makes you feel more heroic when you beat him and less unworthy in defeat. That's the way it is on the field, ant that's the way it should be reported. It's an extremely difficult game and major league players make it look too easy.

To that end, one of the best things a color announcer can do is to explain why certain plays are exceptional even though they may look routine. Another thing that an analyst can do is teach—that's why the color man is more important on TV than on radio. It's almost impossible to teach on radio: You really need the pictures, especially the replays, to explain many things about the game.

Sometimes, however, you don't get all the pictures you would like, or, as is more often the case, you get replays that you don't want. One time we were doing a series in Atlanta and the director kept showing replays of routine outs. My preference was to speak only when I could add something to the play-by-play description. After the game, the director was annoyed with me because I didn't talk about all the replays. I'm pretty sure he felt that I was showing him up, though he didn't say those words. He simply stated that the replays were the responsibility of the analyst. He wanted me to talk about every replay. "What if it's a routine two-hop ground ball to short?" I asked. "If there is nothing special about the play, should I just restate what my partner has just said?"

"Yes," he replied.

A meeting halfway was the best solution to this problem and I think this type of policy was written without words. We both made our points—we didn't replay so many easy plays after that and, when we did, I talked about them.

Talking to players was another thing entirely. It seems like interviews would be easy, but they can be difficult, especially at first. There is the natural fear that you will forget the questions you planned to ask and end up uttering incoherent platitudes. This happened to me a few times at first, but less once I learned that the purpose of the interview is to listen to the player, coach, or manager. The announcer should try to stay out of it, something I learned from Jack Buck, the legendary former Cardinals announcer and Hall of Famer.

BUCK: Interview with Larry Dierker in 3-2-1 . . . Back at the ballpark, I have the skipper of the Astros, Larry Dierker. How's it going?

DIERKER: Uh. Fine. I mean we've been playing good ball and blah, blah, blah. (I wasn't prepared to jump right in that quickly.)

BUCK: Has the talk about going from the booth to the dugout subsided?

DIERKER: Blahblahblahblahblahblahblahblah . . .

You get the point; he presents his guest to the audience and lets him do the talking. This is really effective when your guest speaks well, but that's not always the case. Sometimes you get a young Latino kid who doesn't speak English very well; sometimes you get the strong, silent type. The worst is what you get most often, the guy who tries to give a good interview but ends up saying the same thing about how his teammates put him in position to get the big hit, or his fielders made unbelievable plays to help him win the game. After a while, it seems like the movie *Groundhog Day*, where the same day keeps coming again and again.

I had a couple of interviews that taught me some practical lessons early in my broadcasting career. The first one came when I was interviewing then Astros manager Bill Virdon. We started the interview between the dugout and the first base line at Wrigley Field, but as we spoke, Bill kept shuffling his feet and moving back toward the foul line. I moved with him until I ran out of slack in the cord to my microphone. At that point, I had to stop. Thankfully, Bill stopped moving too and came back toward me. From that point on I never moved when I was interviewing someone. If you keep the mike in one place, your guest will stay put unless you drive him back by putting it too close to him.

On another occasion, I was interviewing Don Sutton in San Diego after he had pitched a complete game victory. While we were in commercial break, we checked the IFB (interrupt feedback), the earpiece that allows the announcer to get directions from the truck. On this night, it wasn't working; I would not be able to get instructions electronically, so we had to go with hand signals.

"Look, I'll count you down from a minute," the AD (assistant director) said.

"How long are we going?" I asked.

"About three minutes."

"Will you give me thirty seconds?"

"Yes and I'll count you down from ten."

After I fooled around with the volume control on my IFB and couldn't get it to work, I didn't have time to take it out. So I conducted the interview, watching the AD for signs. We weren't even close to the end of the interview when the IFB suddenly started working. I had left the volume control all the way up. So when it kicked in it was so loud it almost knocked me off my feet. I must have looked foolish as I frantically reached for the switch to turn it down. I could see that the AD and cameraman were laughing, and Sutton cracked a smile too. Even then, he knew a lot about broadcasting.

Most announcers like doing the game better than the interviews. One interview is about as good as another, but the games are always different. I operated under the assumption that the game I was doing was more important than games already played. I liked to go back and retrieve things from the past when they were pertinent, but, as a listener, I don't really like the "back when I played" and "we used to do it this way" routine. I find it unbecoming. I tried not to pontificate, only to add insight and help the listener understand. When a fan came up to me and told me that they learned a lot about baseball listening to our broadcast or reading my column, I was flattered. It was the nicest thing he could say to me. Much nicer than "I used to watch you pitch and you were a helluva pitcher." That type of compliment is also welcome, but I care more about what I'm doing right now.

When I went from the field to the booth, I studied my partners, Gene Elston and Dewayne Staats. Before the game, I followed them around the ballpark like a duckling, watching how they prepared and asking them questions. I studied how they scored the game and presented the out-of-town scores. Sometime around the All-Star break of my first season, I realized that I was using their material too much and I needed to get some of my own. While I still did many of the things they did, I started a couple of new projects: Whenever I came across a quote I liked, I jotted it down, and when I saw a listing of things that happened on any particular day during the season, I cut it out and pasted it in a book. Now I have these things in my computer; all I have to do is punch a couple of buttons and I can access this information. I can preview the this-day-in-baseball material before the game and then if something in the game seems relevant to something that happened in another season on that date, I can use it.

The key is relevance: I have heard many announcers jump the

gun because they have done all this great research and, by God, they are going to get everything in whether it makes sense or not. Say a player has stolen eight bases in the last two weeks without being caught. If you use that fact the first time he steps into the batter's box, you don't have any impact with it after he gets on base. If he doesn't get on, so be it. It's okay if you don't get it all in. He'll probably get on base tomorrow.

All these things are easy to say, but there are nets out for the unwary. Even the big fish get caught in them once in a while. One time, I was watching a playoff game between the Cardinals and the Braves. Vin Scully was doing the play-by-play and he had prepared a long list of quotes from Mark Twain, which was a masterstroke since the game was in St. Louis, right there on the Mississippi River. After the first quote, I thought, "What a great thing to say. You're the best, Vinny, the best." Unfortunately, the game soon turned south and became one of those ugly 13–2 affairs that take forever and have about as much drama as Huck and Jim floating lazily downstream. But Vinny kept hustling: He had the Twain quotes ready and he used them—all of them.

"No, Vinny, no," I said. By the fifth inning I was cringing.

This is where the color man is supposed to come to the rescue by offering some interesting asides, by telling some stories, or by just starting a conversation about events in the world of baseball. Unfortunately, this is usually when the color man drifts off on the wings of reverie, or checks his watch to determine if the game will end in time for him to keep his dinner reservations. When I was young, I listened to Vin Scully virtually every day as the Dodgers played their part in the American epic, summer after summer. He really was—and probably still is—the best, but even he can't make something out of nothing.

My all-time broadcast blooper came in San Diego (where, it seems, many of the oddest moments of my career took place); luckily for me it was toward the end of a night game, probably about midnight in Houston, and I don't think many people heard it, but it was all we could do in the booth to finish the inning without exploding into laughter.

Larry Andersen had come on to pitch for the Padres. Andy had spent most of his career with the Astros and was very popular. He became even more popular after Astros fans realized what they got when they traded him to Boston—Jeff Bagwell. Larry signed with the Padres after helping the Red Sox into the playoffs in 1991. He subsequently injured his neck and was just coming off the disabled list. Bill Brown said something like "Andersen hasn't pitched in three weeks. He has had a disc problem in his neck and the Padres don't know if he will be able to play next year, even though he is under contract."

I said, "The amazing thing is that Andy has pitched better than anyone else who has had a sore neck could imagine. Even though he has been on the DL twice, for a total of forty days, he is still 4-2 with seven saves—not bad for a guy who has been pitching all year with a bulging dick, uh, disc, in his neck."

We looked at each other and barely stifled our mirth. When the inning ended, the booth erupted in riotous laughter. I said that Andy must be a real ladies' man, what with the extra appendage and all.

During my last season as a player in St. Louis, I got to know the late Jack Buck, a real class act, and another of the best announcers in the business. If he knew how to conduct an interview, he was even better during the game. Jack wasn't a screamer; he didn't use coined phrases or give you the huckster routine. He simply offered an intelligent and witty interpretation of the game, with a dry, ironic voice. He was in Scully's league, no doubt. I really haven't heard many other announcers because I was either playing or not tuned in. Elston and Staats were good professionals; they were my early mentors and they were terrific. The last few years, I worked TV with another real pro, Bill Brown.

For most of my broadcasting career I shared the booth with Milo Hamilton, who loves the game almost as much as he loves to hear himself describe it. He is a shameless homer, a second guesser, and an umpire baiter extraordinaire. His routine is so predictable that I frequently knew what he was going to say before he said it: "Split the plate in two at the knees . . . right in at the belt buckle . . .

he's hotter than a depot stove . . . that may not be a record but it's way above average . . . he's got the guts of a government mule." And so on and so forth . . .

Every time Milo is asked for an autograph, he signs, "Milo Hamilton, H.O.F. [Hall of Fame] '92, Holy Toledo." He has a Hall of Fame pin for his sport coat and has had his own baseball cards printed so he always has something to sign. He keeps a goodly supply of these cards in his pocket just in case someone wants an autograph. If nobody asks for it, he'll offer. One night in Philadelphia, he was talking with Brownie and me, when our AD, a girl named Karen, came into the booth. He immediately offered a personally autographed card to her and she couldn't say no. Nor could she read his writing. She looked at the Holy Toledo part and said, "Isn't that nice. 'Happy Trails,' how sweet."

We all got a good grin out of that one and when we flew to Atlanta that night, Brownie and I described the incident for a couple of other folks. "I'm going to use that phrase tomorrow night," Brownie said. It was clearly out of character for him, as he is not a comedian, just a good reporter. As it turned out, Jeff Bagwell hit a home run the next night and Brownie said, "Happy Trails! That ball is outta here!"

Milo is obsessed with protecting his own verbal turf. Once, I was doing radio play-by-play on a sunny day in Florida and Milo was off mike. A batter lofted a fly ball into medium-deep center field. I said that the outfielder looked up, "glasses gleaming," and made the catch. Well, the "glasses gleaming" part was an expression I learned from Milo. It was a good one, because if you're sitting at home, you can really picture the scene. As soon as I said it, I looked over at Milo and smiled, but he just shook his head, muttering, "No, no, no." His trademark phrase is "Holy Toledo." I guess he feels he's got the copyright on that one, but my dad used to say it when I was a kid and I know he had never heard of Milo Hamilton.

One time, he came up with something on the spur of the moment that cracked me up and still elicits a grin when I think about it. One of our outfielders, Richard Hidalgo, was having a good year. For some reason, people tend to pronounce his name as if it was spelled Hildago (Hil-dog-o), and, as a result, he acquired the nick-name "Doggy."

One night at the Astrodome, Doggy was having a good game at the plate. Every time he came up, a fan down below our broadcast booth started barking like a dog and doing a darn good job of it. We could tell that the sound was coming through on the air because we could hear it in our headsets. After one particularly loud sequence of ruffing and woofing, Milo said, "Somebody get that guy some Alpo."

Milo is a character, almost a caricature; he is also a dedicated professional. He keeps books on things like multiple steals and multiple home runs. He frequently comes up with information that is not disseminated by the PR departments before the game. After an average 5–4 game, it takes him about two hours to finish his record keeping. Sometimes, when we play a high-scoring extra-inning game at night, and have a day game the next afternoon, he sacrifices sleep to finish his preparation. He also calls in a report to our flagship station every morning. When we are on the West Coast, he has to get up at 6:00 A.M. to call the station. When it comes to energy, he is the best I have ever seen. He's the Pete Rose of the broadcast booth. One time, when we had a sluggish extra-inning game going, I offered to take the play-by-play for an inning to let him rest. This was perhaps the fourteenth inning and we had been on the air for at least four hours. "I'm all right," he said, and he was: He kept blasting away for three more innings until the game was mercifully over.

Milo did a lot of doubleheaders when he first broke into the business in the 1950s. Back then there were more open dates and more doubleheaders on the schedule. Like Ernie Banks, he views a twin bill as an opportunity to have more fun. But even Milo has his limit. One time we had an afternoon double-dip in San Francisco; at that time, I was doing all the color on television and Milo and Gene Elston were alternating, doing the whole game on radio one day, and TV the next. On the television side we were committed to stay on the air between games and Milo had game 2. Before the game we discussed how we would handle it, and it was decided that I would recap the game to give Milo the time to change booths and get hooked up with his earpiece. After I threw it to a commercial break, Milo and I would set the scene for the second game together. He wasn't happy about this arrangement because he wouldn't have time to take a breather and write down the lineups for the second game. He was right to have been annoyed: The station should have provided some programming to help us get ready for the second game.

Well, the first game was a long one. We lost it and Milo was not in a good mood when he came in to join me. He needed help getting hooked up, but our AD in the booth was busy trying to help me and communicate with the TV truck. When we came back from the break the camera was on me because Milo still didn't have his coat on. He was, however, wired into the truck and did have a microphone in his hand. I talked for a while until he got suited up and then tossed it to him. He was angry with Joe O'Rourke, our director, and so he opened up with something like, "Well here we are back in San Francisco. I don't know if we are doing a ball game or a circus here, because it seems like Bozo the Clown is down in the truck." Well, that detonated Joe's Irish temper.

"If you're looking for a clown you should look in the mirror," Joe said, knowing that only Milo and I could hear him.

"We'll give you the lineups for the second game when we have time to write them down—maybe in the second or third inning," Milo fired back, knowing that everyone *could* hear him. "Right now we're standing here filling time because your friendly station back home doesn't have anything else for you to watch."

"Dierk, take over," Joe said. "I don't need any fucking prima donnas on the air right now!"

I started to backpedal, trying not to laugh because I knew the viewers back home were only hearing half the conversation, if you could call it that. I talked a little more and threw it to a break and then listened as Milo and Joe had it out in full fury.

By the time we came back, Milo had composed himself and we moved into the second game with some semblance of order. But, afterward, when we got on the team bus, the chill factor between Milo and Joe made Candlestick Park feel like a sauna bath.

A few years ago, Milo exited the television side of the business. He didn't like taking directions from a young whippersnapper or an old coot in the truck, preferring to dictate the flow of the game himself. Honestly, he does a much better job of it than the TV guys—he knows when to stick with the action and how to depart from it when it drags.

Now that I have spent a summer at home, I can more easily understand the way the broadcast competes with ticket sales. The owners make so much money from TV that they almost have to take it, the crowd be damned. I thought I would attend about one game every home stand, but I didn't go that often. In fact, I didn't go at all unless I had something else to do at the ballpark. At home, I can listen to the announcers, who are more up-to-date on the team than I am. I can also go to the bathroom without standing in line and go to the refrigerator between innings. It's convenient and I don't have to miss a single pitch—sort of.

Last summer, I was working with my son, Ryan, on his pitching delivery. I wanted him to watch Carlos Hernandez because his abbreviated windup is a lot like the one I would like to see Ryan use. Unfortunately, the director of the telecast was more interested in Carlos's facial expression, a kid in the stands, or the batter's glare. With everything at portrait range we seldom saw the full windup. As a result, we only got to see Carlos's entire motion a time or two in three innings. What we typically saw was the tail end of his delivery, just before he released the ball. I can't really complain about the way the director was shooting the game because it was very dramatic: He set the scene with crowd shots and portrayed the emotions of the competitors by zooming in tight on their faces. Still, I was frustrated because we weren't able to watch the whole game, just bits and pieces of it. I know the telecast moves along better when the camera shots come quickly, one after the other. But I still like the centerfield shot of the catcher giving the sign followed by the pitcher delivering the pitch. But I guess I shouldn't worry— if something eventful happens on one particular pitch, they can always show me the replay.

CHAPTER 6

Umpires

When I'm right, no one remembers, when I'm wrong,
no one forgets.

—DOUG HARVEY, NATIONAL LEAGUE UMPIRE

I'LL NEVER FORGET the first argument I had with an umpire. It occurred just after a high school game; the umpire was working solo that day. He had to stay at home plate as the tying runner raced around the bases on a ball in the gap. The runner scored easily to tie the game, but we were able to make a play on the batter as he tried for a triple. I was near third base. The umpire wasn't. He called the runner safe at third when he was obviously out and I protested, but to no avail. It was the bottom of the seventh, the last inning in a high school game.

When the next batter got a hit to beat me I rushed the umpire, like George Brett when they called him out for having pine tar too high on his bat after he hit a game-winning home run against the Yankees. George was demon-possessed and so was I. As I argued, the umpire kept turning around. I kept going around too, trying to get in his face. I remembered what my father demanded of me when he was bawling me out and, borrowing his words, I commanded the umpire: "Look at me when I'm talking to you." This didn't work and I finally got so frustrated that I grabbed him by the shoulders and tried to spin him around. When I did this, he lost his balance and fell to the ground. I stood there for a moment and then walked away. I knew I was in big trouble and I was; I ended up getting suspended for our next game.

I was a hothead in high school. I got suspended another time for throwing my bat and got kicked out of a basketball game too. Over the years, though, I learned to contain myself. About thirty years after I was suspended for slamming the umpire, I got invited to play a round of golf at Lakeside Country Club in Los Angeles. That suited me fine because the golf course is right on the way from my mother's house to Dodger Stadium. As I gathered with my brother Rick, his friend Craig, and one of Craig's clients at the first hole, the client said, "You don't remember me, do you?"

I said that I didn't, wondering why I should. "My name is Connie Gonzalez," he said. "I'm the umpire you threw on the ground at Chatsworth back when you were in high school." I didn't remember his face but I did remember the incident. We laughed about it then, and as we played golf and shot the breeze, I found Connie to be a friendly fellow and a very fine golfer. I wondered how I could have been so crazy when I first met him.

Arguing with umpires is still a part of the attraction in baseball. A good rhubarb offers just a trace of the outrageous behavior that has vaulted the World Wrestling Entertainment into prominence in recent years. Ice hockey is the same way: The NHL, where they simply duke it out rather than argue, makes MLB look sedate.

In the days of the horseless carriage, baseball managers gesticulated and fumed, partly out of anger and partly because the umpires allowed it. It became part of the entertainment value of the sport. But, because baseball is the self-proclaimed National Pastime, those who run it feel a certain pious obligation to meld the game's past with their version of its future. The kicking, snorting, and hat spiking often includes epithets that can be heard over the sensitive crowd mikes of television. This breach of propriety has made some executives in the league office squirm—it seems so, well, uncivilized.

Expert fans can appreciate the undercurrent of violence in a 95 mph fastball under the chin, but anyone can understand the football-like violence of a runner barreling into an infielder or catcher. Real baseball fans don't need the hockey-style brawls. Some people fail to see the need for any violence whatsoever. But a mound-charging melee certainly brings the underlying emotion to the surface. Sometimes the players seem so businesslike that they appear not to care. In almost every case, the players are much more emotional than they seem to be when you watch them play.

As a pitcher, I exercised my right to pitch tight on a hitter, but after the first few years I did not feel the need to protect my turf. I would hit a guy if I had to, but I certainly didn't like it. Still, I didn't mind coming inside at all and that philosophy carried over into my managing career. I told our pitchers time and again that they needed to pitch inside of the inside corner and I challenged our starters to push every hitter back from the plate the first or second time he faced him. Hitting batters is unavoidable—no pitcher has good enough control to pitch 200 innings without unintentionally hitting someone.

I seem to have developed a reputation for pitching inside and yet I only hit five or six guys a year. To me, it was the same as a walk. It didn't bother me except as it affected the other team's chance of scoring. Still, I never tried to throw at a batter's head. Until a few years ago when I was talking with Hawk Harrelson, I thought I had pitched for thirteen years without ever beaning anyone. But Hawk told me that I hit him smack on the helmet when he was trying to bunt in a spring training game at Winter Haven. I didn't remember that so maybe I hit someone else in the head too. I know I definitely didn't damage anyone's career with a head-shot. But I did break two wrists, Roberto Clemente's and Ron Santo's. I saw Clemente that same night at a function in our team hotel. I told him I was sorry and he said not to worry about it. In Santo's case, he was in the hospital with a cast on his arm, listening to the game as we won. "They put you on the postgame show," he told me, "and I was fit to be tied when you said that you didn't hit me on purpose and that we were good friends." We were good friends, however, and still are, even though Santo hit a grand slam off me later on.

I never had a hitter charge the mound on me, but I was in the National League. I believe most of the fighting started in the American League with the advent of the designated hitter. It used to be that you could get even with a beanball artist by affording him the opportunity to see how the pitch looks from the hitter's point of view. After 1973, when the pitcher stopped going to the plate in the American League, hitters started charging the mound because it was their only means of retribution. This overt display of machismo came at a time when we as a society were giving the two-fingered peace sign more than its one-fingered opposite. These days, the power brokers in the modern game seem to be appalled over the notion that a pitcher would actually try to strike a batter with a pitch. This indignation has made its way into the rulebook, giving umpires the right to kick a player out of a game for hitting a batter. It doesn't have to be retaliatory, just suspicious.

One day in Kansas City, our starting pitcher, Scott Elarton, was ejected in the first inning for hitting Rey Sanchez with a pitch. In the top of the inning the Royals pitcher, a kid just up from the minors, hit our first two batters. But he was as wild as a cowlick, hitting our second batter with a curveball. Nobody on either team thought the beanings were intentional, but umpire Jeff Nelson ejected Elarton in the bottom of the inning just the same when after four straight pitches away, Elly came in and nicked Sanchez, who ran down to first base without even looking sideways. I argued with Nelson throughout the time it took Ron Villone to warm up, at least five minutes. What Nelson kept telling me was that he didn't have any choice in the matter; the league office wanted to curb the violence.

"Do you think he was throwing at him?" I asked.

"That's not the point," he said. "They want us to clean it up."

As we spoke, I continued to ask Nelson if he thought Elarton intentionally hit Sanchez. I think Jeff realized where I was going with this line of questioning and he finally said yes, which was his only defense if I protested his decision. This incident as much as any other illustrates the current relationship between players and umpires. They are both subject to the wishes of the league officials in New York. The umpires don't feel that they can police the game as they see fit and the players feel vulnerable to the disposition of the umpires. I questioned Jeff Nelson's judgment and a few weeks later Gerry and I met with Ralph Nelson (no relation), the league's director of umpires. Ralph assured us that the umpire was not supposed to interpret the league's desire to cut down on fighting exactly that way. (As the manager, I was ejected with Elarton due to the league rule, but I was never fined.)

Elarton argued vehemently that day in Kansas City and I kept trying to move him away from the scene. Arguing with umpires can be suicidal for a pitcher. You can get kicked out of a game for bickering over balls and strikes. Or you can just make the umpire mad, and have borderline pitches called balls. I guess every pitcher has a way to let the umpire know when he disagrees with a call. Mine, when I was pitching, was to look back at the scoreboard to verify that the pitch was, indeed, called a ball, and to show disbelief on my face. The umpires knew what I was doing but the fans didn't. I wasn't showing up the umpire.

A pitcher should never show an umpire up. It's not so much that the ump will stick it to you, as that he will subconsciously hope you fail. Since you will typically throw 100 or more pitches in a game and try to hit corners with most of them, the home plate umpire can have a great impact on your success or failure. When I came up to the plate to hit, I spoke to the umpire in a friendly way, hoping he would like me or, at least, not dislike me.

During my entire thirteen-year pitching career, I failed to follow the friendly approach only once. That was when Hank Aaron hit a three-run homer off me in the first inning of a game in Atlanta. The ball was foul by at least ten feet and I got to third base way ahead of Aaron. He was trotting—I was dashing. Al Barlick was the umpire at third. I considered him to be the best umpire in the league, but best doesn't mean perfect. When I got to Barlick I pointed to the foul pole where a fan in the first row of seats was jumping up and down with the ball. "Look at the fan with the ball," I told Barlick. "He's in foul territory."

Al told me that the ball had gone over the foul pole, which was ridiculous because it wasn't hit that well. "Are you telling me that the ball went over the pole, made a left turn, and came straight down in the first row of seats?" I asked.

"That's the way I saw it," he said. And that's the way I lost the game. I don't know how he missed the call, but I do know that Aaron had not really broken Babe Ruth's record until he hit his 716th homer.

One of my teammates with the Cardinals, John Denny, argued balls and strikes all the time. I bet the umpires hated to work home plate when he was pitching. One time he went so far as to charge home plate, cussing up a storm. He got tossed from that game and it was a start he could have won. Later in the year, the same umpire was working in St. Louis, and when he came out on the field before the game, Denny was signing autographs along the side of the dugout. This fan-friendly gesture is common with players who are not in the lineup, but it was, and is, against the rules. Players are supposed to leave the field fifteen minutes before game time. This is a rule that was never enforced—until this time. The umpire who got Denny the first time got him again. He was kicked out of the game before it even started! This outrageous call speaks to the attitude of a lot of umpires. They want to maintain control of the game, which means they feel compelled to discipline the guys who protest too much. But most pitchers are not like Denny. They adopt the respectful son approach when dealing with the men in blue. I think the friendly approach helped me a little with the umpires who called my games both when I was a pitcher and a manager.

I think the thing I dreaded most when I took over as manager of the Astros was my first argument. I knew it was inevitable and I worried about it all winter. I knew I would have no appetite for it because it doesn't help you win; umpires almost never change their calls, especially if you are yelling at them. My first confrontation

THIS AIN'T BRAIN SURGERY

came in San Diego: Greg Bonin was the second base umpire and he called our runner out on a throw from the left field corner. I thought I saw the ball on the ground as Quilvio Veras applied the tag. Since the out ended our half of the inning, I went running out to protest as our players ran out to begin the bottom of the inning. Bonin turned his back and walked into short right field and didn't see me coming. I had to run a long way to get to him, and I think I scared him when I came screaming up from behind. He seemed incredulous that I would argue such an obvious out call. When I told him that the ball was on the ground, he told me that Veras took it out of his glove after the tag.

As I walked back to the dugout, our third baseman, Bill Spiers, told me that he thought Veras had snow-coned the ball (caught it half in the glove and half sticking out of the webbing). A cameraman down at the end of the dugout showed a replay to several of our players. It was a snow cone all the way—I was wrong! Well at least the confrontation that I dreaded was over. I was glad of that. But my heart was beating like crazy. I wondered if I would get used to it or if it would be like a car wreck every time. I tried not to get emotional when I was pitching because I wanted to maintain my mental faculties, and as a manager this was even more important. But how could I do it?

After that, I made a mental note not to argue unless I was certain the call was wrong or I felt the need to get kicked out of the game in order to send the team a wake-up call. During the rest of my years in the dugout, I never wavered from that way of thinking and I don't think I was wrong more than once or twice. It had to be pretty obvious before I would leave the dugout. Sometimes a call would elicit a response from a few guys on the bench; other times everyone sprang to the railing of the dugout simultaneously. On those occasions, I was compelled to go out and argue. Fortunately, those were times when the call was obviously wrong and I would have gone out anyway. There were more than a few calls that I didn't protest even though I knew they were wrong, because they had no bearing on the game. If you are up by six or seven runs in the eighth, or way behind, what's the point? I realize I wasn't as combative as some managers and I sensed a few times that our players wanted me to be more aggressive with the umpires. But I remembered that when I was playing I didn't think the rhubarbs did much good. I imagined most of the players still feel the same way about it. I guess I should have gone out more, but that isn't my personality. It's hard to put on a show if you're not an actor. The fans love it though. They want you to stick up for the team. I wonder how they would like it if they actually had to do it. It's like beating your head against a wall to alleviate a headache. To this day, I am amazed that Bobby Cox and a few others can rage against the heavens one minute and be back in the dugout, cool as a cucumber, the next.

One night in Los Angeles, Joe West made a curious call that really had me puzzled. The Dodgers had a runner on first and he broke for second to steal. The batter hit the ball and it struck the runner when he was about halfway to second base. In this case, the runner is always called out, but West called him safe. As I was heading out to argue, Mike Cubbage told me that there was a rule regarding a fielder being in front of the runner. Well, when I got to first base, Joe told me the same thing. He said that Bagwell, who had been holding the runner on first, was in front of the base runner on the play. I maintained that Bagwell had nothing to do with the play. He agreed, but refused to reverse his call. "A rule is a rule," he told me. We lost the game and afterward I checked the rulebook and found rule No. 7.04b, which states that the runner is not responsible for being hit with a batted ball if it has passed by a fielder before it hit him. It is clear that the rule is intended to cover situations where a fielder might block the runner's view of the ball. But in this case, the runner was a good thirty feet away from Bagwell. I understood the rule but did not think it was interpreted properly. I should have protested right then and there but I didn't because I wasn't sure how the rule was written. We checked with the league office anyway and were told that the rule had, in fact, been interpreted improperly. It was a hollow victory, but does demonstrate the best way to learn a rule—to have it happen in a game and affect the outcome. I'm not sure we could have won that game anyway, but I am sure that if it happened again, I would know the rule. When I got back to the dugout that night, after arguing the call, Cubby told me that the only reason he knew there was such a rule was that it was called against him when he was managing a minor league game.

Honestly, I think Joe was just trying to bust my chops because I was a rookie manager. He was the home plate umpire in my managerial debut game against the Braves in the Astrodome. When we met at home plate, he asked me to review the ground rules, which is the responsibility of the home manager. I was suitably embarrassed, for I had not read them myself. Both encounters with West taught me something and both lessons stuck. He got me fair and square on the ground rules; he got me in L.A. just by being a jerk. I didn't let these incidents bother me and I don't think Joe did either. For the most part, I found the umpires to be expert in their knowledge of the rules. I was also impressed with their level of concentration and the way they hustled to get into position to call a play.

From the dugout, with your head at ground level, it's tough to see a play well enough to argue it unless it is at home plate or at first or third base depending on which dugout you're in. Generally speaking, it's impossible to see a tag play at third base if you're in the first base dugout. There was one play at third, however, that got me into the most strident screaming match I had with an umpire. The game was at the Astrodome at the end of the 1997 season, when we were trying to clinch the division title and qualify for the playoffs.

We were threatening a comeback in the seventh inning when our left fielder, Thomas "Tank" Howard, took off for third on a double steal with one out. He appeared to be safe, but Eric Gregg called him out. Tank grabbed his helmet in disbelief and Cubby started arguing.

I walked out deliberately, thinking, This might not be a bad time to get thrown out. I started yelling at Gregg when I was still twenty feet away. I gestured with my arms and used every expletive in the book. Luckily for me, he got right in my face and screamed back. At one point I said, "It wasn't even fucking close." He said, "You're right, it wasn't even fucking close." We both repeated that line, like children, four or five times. Finally he said, "When you watch the replay, you're going to have to apologize to me."

"I'll tell you what, Eric," I said. "When I see the replay, if you're right, I'll apologize." He seemed satisfied with this and I was about spent. I turned to walk back to the dugout and got a standing ovation. I watched the replay that night, and didn't have to eat crow the next day. I don't know why Eric let me persist so long. As irate as he seemed, he sure showed a lot of patience. By going toe-to-toe with me, he made it possible for me to show some passion. The way we were playing at the time, and with the division in the balance, I didn't have to fake it. Still, I don't know if I could have raged for that long if he had just turned away and shrugged me off, which is what most umpires do. But Eric is an old-school guy. Maniacal arguments provide good entertainment, which is why they are still part of the sport.

But now we have rules for arguing. You're supposed to keep your distance and hold your arms by your side—very polite. If you argue that way, the fans won't cheer for you and your players will think you don't have any guts. I would have been happy to have a rule, like in basketball and football, where you can't even enter the field of play—most managers would. But the "in your face" method is good theater and if it's part of the price of admission, we should do it the old-fashioned way.

A lot of times, I did not go out while we were in the field because our pitcher was in a good rhythm and I didn't want to interrupt the flow. I knew the umpire had missed a call, but I also knew he was not going to change it and, moreover, I thought our pitcher could overcome it, especially if he could just keep pitching and not have to wait for me to finish arguing and get back in the dugout. If I were pitching in a good rhythm, I wouldn't want to wait. I would want to keep pitching.

When I did argue, I usually ended up saying, "Check the replay." Perhaps the first time I said this was when Bill Spiers slid in ahead of a tag at third base in St. Louis. This was in the early stages of the game and we were in position to score. Since I was in the third base dugout I had a very good view of the play, but the umpire, Dan Iasonga, did not have a clear line of sight. He was posi-

tioned right behind the fielder so that his view of the tag was ob-
scured by the third baseman. The first thing I did was to walk over
to the bag and gesture to show him what happened.

"Get away from that bag," he commanded me.

"What do you mean?" I said. "This is where the play was."

"Just get away from there and quit motioning with your
arms."

"What are you talking about?" I said.

"I'm telling you to get away from that bag and quit moving
your arms. It looks like shit."

"You know what looks like shit?" I said.

With that, he walked over to where I was standing near the
bag and got on his tiptoes so he could get right in my face and said,
"No, I don't know what looks like shit. You tell me."

I knew I was on the brink of getting tossed and since it was still
early, I walked away saying, "I think you already know."

I suppose every manager has an umpire who gives him problems. The rhubarbs involving Earl Weaver and Ron Luciano are
legendary. My guy was Iasonga. He was behind home plate in Arizona one night and our catcher, Mitch Meluskey, was having words
with him throughout the game. Mitch kept holding pitches where
he caught them on the corner after Iasonga called them balls.
About halfway through the game, we had a sizable lead and Mitch
kept holding the ball. Iasonga told Mitch to stop holding the ball.
"It looks like shit," he said, using the same words he had used
on me.

With two outs in the bottom of the ninth, Mitch thought we
had strike three. Iasonga didn't agree. On the next pitch, the batter
hit a double down the left field line, driving in two meaningless
runs. But Mitch had all he could take; he turned around and told
Iasonga exactly what he thought about his umpiring. Mitch got
tossed, and our pitcher, Jose Cabrera, was pacing around the mound
like a tiger as the new catcher donned the gear. After the last out,
Cabrera started screaming and gesturing toward home plate. At
that point, second base umpire Wally Bell kicked Jose out of the
game. It was a nitpicky thing to do—it would cost Cabrera a few

hundred dollars. But it had absolutely no bearing on the outcome of the game or Cabrera's availability the next day.

I guess I must be one of a select few who have seen a player ejected before the start of one game and after the end of another.

Bell was sticking up for Iasonga when he tossed Cabrera and I understand that. As an umpire you are generally belittled by the contestants and reviled by the fans. If you did not have each other, you would have no one. A lot of times, a veteran like Bell supports a young umpire like Iasonga in order to show solidarity and I appreciate that too. In 2001 the umps had a real need to circle the wagons. Even the league, it seemed, was against them. Many of the big-name umpires had recently lost their jobs over a labor issue when their negotiator, Richie Phillips, threatened to stage a strike in the playoffs if the league didn't meet the umpire's demands. The league called their bluff and about half of the veteran umpires lost their jobs over it. What's more, the league office, principally Bud Selig and Sandy Alderson, was determined to change the way balls and strikes were called.

I'll never forget the meeting we major league managers had with the league officials and umpires in the huge conference room at the Loews Anatole hotel in Dallas at the winter meetings before the 2001 season. The grandeur of the room and the occasion made it seem like the United Nations. Along one side of the long, linen-clad rectangle of tables in the center of the room were chairs for the thirty major league managers. There was a new legal pad on the table in front of each seat. On the other side, a similar number of veteran umpires were already seated. All the accoutrements of style were laid out neatly, including a silver tray of pastries and coffee and large urns of water and tea. The CEO of baseball, Sandy Alderson, sat with league officials Frank Robinson and Bob Watson at the head of the table with a slide projector for his dog-and-pony show. In this setting, the sight of a bunch of old ballplayers and umpires seemed somehow, somewhat ludicrous, but Sandy, an attorney, looked right at home.

Prior to the summit in Dallas, Alderson had met with most of the crew chiefs concerning the commissioner's pledge to the fans of America that the strike zone would be called as it is written, meaning at least a foot higher than the current practice. In our meeting with them, the umpires gave the proposal strong, unwavering support. But as some of my comrades (notably Tom Kelly and Bobby Cox) put up a squawk, the umpires' ranks started to break too. Despite some equivocating but not much, it was clear that Sandy had his marching orders from commissioner Bud Selig and that this was a done deal. Still, I don't think any of us actually thought it was practical.

Personally, I didn't care how they called the strike zone as long as they called it the same way for both teams. With a larger zone, there would be more strikeouts, fewer walks, and probably more home runs. I think the zone was being called a little lower than when I pitched, but not much. As a broadcaster, I said the top of the zone was the catcher's shoulders or the batter's waist, which was about the same place. I would have loved it if the zone was called by the rulebook definition when I was pitching, but I don't think any of us were as consumed with delivering the game as per the rulebook as much as Selig was.

We were not dealing with practicalities in this meeting, however, but ideals. The league was going to support the umpires all the way, but the umpires themselves had to take a stand they were unsure about. They stood squarely on the fault line, with the players. The players and the umps against the league—who woulda thunk it?

We managers were expected to be tolerant and to help reduce the players' complaints. I am not a social Neanderthal, but I had my doubts about lawyers legislating the play of a ball game the same way they might legislate the distribution of food stamps from Washington, D.C.

What is going to happen, I thought, is that we are all going to get out there and start sweating and spitting and cussing and playing ball. And when the new strike zone takes effect, there's going to be a lot of grousing. Finally, each umpire's zone will slowly go back to where it was in the first place and we'll all go home for Thanksgiving. You can flash all the mahogany paneling and sterling silver you want, but you're still dealing with umpires and ballplayers. In the end, the umpires paid the highest price, as usual. They were required to practice the new strike zone in winter leagues and to watch instructional videos.

The players grumbled but there was no major disruption. I think the zone is a bit higher now, which is good for the sport, as it cuts down on walks and promotes home run hitting. That, in combination with the relaxing of the "full stop" rule with regard to balks, helped the games move along a little faster. There are a few hard-throwing pitchers, like Curt Schilling, who have good enough control to pitch effectively across the top of the strike zone, but most of the guys in the big leagues these days have been trained to pitch under aluminum bats. They only hurt themselves when they try to pitch upstairs. Most of the extra-base hits come off high pitches. If you're going to pitch upstairs effectively, you have to be able to throw hard and to pitch low too.

What really bothered me once we got into the season was that the umpires failed to carry out another goal that was clearly stated in that meeting: the assertion by the league that the most important thing was to "get the call right." It was specifically mandated that if a manager had a beef with a call he could ask an umpire to consult one of his comrades who may have had a better view of the play. I took this to mean that an umpire would be required to seek help from another member of his crew if I asked him to. They seemed to be trying to call higher strikes according to the rulebook description of the strike zone, but when there was a meeting on the infield as to a ball that was either fair or foul, or a close play that was either out or safe on the bases, the result was invariably to support the original call, even though many times they got it wrong.

One time, we were in Milwaukee and the Brewers second baseman (I believe it was Ron Belliard) came across the bag to make a double play. He bobbled the ball as he made the pivot and never really got hold of it until he was well past the bag. Everyone in the park could see it but the second base umpire called our runner out. I tried to get the umpire to solicit another opinion, but the more I talked, the more stubborn he became. It's just like asking the home plate umpire to seek assistance on a checked swing. If the guy doesn't want to ask for help, he doesn't have to. And many times he won't. But even when he does, if there is any intimation in his body language that he feels forced to ask, his cohort will support the original call every time.

I think, for the umpires' and the game's sake, the way a checked swing is called should be changed. A hitter can be called out on the appeal of a swing, but he cannot be called safe: In other words, if you ask the home plate ump to check with the first or third base umpire, the call can be changed from a ball to a strike. If the home plate umpire asks for help right away, the base ump will render his honest decision. If there is a delay, the home plate umpire's call will stand every time. Sometimes the home plate umpire calls a swing when the batter seems to have checked in time. In this case, the batter cannot ask for an appeal. As a pitcher I probably shouldn't say this, but I don't think a hitter should be vulnerable to a strike call on a checked swing with no right to appeal. I feel that the home plate umpires should ask for help from the base umpires every time there is a checked swing. That way, the pitcher and the hitter are on equal footing.

In the thirty-eight years I've been in baseball the idea of both umpires and players earning their stripes has been prevalent. As a young pitcher, I threw at a lot of batters in order to defend my teammates and establish my toughness. Later, I knew that some of our batters were hit by accident and I was not willing to put a guy on base every time someone got hit just to extract a pound of flesh.

Umpires are the same way: When they first come into the league they want to prove they are in charge; they don't want to be shown up and they think every argument makes them "look like shit." They toss a lot of people out of games to establish their authority. But after a few years on the lines they are less likely to eject a player or manager. Bruce Froemming was an absolute terror at first—a cross between Napoleon and Hitler. Now he is reasonable most of the time, unless it's a day game after a midsummer's night contest and he has to umpire behind the plate.

One night we were playing the Rockies and they had the bases loaded with two outs. One of their batters (I believe it was Todd Helton) took a healthy half-swing at a breaking ball in the dirt for strike three, which would have ended the inning. The home plate umpire called the pitch a ball, however, and we asked for an appeal. The third base umpire was just up from the minors to replace a major league umpire who was on vacation, and apparently wanting to support his comrade he called it a ball, even though everyone in the ballpark saw the swing. Helton ended up walking. I was out of shouting distance, in the front of the third base dugout. I also had a pitcher warming up and I had to decide if I wanted to make a change, and if so, if I wanted to double-switch. I was talking with my bench coach, Mike Cubbage, and my pitching coach, Burt Hooton, trying to make the right decision and so I didn't have time to walk to the opposite end of the dugout to argue. It turned out that the next two hitters got base hits before we finally got the third out. The Rockies scored four runs when they should have scored none. I didn't go to the bullpen for a relief pitcher, but you can imagine how hot I was at the end of the frame.

When the inning was over, I walked down to the far end of the dugout to complain. By that time, the third base ump had walked into the outfield, just like Bonin in San Diego. I didn't know his name and I didn't want to create a scene by running into the out-field between innings . . . so I waited. And waited. I knew he could see me there, and he didn't want to hear what I had to say, but as the inning was starting, he had to come back to the infield. When he was within earshot, I yelled, "Next time, watch the game."

He said, "What did you say?"

I said, "Watch the game. You just cost us four runs!"

With that, he kicked me out. I burst onto the field screaming and cussing. The other veteran umpires had to intercede and one of them, Jim Joyce, gave me a knowing look as if to say, "This guy is new and we can't do anything about it." What he actually said though was, "We can't do anything about it and you have to leave the field."

A week later, we were on the same trip, in Minnesota. Iasonga missed a call at first base and we were in the first base dugout. If our runner were safe, which we were sure he was, our guy on third would have scored, but, as it was, the inning was over. Our bench erupted in outrage and I had to argue. Because of my previous problems with Dan, and because it was early in the game, I was determined not to curse.

So it went like this: "He was safe."

"No, he was out."

"He was safe."

"He was out."

"Safe."

"Out."

"He was safe, Dan. Check the replay."

"You're always telling me to check the replay. I don't have to check the replay. And you're outta here," he said, giving me the thumb.

I was ejected twice on that trip without uttering a single epithet. The first time, I didn't even leave the dugout. The second time, I didn't even raise my voice. The point here is that an umpire's attitude is just as important, if not more important, than his knowledge of the rules and the accuracy of his calls. When I was playing, Tom Gorman was the best at controlling the mood of the game. He was a huge guy, tall and heavy, but he was like a big teddy bear when he was umpiring. He was almost impossible to argue with—it takes two to tango and Tommy wouldn't lead or follow. He would flap his jowls a time or two and look at his watch. "You've got one minute," he would say, and that is the last thing he would say. When he looked at his watch again, it was time to leave and most managers left. But when they did not and the minute was up, Tommy just kicked them out of the game. He seldom argued at all. I mentioned this to another umpire, Doug Harvey, and Doug went off on Tommy, saying he didn't have any guts, wouldn't stand behind his calls, made it tough on the other umpires, and a few more choice criticisms. Harvey may have missed fewer calls, but I liked Gorman better.

One thing Harvey did when I first came into the league that really irked me was when I threw a pitch I thought was a strike and he called it a ball, he would hold his thumb and index finger about an inch apart to show me how close it was. I was a young guy and never said anything about it, but our veteran pitchers hated it. They thought he was officious and they were right. No umpire can mince inches at home plate; the pitches come in with a lot of movement and the best an umpire can realistically do is to call them balls or strikes and leave it at that. Later in his career, Harvey stopped gesturing. I guess at that point he felt that his decisions were rendered from on high. He was good, no question. But he was nowhere near as good as he thought he was.

In fact, none of the umpires are as good as they think they are. As a rule, they are pretty bad. I can say this without hesitation now because I have watched them a lot on television where bad calls are almost always exposed. Hall of Fame umpire Bill Klem was at the end of a long career when he said, "In my heart, I never missed a call." I doubt that he could have said that if the watchful eye of television had scoped his heart.

During my first three years managing, I thought the umpires were a lot better than they were when I played. Now, I believe that the only reason I thought they were better is that I didn't have as good a view of the plays as I did when I was on the mound. After I had my seizure in 1999, I had to rest up for a month and I watched a lot of games on TV. I was surprised to see so many bad calls. I bet most of them went unnoticed by the players and coaches in the dugout—you almost have to be on the field or in front of a television set to see how bad the umpires really are. I do believe, however, that the umpires are doing their best. They hustle to try to get a good view of the play and they know the rules. I have come to believe that judgment calls are a lot more difficult than they look. I used to think I could do a better job than most major league umpires without any training, but I don't feel that way anymore. They may miss a lot of calls, but they get most of them right. When they're right, no one remembers.

I do think, however, that most modern umpires are better than their predecessors in the area of comportment. One night, Angel Hernandez was umpiring at third base in Phoenix: The D-Backs had a runner at second base. When the ball was hit to shortstop, he tried to advance to third. The throw was there in plenty of time, but I couldn't see the tag from the first base dugout. Bill Spiers could have missed the tag, but he jumped up in the air in disbelief when Angel called the runner safe and that was good enough for me. I tore out onto the field in a rage. Most umpires would make the out call regardless of the tag if the throw came in ahead of the runner, which this one clearly did. The umpires know the game. Angel knew the runner made a bonehead play; it would have been easy for him to make the out call and no one would have complained. But when Angel called him safe, he had to know I would come out to argue. I was really frustrated at the time, as it was late in the season and our lead in the N.L. Central was shrinking. I was looking for a reason to get ejected—a way to wake up a slumbering ball club. Well, I argued and argued, I used every filthy word I knew, and still, he wouldn't kick me out. I have been raised not to call people names and the one thing I had not done was to say, "You're an asshole." I finally realized that I was going to have to call him a name to get the hook and the minute I did it, he thumbed me— thank you very much. My memory might be hazy, but I don't recall any other umpire putting up with so much invective. Perhaps Gorman would have, but there weren't many reasonable umpires back then. Now that the league has come down on them, they aren't quite as tough. The fact that almost every game is televised and that all the viewers will see the replay may have something to do with their equanimity.

There are several things I think the league could do to help the umpires. The first is to insist that they take an outfield position at second base with a man on first. When I was a broadcaster, I used to say this all the time because we used the view from the center field camera to replay a stolen base attempt and we always got a good view from that angle because the infielders caught the catcher's throw in front of the bag. Oftentimes they turned toward the bag while applying the tag and blocked the umpire's view. I know beyond doubt that the outfield side gives the umpire a better view of the tag on the steal, but I have been told by several umpires that the view is better from the infield. That's probably true if the ball is coming in from the outfield, with the infielder on the outside of the bag, but in that case, the umpire would have time to get an inside position during the play even if he were behind the bag on the pitch.

My biggest complaint, however, is with the balk rule, which is intended to prevent the pitcher from deceiving the runner. If this is the case, why can a pitcher go into his delivery and swing his leg all the way around and fake a throw to second base? Why can he fake to third and throw to first or fake to third and fake to first? All this faking is done solely to deceive the runner but these tactics are allowed by the rules. With runners at first and third, it is almost impossible to steal second if the pitcher keeps using the double fake routine. In the late stages of a ball game, when one run can win or lose it, pitchers fake constantly and I don't blame them; the way the rule is written, they would be foolish not to. This strategy, however, really slows the game down. If the rule is intended to protect the runner from being deceived, the pitcher should have to throw to a base when he steps in that direction. Most pitchers don't like to throw to bases because there is a chance that they will make a bad throw allowing all runners to advance. I think the pitcher should have to take that risk. Faking to bases has no risk at all; it just consumes a lot of time.

Another thing I found interesting was the umpire calling "foul ball" every time a batter chopped a ball in front of home plate and did not run. A couple of times our catchers felt like the ball didn't hit the batter's foot. When we checked replays, most of the time the ball did nip the batter. But a couple of times it did not. I asked an umpire about this between innings one night because the play cost us a couple of runs. "How can you see the ball hit the guy's foot?" I asked.

"I can't," he said. "I have to go by his reaction. If he jumps up and down holding his foot, I assume the ball hit him. What else can I go on?"

I appreciated his honesty, because I know the ball is faster than the eye, but I told him I was going to tell all of our hitters to jump up and grab their foot every time they chop a ball in front of the plate. "Don't do that," he implored. "It's tough enough as it is with all the replays." Again, I appreciated his point, but I still told the hitters what he said and encouraged them to use the knowledge. What did they have to lose? If they ran, they would be out for sure. If they didn't, there was a good chance it would be called a foul ball.

As a player, I used a similar tactic when I was bunting. If I bunted on top of the ball and it only went a few feet in front of the plate, I intentionally slipped down to my hands and knees as if I had lost my footing, forcing the catcher to go over or around me. I got up and headed for first fairly quickly so it wouldn't look like interference and it worked for me several times. I even told our starting pitchers about it but none of them ever tried it. I don't think the umpire can call interference on you if you make an effort to get up and run.

So many things can, and usually do, happen that the umpire cannot see clearly because of the speed of the game. It is a thankless job, no doubt. The only friends you have at the ballpark are your fellow umpires. Both teams are critical of many of your calls, every game. And the fans, they're the worst. They think they can see the plays better from 100 feet away than the umpire can from five. I have often heard my old broadcast partner, Milo Hamilton, berate an umpire for a call that the replay showed to be correct. That made it tough on me because I had to support Milo or the umpire. Luckily, we were on radio and there were no replays to prove him wrong. What bothered me was that some fans listened to the radio as they watched the game on TV. I almost always let Milo's critique of the umpire slide but felt a tiny twinge of guilt for not getting it right.

I used to think it took an idiot to make an umpire. First, you had to spend many years in the minors with low pay and excessive travel. When you finally made it to the big leagues, the pay was still low, there were more fans to boo, more replays to reveal your mistakes. Now, there is a rule that teams cannot show close plays on

Diamond Vision, the pay is far better, the travel is easier, and there are a few short vacations built into each umpire's schedule. I suppose the extra work Sandy Alderson has prescribed offsets the vacations, but at least the umps make decent money now and they should. Not because they are part of the entertainment, but because they have a very tough job. The salaries have only been good for a few years, so it is too early to judge the impact, but I hope it will have the effect of attracting more good men, or women. Now that we have television, we will have no more perfect umpires like Bill Klem. But even a small improvement would be great. I think Sandy's approach is idealistic, but I also think it is the right approach. He'll have to stay with it until a new generation of umpires gets to the big show. I hope he stays around long enough to see it work.

In the meantime, I have the perfect cure for insomnia: Read the *Official Baseball Rules.* I tried three times and got nine short naps for my effort; God, is that stuff boring. The basic rules are easy but it is hard to imagine how so few rules can blossom into so many pages. The minutiae are connected through the enormousness of the document like the strands of a giant spiderweb, making passage a sticky proposition. I'm glad we never got stuck batting out of turn when I was managing. I have been through that rule a number of times, terrified over the embarrassment it could cause me, but I still can't remember how to reconstruct the lineup.

Let's see now, say the batting order is Abel, Baker, Charles, Daniel, Edward, Frank, George, Hooker, and Irwin. By the rules:

> Play (3) Abel walks. Baker walks. Charles forces Baker. Edward bats in Daniel's turn. While Edward is at-bat, Abel scores and Charles goes to second on a wild pitch. Edward grounds out, sending Charles to third. The defensive team appeals (a) immediately or (b) after a pitch to Daniel. Ruling (a) Abel's run counts and Charles is entitled to second base as these advances were not made because of the improper batter batting a ball or advancing to first base. Charles must return to second base because his advance to third resulted from the improper batter batting a ball. Daniel is called out and Edward is the proper bat-

ter. (b) Abel's run counts and Charles stays on third. The proper batter is Frank.

To understand rules such as this, you may have to be a lawyer, like Tony LaRussa and Hughie Jennings, two of the most successful managers of all time. Compared to the batting-out-of-order rule, the LSAT is a breeze. And, if you fell asleep trying to read this rule, now you know. The rulebook only costs $7.00. It's a lot cheaper than sleeping pills.

CHAPTER 7

Scouts

You just can't keep the friendship out of scouting, because so many of these fellows have been buddies for years. A lot of us have played with each other or against each other, and we go back a long way together. It's a fraternity.

—Ray Scarborough

WHEN I GRADUATED from Taft High School in June of 1964, I was hoping to sign a contract to play professional baseball with either the Cubs or the Colt 45's. Both teams pursued me right up until the end of the semester. I was hoping they would get into a bidding war and jack the price up high enough that my father would allow me to sign. He estimated that the scholarship offers I had from Stanford and UCLA were worth $30,000 and he set that amount of money as a minimum I would accept. He had that power because I was a minor and could not legally sign a contract to play professional baseball unless he co-signed with me.

I was a pretty good student, but a better pitcher. And I promised my father I would attend college during the off-season if he would sign the contract. I was optimistic that the offers would reach $30,000 or more because both teams were aware of the $30,000 price tag and both were posturing, hoping to influence my decision.

As it happened, the thing that kept me from getting a six-figure bonus was a game I pitched against Birmingham High

School. Birmingham had several pro prospects and there were probably twenty scouts at the game when I pitched against them. I can't remember how many of their players signed—I don't think any of them ever made it to the big leagues, but I remember being out of sync that day. It wasn't just one or two guys but the whole team that hit me hard. Tommy Lasorda, then a scout with the Dodgers, still remembers watching that game and still kids me about it.

"They had a guy," he said. "I can't remember his name, but he was a left-handed hitter . . . Pete Lentine, that was his name. Yeah I remember that. And every time you pitched a good game against the Dodgers, I thought about seeing you that day. If you would have gotten Lentine out, we might have signed you."

Based on that game, the Dodgers passed on me. But I still filled out forms for the files of seventeen out of the twenty teams that comprised the major leagues at that time. I did not register with the Dodgers, but the Angels stayed in the hunt until they found out how much it was going to cost. The Twins stayed in the hunt a long time too, but it ended up being just the Cubs and the Colt 45's. I'm not sure I would have wanted to sign with the Dodgers anyway. One of the things the Cubs and Colts kept telling me was that the pathway to the major leagues could be traveled in a short period of time because their organizations were thin in the pitching area. I knew this was not the case with the Dodgers.

The thing that jumped me up beyond $30,000 was a Saturday workout at my high school that was orchestrated by the Colt 45's. The general manager of the team, Paul Richards, flew in to watch. The chief scout on the case, Jim Wilson and his sidekick, Karl Kuehl, must have been peacock proud as I overpowered Willie Crawford and another left-handed hitter they brought up from San Diego. Crawford signed for about $100,000 with the Dodgers and he became a pretty good major league ballplayer. The other young man may have made it too. I just don't remember his name.

I do remember Wilson telling me I could have won a game in the big leagues after a game he watched me pitch in high school that semester though I didn't believe him at the time. I knew I could throw harder than any other high school kid I went up against, but

I also knew that my record was only 3-2, that Birmingham had killed me, and that there were a lot of kids in America who wanted to play pro ball. I assumed many of them were more talented than I. Once I got to the rookie league in Cocoa, Florida, and worked out for a few weeks with all the rookies from four different teams, I knew my ability was way above average. My mother recently told me that I called home one day that first summer and said, "I've got it." Now I know that Wilson was right. I could have pitched in the big leagues that day. Just a few months later, I proved it.

In 1965, the major leagues implemented an amateur draft; but in '64, signing young players was a free-for-all. Bonuses of $80,000 to $100,000 were being offered to more and more top players and the owners were so alarmed that they changed the rules, incorrectly thinking that the draft would hold the bonuses down. I suppose it had that effect at first, but after the agents started working the market, it had the opposite effect. If a team didn't want to pay a six-figure bonus it had to draft a kid who would sign for less; most of the time, this meant signing a player with less talent. Nothing has really changed except the six-figure numbers are now seven.

Gene Hanley was the Cubs' scout in Southern California at the time and he offered me $30,000 immediately after I graduated. He said that I would probably make it to Chicago in a year or two and that I would have a great young team behind me with Ron Santo, Billy Williams, and Kenny Hubbs. My mother told me that she wanted me to sign with the Cubs because she had watched Hanley in the Pacific Coast League and he was one of her favorites. Then, when we got to know him better, she liked him even more. He was a real gentleman.

The Colts took me out to dinner a few times; so did the Cubs. The Colts came with an offer of $35,000 and I told them that I had promised Hanley that I wouldn't sign before he had a chance to talk to the Cubs about upping the ante. Actually it was my dad who told Hanley we would wait. (The Colts took us to dinner, but the Hanleys had us to dinner at their own house. My best friend, Bill Kringlen, told my mom that the scouts must really like to watch us eat.)

After my graduation day, and the initial offers, the Colts kept calling back, offering more. They never told me that I would have a great young team behind me but their money spoke eloquently. The last call came about 10:00 P.M.: They said that their final offer was $55,000 and either a college scholarship that would pay me $1,000 per semester for up to eight semesters or a brand-new Mustang. I was thrilled. I had a little trouble sleeping that night because I knew I was going to sign the next day. Hanley called back and said that the Cubs could only offer $30,000. The Colts could have had me for $35,000. I ended making $20,000 more and getting a scholarship to boot, just by waiting.

The next day, Wilson and Kuehl came over to the house and we signed the papers. I know now that the workout for Richards was the fuel behind the signing fire. It didn't take a genius to see that I had a major league fastball. But the one thing that sticks in my mind about that morning was what Jim Wilson said when I inked the deal.

"Larry," he said. "We think a lot of your ability and I'm certain you'll pitch in the major leagues. How fast you move through the farm system is up to you. But I do want to tell you that I have one major league record that you will never break." He stretched the moment to let the suspense build. How could he have a major league record? I thought. I've never even heard of him.

"I pitched twelve years in the big leagues," he continued. "And I never slid once."

"Never slid once?" I repeated, incredulous.

"Never once," he said. "They paid me to pitch. I hardly ever got a hit. They pay those other guys to hit and slide. Let them do it."

As a high school player, I batted fourth and had to slide all the time. I hit over .400 my senior year. What Jim Wilson was telling me straight off was that I should no longer consider myself a hitter. I was a pro now, and in pro ball pitchers and hitters don't mix. Sometimes they socialize, but there's an edge that's always present on the diamond that separates the guys who make their living with glove and bat and those who make it with the ball. Sometimes the edge can be sharp—especially on a losing team, as the blame is shifted back and forth depending which side you're on. On winning teams, this divide is blurred because there is less blame to toss around.

When I got down to Cocoa to play rookie ball, my manager was Dave Philley. The first few days I called him "Coach Philley" and he got pissed off. "My name is Dave," he said. "This isn't high school." Then I called him "Mr. Philley" and he was still pissed. It was hard for me to get used to calling a grown man, especially a real big-league ballplayer, by his first name. I finally got over it and started referring to him correctly; then I saluted my instant leap into manhood by smoking House of Windsor cigars—the same brand as Dave.

As it turned out, I pitched thirteen years, a year more than Jim Wilson, and I only slid four or five times, all at the plate. My thinking—which was not challenged by any manager or third base coach—was that it wasn't worth the chance of injury just to move up one base. Home, though, was different; with two outs you had to try for the run. Normally, a pitcher has to slide into second to try and break up a double play from time to time. I never did that once. Fact is, I took such a short lead and was so slow afoot I knew that if I could get to second in time to slide, the leadoff hitter would be past first base anyway.

One time we were playing the Pirates at Forbes Field and I had ended up on third base with less than two outs, don't ask me how. "Tag up on a fly ball," third base coach Jim Busby said.

The batter hit a fly ball to short right field. As Roberto Clemente, perhaps the premier throwing outfielder in the history of the game, came jogging in to catch the ball, Busby yelled, "Tag up!" I tagged and when Clemente caught the ball, I ran. Busby wanted me to tag, but I'm sure he didn't want me to go. He was probably yelling, "No, no, no!" But before he could corral me I had set sail for home. Clemente was stunned; he took a double take before firing a laser to the plate. The throw was up the line and high and Jim Pagliaroni, the Pirates catcher, had to leap to catch it. As I slid under, he came down. His spikes slashed my leg, tearing the uniform from the knee to the ankle. I was safe!

While this maneuver may have taught me the value of the

surprise attack and may have influenced my managing, it did not encourage me to further derring-do on the bases. To get a new pair of pants I had to go across the field, through the Pirates dugout, and up to the locker room—and we lost the game anyway. (We *never* won at Forbes.) Why slide? I would have gotten the same result without tearing my pants if I had heeded Jim Wilson's advice.

Looking back, I don't think it was too difficult for Wilson to guess that I would pitch in the major leagues. I was a "can't miss" prospect. I was 6'4" and 190 pounds in 1964. I never got any taller and only gained twenty pounds during my career. I could already throw in the low to mid 90s. I had an aptitude for throwing break-ing pitches and I could get the ball over the plate. With just a little refinement and the right attitude, I would be good enough to com-pete against anyone. It is seldom that a scout can tell a kid "You could pitch in the big leagues right now" or, "You could play short for the Cubs tomorrow." Most of the time, the scouts mine dia-monds in the rough. They know there is a gem inside, but they don't know how many carats they will get or what kind of quality it will be. That is why they have to project improvement. They sel-dom see a "can't miss" prospect in high school. Finding a prospect with all the tools (including the most overlooked one, the brain) at age eighteen is like finding money in the street.

Usually a scout looks at a kid's parents to get a feel for the bloodlines. Are the mother and father well built? Are they success-ful, motivated people? Does the kid have big hands, big feet? How much will he grow? How much harder will he throw in the future? If he is a hitter, how much more power can you project? I'm sure the scouts got positive vibrations from my mom and dad. She was a high school teacher, a swimming and gymnastics coach; he was a bit overweight but had large strong hands.

When Al Campanis was the general manager of the Dodgers he encouraged scouts to "look the prospect in the eye." Campanis believed that it was possible to determine mental toughness, con-centration, confidence, and other intangible qualities in a player's visage. Scouts started telling him that this or that player either had the "good face" or lacked it.

Paul Richards was a sly, cocky sort of character. He thought of himself as a latter-day Branch Rickey—a baseball genius. When he was with the Colt 45's he signed a lot of good players in a short period of time; guys like Rusty Staub, Jimmy Wynn, Joe Morgan, Bob Watson, Doug Rader, Jerry Grote, Don Wilson, and me. That's almost an All-Star at every position, and all signed in a three-year span. But Richards got crosswise with Judge Hofheinz. Two geniuses were one too many and Richards got the ax and took over as general manager of the Braves.

I don't know if Richards ever consorted with Campanis but I believe he looked me in the eye during that workout at my high school. Before he left Houston and went to the Braves, Richards asked me to lunch and encouraged me to hold out for way more money than I would have asked for when my I got my original contract. He said that the Astros had to sign me because of my youth and my potential to become an All-Star caliber pitcher. I asked how much I should demand and he advised me to sign for something like $20,000. I settled for $17,000 and thought it was great. Several years later, in 1969, we went to Atlanta in early September and we were just two games behind the Braves with a good chance to win the pennant. In the first game of the series I hooked up with Phil Niekro. I pitched twelve shutout innings against the Braves in that game and had a no-hitter broken up on an infield hit with two outs in the ninth. Niekro matched zeros with me and the Braves won the game. We scored two runs in the thirteenth. They scored three.

Richards was quoted in the newspaper the next day. "I'd rather have Dierker for a big game right now than any other pitcher in the league," he said. "He's a cold-blooded, fishy-eyed, son-of-a-bitch." It was easy for him to be glib—after all, he signed me and his new team won the game. As for the eyes, I wonder if he saw something fishy when he looked at my mom and dad and projected that I would become a cold blooded SOB? I felt like $17,000 was adequate compensation, but what did I know?

After I won twenty games in 1969, I got my first practical lesson in negotiating without leverage. I had made $27,000 in 1968 and I held out for $54,000 in 1969. I had no compunction about asking the Astros to double my salary because I was one of the best pitchers in the league at that time although I was certainly *not* among the highest paid. During that winter, I took negotiating advice from a friend, Bill Sherrill, who was a governor on the Federal Reserve Board. We organized an argument that would unfold in stages, saving the best ammunition for last. After a few sessions, I had Astros general manager Spec Richardson up to $47,000. That is where he made his stand. As spring training approached, it was obvious that I would have to make a deal or hold out by not reporting to camp. I was only twenty-three years old and I was champing at the bit to go to Florida. I'm sure Spec knew that. The week before he departed for Cocoa we had two meetings. The first went just like I thought it would: I made my point; he made his. I saved my strongest argument, an independent statistical study that named me the best pitcher in the league that year, for the end of the meeting. When I made my point and placed the study on his desk, he wheeled around, facing away from me and toward the wall. Then he slowly lit a cigar and kept staring at the wall, as if in contemplation. I got tired of waiting for him to respond and weakened my position by blurting out some other arguments that were less compelling. The meeting ended with no deal and when I told Bill about it, he laughed.

"You know what you should have done when he lit that cigar?" he asked.

I had no clue.

"You should have pulled a cigar out of your pocket and lit it and remained silent."

I had my strategy planned for our next confrontation and I had a cigar too. Once again, I felt like the drift of the conversation was going my way. Once again, he lit a cigar. This time, I lit one too. We still failed to get the deal done.

Spec called me in right before he left for spring training and made his final offer, $48,000 plus a $1,000 bonus for each game I won beyond fourteen.

"If you're so good, you'll win twenty games again and get your $54,000," he said. I declined, but afterward I told Bill that the pen was dripping in my pocket.

After two weeks of holding out while the rest of the guys practiced, I finally signed for $48,000 with a $1,000 bonus for every win beyond ten. I had only eleven wins as the season turned to September, but then won my last five games to get to $54,000.

This process gave me an object lesson in the strength of the reserve clause. This part of the uniform players contract specified that if a player refused to sign a contract, his team could renew the contract for another year. In other words, you had to sign for what the team wanted to pay you, or quit baseball. Obviously, no team wanted a key player to quit, but it was also patently clear that no player would. Prior to arbitration and free agency, a team had control of each of its players for life: If they misjudged him, they could release him, but if they ended up with a superstar, they could keep him for his entire career and pay him whatever salary they deemed appropriate.

Knowing that the team could keep a player for his entire career made amateur scouting more important than it is now. These days, a team can make up for a mistake or fill a need by signing a free agent, without having to wait for—and gamble on—a kid maturing into a solid major leaguer (although, on the other hand, teams *are* now vulnerable to losing a great young player on the open market after the player has six years of major league service).

The current system, with arbitration and free agency, creates a lot of mobility. Some players sign with other teams when they become free agents; others just aren't pursued by their current club. When a team isn't willing to pay a player what an arbitrator would likely award him, it simply doesn't tender a contract and forces the player to become a free agent, where his value to a team would be established by the open market. Most of the time, the player ends up signing for far less money than he could have gotten in an arbitration hearing.

Most teams separate amateur and professional scouting because most amateur players do not look like big leaguers, either in the face or on the field. Frame of reference is important in scouting: If you watch major league players most of the time, almost none of the youngsters will look good; but if you only scout kids, you will judge them in their own environment and be able to compare and contrast their talents.

In 1967, I played winter ball in the Dominican Republic. A sixteen-year-old Dominican kid kept coming to the ballpark and taking grounders at third base and batting practice. He obviously could run fast and throw hard; but I didn't think he would ever be able to hit. Why do they keep bringing this kid out here? I thought. He's never going to make it. Three years later, that kid was a teammate of mine. He is still the best young player I have ever seen come into the major leagues. His name is Cesar Cedeno; and he was, according to Leo Durocher, the next Willie Mays. That much was obvious to Leo and to me when Cedeno was nineteen. When he was sixteen, another scout did some good projecting. I bet Cedeno was pretty impressive when he played against other kids his own age. I'm sure this was obvious to the scout.

Sometimes you can project more from a young player even after he reaches the major leagues; sometimes you can't. I have to admit I don't know where Luis Gonzalez found his power stroke in 2001 when he hit 57 home runs for the Diamondbacks. Ordinarily, I can see power potential during batting practice: When the Astros got Steve Finley in a trade with the Orioles, he was a slap-and-dash hitter—a speed and defense guy. Most of the time, he tried to hit to the opposite field and race down the line. But I saw him hit some long balls in batting practice when he was with the Astros, and once in a while he would connect in the game. He was a lot stronger than his body frame would suggest—a lot like Gonzo. I saw Luis hit a lot of home runs, but I never saw him hit a tape measure shot, even though he had the classic home run hitter's swing. One time, in the company of several media guys, I said that Finley would hit twenty-five or thirty home runs in a season one year. They looked at me like I was crazy. But guess what? He did it. On the other hand, I never said Gonzo would do it; I just didn't think he had the pop in his bat. I was happy to see him hit all those runs for more than one reason: First, I like him and was happy for him. Second, he didn't look like he had spent the winter in the weight room like Sammy Sosa, Mark McGwire, and Barry Bonds. He was the same old skinny Gonzo.

Gonzo and Finley are both great guys. When you see a player day after day, during streaks and during slumps, you can assess his character and get a better feel for his resiliency. It is difficult to get a read on a guy when he is an amateur free agent. With free agency, as opposed to a draft system, a scout can start doing background work as soon as he decides that he likes the player's ability: He can check with coaches, teachers, and friends. He can take the family out to dinner and watch them eat. One night, one of the Houston scouts, I think it was Karl Kuehl, made an offhand comment about my appetite. "He even eats the vegetables," he said, mentally adding good diet to the plus side of his appraisal of me.

Once a scout gets to know a kid, he has a much better chance to evaluate intangibles such as desire and intelligence. It's all a matter of projection. These days, scouts still do in-depth research on guys who might go in the first few rounds, but they can't afford to spend too much time on a lesser prospect because they don't know if he will be available when it's time to choose him. You frequently hear a scout compare a young player to an older one. To me, Vladimir Guerrero looked like Andre Dawson the first time I saw him play and I haven't changed my mind. Cedeno never became Willie Mays and I never became Don Drysdale. But we reminded scouts of great players they had seen. Even though Cedeno and I did not become Hall of Famers, we proved to be valuable players and were well worth the investment. The year after I signed, 1965, the amateur draft system was adopted. A few years later, the Colts drafted a kid named Marty Cott in the first round. Marty was a catcher and he had all the tools but he didn't really like baseball that much. He collected a sizable bonus check, played for one season in the minors, and hung up his spikes. What a waste of time and money.

For the sake of the scouts, I favor a return to the free agent system. An open signing system for amateurs would probably help the big-money teams more than the smaller franchises. But at least the scouts would be able do their jobs from start to finish. They would have to sell their team to the young men the same way the Cubs and Colts did with me. The scout's job in evaluating talent would be the same, but his ability to negotiate a good deal for his team would require more than an eye for talent. Most scouts I know would prefer this system. For one thing, they could make more money. These days, most scouts work on straight salary. Back when I signed, many scouts had bonus clauses that gave them a chance to cash in when a player they signed made it to the majors.

I don't know if it would help the *game* to return to a free agent system. My opinion is that it would bring signing bonuses back down a notch and would allow a team to feel more comfortable with the players it selects. In the old days, teams competed with one another for prospects. If they lost one player, they could go to plan B and sign another. Now, if you draft a kid in the first round and fail to sign him, you just lose your top pick. There is no plan B. In this environment, many small-market teams draft players they deem signable, passing up better prospects that they know will command a higher signing bonus. The Astros drafted Phil Nevin in the first round because they thought he would be a good hitter, though his fielding tools and foot speed were not as highly rated. There were other players, like Jeffrey Hammonds, who were rated higher in that draft; the Astros might have drafted Hammonds but they were afraid they couldn't sign him. Nevin was a college senior; he couldn't say he was going to go back to college so they were just about sure they could afford to sign him. (Under the current system, all players except the college seniors have the leverage of returning to school and trying to improve their draft position or signing bonus the next year.) Nevin turned out to be a good selection, but because he was a late bloomer, he didn't help his first two teams, the Astros and the Tigers, at all.

The Astros hit paydirt with Lance Berkman, signing him under the same scenario as Nevin. Lance did not bargain that hard: He assumed that if he made it as a major league player, the rest of the money would flow naturally to him, and he was right. He was also a local kid, a product of Rice University. When he came out to take batting practice with us, he littered the outfield pavilion with home run balls, hitting both left- and right-handed. (His power potential was easy to see.) Houston was a perfect fit for him and vice versa. Conversely, we signed another first round pick from San Diego in 1989 or 1990, and when he came out for batting practice, he could barely get the ball out of the batting cage. Somebody saw something in him that wasn't there when I saw him. If the kid had ever made it I would remember his name. I think he hit the end of the line in AA ball.

Some scouts are looking for prospects, some are looking at minor league players that their teams might be interested in trading for and still others are acting as major league talent scouts and advance scouts. When I was managing, I received a report on the team we were preparing to play the day before the start of our next series, which the advance scout compiled to help us prepare. His input was somewhat limited because he had to watch games and write them up immediately; there was no time to study videotape. He might warn us to be careful with a certain hitter because he was swinging the bat well. Sometimes this sort of information is inadequate because hitters go from hot to cold and vice versa all year long.

One report, though, did help me when I was pitching. The scout said that Tony Perez was having trouble with off-speed pitches. I had to laugh when I heard that: I thought Tony was one of the best off-speed hitters in the league. Well, the first time up I got ahead of him with two strikes and decided to throw a change-up in the dirt, just to see how he would react. Well, what do you know, old Tony took a foolish, lunging swing at the pitch and struck out. I used the change-up successfully on him the rest of the game. I did not, however, try it on him after that contest, except as a show pitch—I never had any intention of throwing him a slow pitch for a strike, and I don't ever remember him chasing one in the dirt again either.

It usually took us about fifteen minutes to go over how we were going to try to pitch to the other team's hitters and determine where the fielders were going to play. The fielding positioning was the easiest—we got it straight from ESPN. They posted a hit chart on every hitter on the Internet and updated it daily. It was a diagram of the field with color-coded dots where each ball was hit. It was divided by line drives, ground balls, and fly balls. The information was almost too detailed: It broke the chart down based upon whether the hitter was even, ahead, or behind in the count. Most players' tendencies were similar regardless of the count. Time and again, our advance scout told us that a hitter would try to go the other way when he was behind in the count. Time and again, ESPN would show us that though he might be trying to go to the other field, he was not succeeding.

One time we were playing the Indians in Cleveland about mid-season. The ESPN hit chart showed that Jim Thome had hit no ground balls to the left side of the infield all year and by that stage of the season he would have had 300 at bats or so. Accordingly, we decided to play our shortstop on the second base side in that series and the shift worked well. Thome grounded out to the shortstop, who was playing up the middle on the second base side, and to the second baseman, who was way over in the hole. Positioning depends upon knowledge of the hitter, the pitcher, and what the hitter may be trying to do in each separate situation, and that is why it is so important to have players who can think. If a guy is really throwing hard, they need to shade almost every hitter to the opposite field; if a guy is a knuckleball pitcher, they should shade the hitters to pull. With a man on second and no outs everyone knows the hitter is going to try to hit to the right side of the field. Most teams have a coach who does almost nothing but check his team's defensive alignment. When he wants a player to move over, he uses the high-tech approach of waving a towel and motioning for fielders to move one way or the other. I preferred having players who were as smart as my coaches, and most of the time we had guys who could read the game and position themselves accordingly. Our coaching staff repositioned players from time to time, but not as often as most of our opponents did.

The thing our players liked to do most was to get their own scouting report by watching TV. Before each game, we always had a tape playing in the clubhouse that showed video of the pitcher we were getting ready to face, both in his last start and his last start against us. Back when I played, we didn't have video. As a matter of fact, I have only one tape of myself pitching and it was shot not on videotape, but on film from behind home plate, from high first and high third. I never got to look at myself facing another hitter from the center field angle and they didn't get to look at me either. I'm not sure it made much difference. As a manager, I regarded advance and video scouting to be somewhat helpful, but I was more attuned to our internal chemistry and the intelligence with which we played the game. We had good talent throughout my tenure and I always felt that if we just played our own game, we would win more often than not.

Frankly, baseball is so unpredictable that all the scouting in the world can be unavailing. For example, some teams just can't hit some pitchers. Larry Jaster used to beat the Dodgers every time and he was just an average pitcher. Do you think the Dodgers could have figured out how to hit him if they had had video? Well, we had video when Francisco Cordova pitched a one-hitter against us. The next time we faced him, we watched the video and he pitched a no-hitter! Cordova is a side-arming right-hander with good sinking action on his fastball and great control of a knee-buckling breaking ball. Left-handed hitters had a lot better chance against him but we didn't have many left-handed hitters.

One of the best books on scouting is *Dollar Sign on the Muscle* by Kevin Kerrane. From it, I learned that in the old days a scout could be fired if he was caught with golf clubs in the trunk of his car. The theory was that if he wanted to, a scout could find a game to watch every day and every night. I would never make it as a scout because I prefer to watch only one game a day unless I have to participate in a doubleheader. Times have changed, though: Last year, I entertained two of my scout friends on the golf course. Now you can play golf and still watch two games if you can figure out how to program a VCR. Scouts used to send written reports. Now they use the Internet. The young guys could probably file a report using their PalmPilots while waiting to tee off. The older guys agonize over the keyboard as if they were disarming a land mine.

Somehow, I have a hard time imagining Howie Haak chewing a plug of Red Man and sipping Jack Daniel's Black while typing notes into a laptop. Howie's claim to fame was that he got the inside information on Roberto Clemente when the Dodgers were trying to hide him from the minor league draft of 1954. Branch Rickey, then with the Pirates, sent Howie to Montreal to see Clemente but the Dodgers didn't play him. Howie watched him take batting practice and infield practice and was impressed enough to follow him to his native Puerto Rico where he was playing winter ball and the rest is history. But Howie never sent Rickey an e-mail. He was a great scout, but I don't think he could have managed a computer with the mangled hands that fought so many battles behind the plate as a middling minor league catcher.

At the end of his scouting career, Howie was a special assignment scout for the Astros. Sometimes this position carries the title of assistant general manager. It is the top rung on the scouting ladder. Howie would watch our Triple A team for a week and report back on a kid we were thinking about bringing up to the majors. He might follow a player on another major league team for a week if there was the possibility of trading for him.

Another special assignment in scouting is cross-checking amateur players. This too is near the top of the scouting ladder. A cross-checker looks at a kid after an area scout has filed a report on him. If the cross-checker sees what the other scout saw, the player is rated as to where he should go in the draft. If he is projected as a third-round pick and is still around in the fourth round, the team will probably draft him.

Scouts have always been undervalued and underpaid, but some of them were creative enough to make an extra dollar or two on their expense reports. Leon Hamilton, for example, learned all the tricks in his fifty years in the business. He used a pad of receipts from a motel for three years after the lodging burned down. One time, he was scouting down South and the weather was especially hot so he bought a straw hat, probably as much to cat around in as anything, and he put it on his expense report as a sunhat. When the expense was denied, he filed another report for the same trip, without the hat, but in the same amount as the first report. At the bottom was a note that said, "You find the sunhat."

Truthfully, all of us in the professional baseball business are scouts, but most of us don't get paid for it. One day in March, we had an exhibition game with the Royals at Baseball City and Bo Jackson was playing right field for them. In the top of the first, a ball was hit into the corner—he retrieved it and threw it all the way to third base in the air, almost in time to get a runner advancing from first. Then in the bottom of the first, he hit a one-hop shot to short with a man on first. Our shortstop caught the ball out of self-defense and shoveled it to second, but the relay throw to first was late. Bo beat it out! After watching one inning, I knew for sure that he had a great arm, great speed, and home run power. Later in the spring, I was watching him take batting practice and he hit a ball so hard that even though it glanced off the tubing of the cage, it still carried all the way over the fence in left center. That is raw power to the max. There is no doubt in my mind Bo Jackson would have been a Hall of Fame outfielder if he had not injured his hip playing football.

Most of the time it isn't that easy to pick the future big leaguers out of an amateur game, even if you get to look them all in the eye. Moments like mine with Jackson, Haak's with Clemente, Cy Slapnicka's with Bob Feller, Paul Krichell's with Lou Gehrig, Joe Devine's with Joe DiMaggio, and Tom Greenwade's with Mickey Mantle come once in a lifetime. If I had developed into a Hall of Fame pitcher, Paul Richards may have professed such an epiphany with me.

CHAPTER 8
Farm System

Rickey had both money and players. He just didn't like to see the two of them mix.

—CHUCK CONNORS, ACTOR AND FORMER BROOKLYN
DODGERS PROSPECT, ON BRANCH RICKEY

PROFESSIONAL BASEBALL IS BOTH a sport and a business. In the first half of the twentieth century, the robber baron mentality prevailed and ballplayers got the labor end of the stick. Ironically, though they barely made a living wage, they were expected to dress and act like gentlemen. While the sport was growing into America's National Pastime, owners like Charles Comiskey (a former player) made a handsome profit. Back then, minor league teams operated independently; they signed kids and often made more money selling them than they made selling tickets. If the owner of a major league club wanted a minor league player he would simply try to buy him.

In the 1920s Branch Rickey took over as manager of the hapless St. Louis Cardinals. Rickey must have been frustrated—he had a great eye for talent, but he was unable to field a winning team. Since he was parsimonious by nature and wasn't prepared to pay a minor league operator top dollar, he started buying entire minor league teams instead of players, spending money in the short term to save it in the long run. To fill the rosters for these teams, he held tryout camps all over the country and signed the best players he could find using the logic that from quantity comes quality. It didn't matter much to him if most of the players he signed never made it to the show; he just wanted to have control over as many young players as possible so that he could, in turn, buy them for the Cardinals once they were developed. By 1926, Rickey operated the Cardinals from the front office, and though he was no longer the field manager, his farm system paid its first dividend—a Cardinals pennant. Rickey continued to purchase teams until the Cardinals controlled thirty-two minor league clubs and over 600 players. With this system, he turned the Redbirds' fortunes around and made a fortune of his own selling players from his farm teams to other ball clubs and paying himself a commission. (As far as I know, Rickey was the last executive to take a piece of the action on the sale of a player. Branch Rickey liked his bread buttered on both sides— as author Roger Kahn wrote, "He had a Puritan distaste for money in someone else's hands.")

Judge Kenesaw Mountain Landis was the commissioner of baseball at the time. Landis, an avowed labor advocate, was firmly opposed to Rickey's maneuvering. He felt that the Cardinals were cornering the market on talent to the detriment of other big league clubs, not to mention minor league players and owners.

Landis, with his jutting jaw and shock of unruly silver hair, quarreled with Rickey constantly. Landis had no legal power to prevent Rickey from buying franchises, but finally, in 1937, after repeated warnings, the old judge turned ninety-one Cardinals farmhands loose to seek better offers. This was a body blow to the Cardinals. Rickey moved from St. Louis to Brooklyn shortly thereafter and brought his farm system concept to the Dodgers. He reaped a few more pennants in Brooklyn, and the Dodgers and Cardinals became archrivals. By this time his cat, as they say, was out of the bag.

Once the other teams saw what Rickey was doing and how well it worked, many of them started buying into minor league franchises. The farm system became a part of every big league team, and it continued to grow, despite the objections of the commissioner. As baseball turned to a new century three years ago, most minor league teams were privately owned again but had working agreements with a big league, or parent, club. Accordingly, they are supplied with players and an operating subsidy, but the big league team controls the movement of players within the system and the big league club pays their salaries. This has proven to be a workable system, but it has developed in a way that would have made Rickey's skin crawl. In the last two decades, signing bonuses for amateur players have grown as fast as big league salaries—the farm system Rickey conceived to gain competitive advantage and save money does not do either these days.

The concept of developing players by "farming them out" to minor league affiliates is unique to baseball. In this sense, baseball is a lot different from the other major sports in America. Most of the time, basketball and football players go straight from college to the top level of their sport. In baseball there are many levels of play from rookie leagues, to A ball, AA, and AAA; and most major league teams have at least five minor league affiliates. More often than not, players have to work their way up the ladder, one rung at a time. A player fresh out of high school almost always starts at the rookie league level. A good college player usually starts no higher than AA. Seldom will a player rise to the majors without spending at least two years in the bushes. One thousand at bats or 400 innings pitched are rule-of-thumb minimum requirements for advancement to the major leagues. In the lower levels, youngsters don't make much money. But in Triple A, many teams stockpile a few players with major league experience and pay them a considerable amount of money.

Only a few players have made it to the major leagues without working their way up from a minor league team. I am one of them. Actually, I did play in a rookie league, but it was more like an instruction league. All the players that signed professional contracts with the Colt 45's, Tigers, Mets, and Twins in June of 1964 were sent to Cocoa, Florida, where the Colt 45's had built a spring training complex, complete with a dormitory. I did pitch thirty-nine innings in that league, but we never took a bus ride. For practical purposes, I can say that I don't have any firsthand knowledge about life on the farm.

I got to the big leagues ahead of schedule because the Colt 45's were an expansion team consisting mostly of over-the-hill veterans. The Colts' fledgling farm system was barren back then and I didn't have many bodies to leap over in my ascent to Houston; Dave Winfield and Bob Horner went directly to the major leagues out of college for the same reason. These are exceptional cases. Even Lance Berkman, the Astros' All-Star outfielder, had to spend a couple of years in the minor leagues developing his skills. Barry Bonds and Randy Johnson played minor league ball too.

In a way, coming to the big leagues with little minor league experience helped me. I didn't know how many good players there were down below and I didn't bother to think about it. I only knew that the other pitchers on the Colts didn't throw as hard as I did. Once I knew that, I gained a lot of confidence. After I had pitched twenty or thirty innings, I knew I could carry my weight on the team. Houston was an expansion franchise, so no one expected us to field a championship team. As a result, I felt very little pressure. Since that time, I have noticed how nervous most players become when they get their first taste of major league competition. I think there is more pressure on a guy who has apprenticed for five or six years because he is usually in his mid- to late twenties and doesn't know if he'll ever get another chance.

Oftentimes, a youngster comes into professional baseball at one position and makes it to the majors at another. Jeff Bagwell was a Double A third baseman when he was traded from Boston to Houston. Since Ken Caminiti was young, talented, and already playing third for the Astros, Bagwell had to learn to play first base to climb to the top rung of the ladder.

Although there is no way to predict a player's advancement through the system, the process is as scientific as it can be. Each minor league team has a manager and a pitching coach that are handpicked by the major league general manager. In addition, the

GM also hires roving instructors that specialize in hitting, pitching, fielding, and base running. During the course of the summer, each team sends a scout to look at the minor league players in its system. If a particular pitcher is performing well, it is arranged that he will be on the mound when the scout comes to watch. Everyone who sees the player files a report on the team's computer network and the reports are displayed on a universal grading form. In each category there's a place for a numerical grade from 1 to 8. (One is the lowest rating, 8 the highest.) It is rare to find an 8 on any scouting report: For example, the only guys who would get an 8 rating for power hitting at this point in time are Barry Bonds and Sammy Sosa; Mark McGwire would have been rated an 8 a few years ago. The only pitchers who would get an 8 for their fastball would be guys like Nolan Ryan and Billy Wagner, and Randy Johnson, who can throw the ball near 100 miles per hour with good control. I don't recall ever seeing a minor league player with an 8 grade in any category.

Every time a scout or coach sees a player, either on his own team or the opposition, he fills out the form and dials it into the system. (Files are updated daily.) Anyone in the organization who has the ability to access this secure information can check a player out to see how others have rated him over the last several years. There is also a place on the form that calls for a judgment on level of interest in players from other organizations—N for no interest, M for mild, and D for definite. Each category has two fields for numerical grades, one for current ability and the other for future promise. Then there is a space at the bottom of the form for a narrative description of the player. This is where things like attitude and instincts are added to the talent ratings.

When a team makes a trade for a player who has not yet made it to the major leagues, the scouting reports are used to evaluate the deal. For this reason, the general manager has to evaluate the evaluators. He needs to know which scouts tend to give higher marks and which are tough graders. If a scout or minor league coach is wrong too often, he will likely be replaced.

In recent years, more and more players from the Caribbean, Mexico, Central and South America have been signed. For this reason, most minor league teams have a Spanish-speaking member on the permanent staff. Some teams actually help their Latino players learn to speak English and integrate into North American culture. As you might imagine, this system is not a cash cow like the one Branch Rickey started in the 1920s. Conversely, it involves considerable expense, and only pays for itself if it produces major league players. It is, nonetheless, a critical part of every organization.

When you bring a player up at minimum salary and he helps produce wins at the major league level, like Adam Dunn and Austin Kearns of the Reds, you get relatively cheap talent despite the money spent developing him. Every team, including the imperial Yankees, needs to have players at the entry level. It has been said that it took Columbus two years to find America, and George Steinbrenner twenty years to discover Columbus (his Triple A farm team in Ohio). What a discovery that was! After many years of buying a team of veteran free agents and enjoying little success, the Boss found players like Derek Jeter, Bernie Williams, Jorge Posada, Alfonso Soriano, and Andy Pettitte in his own minor league system. When you can develop star players at the up-the-middle positions, you have a great advantage over most other teams. When you add star-caliber free agents at the other positions, you have a World Championship type team. This is how the Yankees dynasty was rebuilt, not from without but from within.

There is an ongoing debate about which aspect of team building is the most important, and although there is universal support for finding and training your own players (especially pitchers), as opposed to signing free agents, the opinions are divided as to whether scouting or development is the most important part of producing major league talent. Some feel that if you get talented players they will rise to the majors with or without good instruction; others believe that the talent issue is moot because every team has scouts and their judgments will be offsetting over time. These folks believe that *teaching* the kids to play baseball properly and to be good teammates is the most important thing.

One thing is certain—it is less expensive to develop players than to sign free agents. The Montreal Expos are a great example of that: They have consistently found and developed good ballplayers but have been unable to win championships because they don't have the wherewithal to retain them. They have parted with players such as Larry Walker, Moises Alou, Pedro Martinez, Cliff Floyd, and Andre Dawson because they couldn't afford to keep them. If the Expos had revenue equal to that of the Atlanta Braves they would quite likely have posted just as good a record over the last ten years.

Back in the 1960s the Colt 45's/Astros produced a surfeit of talent. Unfortunately, they did a bad job of evaluating their own players and traded a lot of them away without getting much in return. Mike Cuellar, Rusty Staub, Jerry Grote, Joe Morgan, Jack Billingham, Cesar Geronimo, Sonny Jackson, Dave Giusti, John Mayberry, and Jerry Reuss helped other teams win championships and I am certain that if they had not been traded away I would have pitched in the World Series sometime in the early 1970s. Even after the ill-advised trades, we had quite a few good players left—players like Doug Rader, Bob Watson, Jimmy Wynn, Cesar Cedeno, Don Wilson, and me stayed in Houston. If the Astros had exercised more patience, they would have fielded a team that looked like this:

Lineup

2B Joe Morgan
SS Sonny Jackson
CF Cesar Cedeno
RF Jimmy Wynn
LF Rusty Staub
1B Bob Watson or John Mayberry
3B Doug Rader
C   Jerry Grote

Starting pitchers

J. R. Richard
Mike Cuellar
Don Wilson

Larry Dierker
Jerry Reuss

Closer

Dave Giusti

Cesar Geronimo could have provided late-inning defense and outfield depth. Jack Billingham probably would have become one of the best setup men in the league.

Most of these players made All-Star teams. All of the starting pitchers became twenty-game winners, except Wilson. And he pitched two no-hitters and had an eighteen-strikeout game. Of course, this team includes several players the Astros traded for (such as Cuellar and Reuss and Billingham) so it's not a pure example of scouting and development. And we did get some useful talent in the deals but none of the players, save Lee May, would have cracked this lineup. As a young player, it didn't bother me when we made a deal: Except for the Curt Blefary for Mike Cuellar exchange, I usually thought that the trades would help us, and besides, it was none of my business. I can second-guess these trades now, but cannot claim to have questioned them at the time they were made. Now I can pan these deals, not just because they didn't work out, but because I know more about building a team than I did when I was younger.

Most of the players on this early Astros all-star team were signed between 1963 and 1970. Most of them became excellent major leaguers and there were several other players in addition to those listed above, like Jim Ray and Tom Griffin, who had solid major league careers. Seldom does a team sign so many outstanding players in such a short period of time. Of course, you won't find many examples of a team trading away so much talent in so few years either. In order to field a championship-caliber team for a long period of time, you have to do almost everything right, from signing and developing to evaluating talent to making good trades. In my estimation, the most important aspect of a farm system is having talented players in it. Good instruction sometimes pays a dividend, but nothing could have prevented Lance Berkman's ascent to the majors and no one could have coached the kid from San Diego beyond AA.

Since the inception of free agency, there has been another aspect of the business in which evaluating and judgment play an important part, and that is in the signing of free agents. Most fans realize that Alex Rodriguez is one of the best shortstops in the history of the sport; most also realize that you cannot win without good pitching. So why did the Rangers sign Ken Caminiti and Andres Galarraga the same year they signed A-Rod, when they already had a good-hitting team and one of the worst pitching staffs in major league baseball? I was in Dallas at the winter meetings of 2000 when this all came down; and major league executives and scouts were shaking their heads in disbelief. It wasn't just the sum of money they paid A-Rod, but their failure to procure any pitchers that amazed the baseball crowd. The crowd was right, as the Rangers have finished last in their division each year with A-Rod. Most kids playing fantasy baseball on their computers could have taken the money the Rangers spent and put together a better team.

One thing that has always made it difficult to put all the pieces together into a neat puzzle is the mistrust between the various departments of a team. During my first few years with the Astros, I heard a lot of grumbling about minor league phenoms. The farm department was extolling the virtues of the kids, and the major league GM, manager, and coaches were skeptical. Most of the farmhands had trouble adjusting to big league competition, and the older players, who would be displaced if a youngster were called up to Houston, were more than skeptical—they were outraged. The fact is that if you bet against a kid making the grade you will be right more often than not. But the development people only see their charges playing against minor league players from other organizations. They have to project what a player might be able to do if he were promoted. There is a lot of uncertainty in these projections because the toughest part of anyone's game to judge is between the ears and in the heart. You can be sure how fast a pitcher can throw or a player can run down the line; you know if a player can hit a ball 400 feet, and if he has good hands and a good throwing arm. But there is no way to know how a kid will succeed competing against bona fide major leaguers until he does it—or, in most cases, doesn't.

One day I was broadcasting a game from Vero Beach. The Astros were playing the Dodgers in spring training and a kid named Darryl Kile was on the mound. DK walked a couple of guys, struck out a couple, and then coughed up a three-run homer. Sandy Koufax was sitting in the booth next to ours and he opened the window between the booths when the inning was over. "What's the story on this kid?" he asked. "It looks like he's got great stuff."

"He does," I said. "But it seems like he has a bout with wildness every start and then he throws one right down the middle to a power hitter. He just doesn't seem to have the knack for pitching."

"Too bad," Sandy said. "It seems like arms and heads seldom come in matched sets."

Actually, Sandy could have identified with Kile better than most former pitchers—he had the same profile in his early years with the Dodgers. He was hard to hit, but was just wild enough to beat himself most of the time. Nolan Ryan was the same way, but both Koufax and Ryan overcame wildness and became Hall of Fame pitchers.

Kile, whose untimely death last summer shocked the baseball world, was still going strong at age thirty-three. He was not going to be another Sandy Koufax or Nolan Ryan—he didn't throw as hard, or strike out as many batters, but he was a dependable pitcher for many years, a workhorse, an innings-eater. When I took the reins of the Astros in 1997, I challenged our starting pitchers to pitch deeper into the game; Darryl Kile stepped up immediately. He wanted to finish every game he started. He was a throwback in that sense and in another—by retaliating when the opposing pitcher threw at one of our players. It is difficult to find guys who will do this distasteful job, but DK never blinked. No, he did not become a Hall of Famer, but he did win nineteen games for us in '97 and he did maintain his dignity and composure while serving hard-labor time with the Rockies in the unfriendly confines of Coors Field. Generally speaking, Koufax was right about arms and heads, but there are many pitchers, like Kile, who eventually put the two elements together. He didn't pitch much in high school and only spent a few years in the minor leagues. He had a good excuse for his spotty performance early in his career, but being the gentleman he was he would never use it.

By the time Kile came to the big leagues, the hazing days of summer were over. Rookies now gain acceptance without having to earn it. It was a little different when I broke in. Back then players didn't make big money. Most of the time, when a veteran player was released, he had to find another job. Most of the time, it was not a job he enjoyed like playing baseball, and most of the time he made far less money. Luckily for me, I was a September call-up so I didn't take anyone's spot on the roster and didn't get the cold shoulder from the veteran players. I will never forget one moment from the time I spent with the Colt 45's in September of 1964.

The Colts were at home and I was not on the twenty-five-man roster, but merely working out with the team during batting practice. When the opposing team started taking batting practice, we went back into the clubhouse at old Colt Stadium. The locker room was rectangular and I had a locker right by the front door. The first week I only talked to two or three of the young guys—I minded my own business. Fact is, though I am not shy by nature, I was more than a little intimidated by my surroundings. I was only seventeen years old at the time, and had very little facial hair and none on my chest. I felt like a lamb in wolf country. The first few days, I just sat on the stool in front of my locker until the last player went out to the dugout. Then I showered, changed into my street clothes, and sat in the box seats behind home plate.

After four or five days, I mustered the courage to walk to the other end of the locker room to get a soda. As I got about halfway there, I looked to my left and saw Dick Farrell, Jim Owens, and Dave Giusti, three of the hairiest, most grizzled guys I had ever seen, huddled together in conversation. Owens noticed my glance and immediately challenged me. "What the fuck are you looking at?" he said. I turned my head, and not wanting to look foolish, continued to the cooler to get the soda and returned to my locker, shaking inside. I didn't pose any immediate threat to these three guys, but Farrell and Owens were on the downside of their careers and I could conceivably displace one of them the next year. Back then (1964) rookies were not warmly welcomed. They had to prove themselves worthy first. I proved myself to some extent by striking out Willie Mays in my first inning of my debut game on my eighteenth birthday. But I knew that one strikeout wasn't enough.

Actually, that strikeout could have been a home run. For some reason, I decided to throw him a change-up, which was my worst pitch. Willie hit it about 450 feet, just foul down the left-field line. At that stage of his career, he didn't want to get beaned by some young hard-throwing kid. With two strikes, I threw a slider and I meant to get it low and away. Instead, it started out right at him and he bailed out. The pitch swerved across the inside of the plate for a called strike. The crowd went nuts.

Luckily for me, or perhaps unluckily, depending on how you look at it, Farrell and Owens took me under their wing in the spring of 1965. Once they knew that I would drink beer, cuss, and chase women, they accepted me and this was before I had won a single game. I had pitched in three games the previous September and given up only two runs in nine innings, and looking back, I realize that my talent must have been obvious enough that the veterans did not begrudge my attempt to make the team. They knew it was inevitable, but I didn't know it at the time—I only knew that I wanted to fit in. As it turned out, I did make the team and ended up winning seven games that year. I won the respect of the veterans because I was not afraid to challenge even the best hitters and I could be depended upon to retaliate.

I did, however, notice that some of the other young guys were flunking their initiation tests. Running with the Dalton Gang (Farrell and Owens) probably wasn't the best idea I ever had. But it seemed right at the time.

My situation was unique—most prospects need more minor league innings to sharpen their skills. Gerry Hunsicker was the assistant general manager with the Mets before he became the GM of the Astros. He saw several young pitchers get called up to New York and sent back down after failing, which convinced him that it was a bad idea to rush a kid through the system. There were several occasions when I would have given a kid a shot even though it seemed premature, and some of my coaches felt the same way. But Gerry held the line. It would be difficult to say he was wrong because almost every kid we called up during my five years did a good job and was ready to help us win.

Still, if I were a general manager, I would probably push some of the most talented players a little faster. My belief is that everyone, including superstars, will have slumps and have to overcome adversity. If a kid, like the Astros' Tim Redding, came up and struggled, he would have to go back down. Usually there's a reason. In Tim's case, he lacked control of breaking balls and off-speed pitches. In the minors, hitters swung at a lot of those pitches and either missed them or hit them weakly for outs. In the big leagues, they didn't swing and he got behind in the count constantly. The hitters were ready for the fastball, and even though he had a good one, they hit him hard. So, we sent him down, he pitched well and came back up. Then he had the same problem and went down again. If he ever makes the grade it will be because he has learned to get his other pitches over the plate. If he hadn't been called up early, he would not have learned this lesson as soon, so did calling him up hurt him? I doubt it. I think it simply showed him something he was going to have to learn anyway, no matter how many years he spent at Triple A. And if a kid like Tim was devastated over being demoted, he probably wasn't going to be the type of tough competitor we were looking for, anyway. The other option is calling up a veteran minor league pitcher who does not possess the lively arm, which is just a stopgap measure, as the team has no long-range plans for him. But when a kid like Roy Oswalt is up to the challenge, the team improves immediately and is better for years to come.

CHAPTER 9

Trades

The reason it is so hard to make a deal is that everyone wants to give you a biscuit for a bag of flour.

—ELLIS CLARY, VETERAN SCOUT

IN THIS ERA OF FREE AGENTS, the impact of a trade isn't quite what it used to be. Even so, as recently as 1976, the Pirates created quite a stir when they traded their catcher, Manny Sanguillen, to the Oakland A's for manager Chuck Tanner. To get a deal this strange you have to have an oddball trader, and A's owner Charlie Finley fit the bill. Typically, when a team wants to interview a coach or manager, it must ask his current employer for permission to speak with him. I can just see it now: The Bucs ask Finley if they can talk to Tanner; Charlie O. says, "You can't have him unless . . ."

When the Tanner for Sanguillen deal came down, most folks thought it was one of the most unusual trades ever. It doubtless dredged up memories of Bill Veeck, who set up a card table in the lobby of the hotel where the owners were having winter meetings, donned a transparent green visor, and put up a sign to the effect that he was open for business. If you look back to Veeck's era and even before, you will find some really weird deals.

In 1956, Tigers Hall of Fame broadcaster Ernie Harwell wrote a story for *Parade* magazine on strange trades, and boy did he ever come up with some beauties. In 1890, when young Cy Young was still a pup, he was traded from Canton to Cleveland for a suit of clothes. I guess you could say the owner of the Canton club wasn't a very good scout.

In 1913, the St. Louis Browns trained in Montgomery, Alabama. When it came time to break camp, they still owed the Montgomery team rent on the field. The Browns satisfied this debt by trading catcher Buzzy Wares for forgiveness of the rent. A similar deal was made with Hall of Famer Tris Speaker. In 1908, Speaker was left at the Red Sox spring training headquarters in Little Rock in exchange for use of the field. When Speaker started tearing up the Southern League, though, the Sox quickly paid the owner of the Little Rock team to get the young outfielder back.

Robert Moses "Lefty" Grove was playing for Martinsburgh when Jack Dunn of the minor league Baltimore Orioles spotted him. Dunn learned that the Martinsburgh club still owed a contractor for the installation of an outfield fence. Several days later, Grove was an Oriole and the fence was paid for. In another doozy, Barney Bunch of the Omaha club had to part with two players to get the airplane he desired.

All of these deals were made out of practical necessity, but some other minor league trades were made out of hunger. The Wichita Falls club of the Texas League traded Euel Moore for a plate of beans; Dallas sent Joe Martina to New Orleans for two barrels of oysters, whereupon Martina was nicknamed Oyster Joe. But just think of how San Francisco's Jack Fenton felt when he was sent to Memphis for a box of prunes. San Antonio owner Homer Hammond got the best of Dallas when he dealt them Mike Dondero for a dozen doughnuts. Hammond reportedly ate the doughnuts before the deal was signed and then decided to keep Dondero.

But for shrewd deals, none can top the one Little Rock Travelers player-owner Willis Hudlin made in the late-summer pennant race of 1944: Hudlin, a veteran of sixteen major league seasons and at that point thirty-eight years old, traded *himself* to the St. Louis Browns. Though he did not pitch in the World Series, he did lose one game in September and he still got a cut of the Browns' share. Then he used part of the money to buy himself back!

Whether it was due to modesty or just a convenient memory lapse, Ernie Harwell left out one of the best deals ever. In 1948, Harwell was broadcasting for the Atlanta Crackers when Dodgers executive Branch Rickey discovered him. In one of the best trades he ever made, the Mahatma sent catcher Cliff Dapper to Atlanta in exchange for a future Hall of Fame broadcaster by the name of Harwell.

Trades are harder to make now than ever before because there are more complications. It used to be rare for a player to have a no-trade clause in his contract but now it's fairly common. It used to be impossible to get a front-line player except by trading for him; now, you can wait for him to become a free agent and sign him without giving up another player. If you sign a player who is rated Type A you lose a choice in the amateur draft the next year, but this seldom has any effect whatsoever on the team signing the free agent because they're looking for immediate help. It will take at least two or three years for a player chosen in the draft to make it to the major leagues, if he makes it at all, so losing a draft pick isn't much of a deterrent to signing free agents.

But trading is still an important part of team building. In baseball, as in life, you usually have too much or not enough. For example, for the last three years the Astros have had three first basemen and have needed a shortstop and a center fielder. Lance Berkman has enough speed to play a corner outfield position and has made the transition smoothly, but Daryle Ward just isn't fast enough to play the outfield well. The Astros have been unable to get a good player in a deal for Ward because he has not had a chance to prove himself to be a good defensive player. We had a contending team almost every year I managed and I didn't even consider playing Daryle at first base to enhance his trade value. The Astros could probably get several good players for Berkman, because he can be used at several positions, but it's for exactly that reason that the Astros don't want to trade him. Bagwell and Berkman fit nicely into the lineup together, and although two is company, three's a crowd.

At one point, in the 1999 season, when we had a lot of injury problems and were in the race, I suggested that we send Daryle to Triple A to play first. "We're never going to get a fair deal for Ward until he proves that he has a position," I told Gerry. "Nobody wants a twenty-two-year-old DH." But Gerry reminded me that Daryle had already proven himself as a major league hitter and was important to us in Houston as a left-handed power bat, either coming off the bench or in an occasional start. He was right, but it was still frustrating because we really needed a strong left-handed hitter in the lineup. The frustration finally ended in February 2003 when the Astros traded Ward to the Dodgers for a double A pitching prospect.

When Ellis Clary said, "The reason it is so hard to make a deal is that everyone wants to give you a biscuit for a bag of flour," he was talking about prospects and suspects. Sometimes a team will give up a good prospect or two for a veteran suspect who can help win a pennant. In 1998, the Astros traded three for one with the Mariners: John Halama, Freddie Garcia, and Carlos Guillen went to Seattle and Randy Johnson came to Houston. We all thought it was worth taking a chance because there were more good players in the Astros' minor league system, and the surplus of minor league prospects justified the deal. But when we got knocked out in the first round of the playoffs by the Padres and Johnson went to Arizona as a free agent, the deal backfired. The three youngsters became important players in the Mariners' rise to prominence, and Johnson, who was having lower back pain, proved not to be a suspect, as he took the Diamondbacks, not the Astros, to the World Series! If we had made it to the World Series, the deal would have paid off nicely, but we probably would have won the division that year without Johnson, and we would have been better prepared for the future if we had kept the three prospects. Still, chances to go to the Fall Classic don't come often and most people feel that you have to strike while the iron is hot.

Eight years earlier, the Astros were not a contending team and the Red Sox were. Houston, the rebuilding team, dealt a day-old biscuit, Larry Andersen, to the Red Sox for a bag of flour named Jeff Bagwell on August 31, the trading deadline. Andy was a hometown favorite in the many cities where he had played—including Houston. His career started in A ball with the Indians. That first year was tough. He loved the lifestyle but his pitching was barely good enough to be called professional. "If I hadn't stayed late and helped the clubhouse kid with the laundry, they probably would have released me," he once said. Actually, it would be hard to release anyone who was so much fun to be around. Andy played ten years in the minors before he finally got established as a big league pitcher. He ended up pitching for all or part of nineteen seasons in the majors, cracking jokes all the way. By the time he got to Houston, his reputation as a prankster was well established and he had developed one of the best sliders in the game. Andy quickly became a great setup man for closer Dave Smith.

He helped the Red Sox make the playoffs in 1990, but they were eliminated by the Oakland A's in the first round of the playoffs. The next year, he signed with the Padres and spent two years in San Diego before finally finishing up in Philadelphia. Meanwhile, Bagwell began his career the next year in Houston. Although Andy was a fine pitcher and a great guy, Baggy is a shoo-in for the Hall of Fame, and, like Babe Ruth, he has become yet another cross to bear in Boston. The point is that you can make a lot of biscuits with a bag of flour, but you must wait for them to bake. Sometimes hunger overcomes patience—just ask Homer Hammond.

While the Bagwell deal is generally regarded to be the best the Astros have ever made, the deal they made for Jose Cruz was just about as good. Toward the end of the 1974 season, the Cardinals were looking for a starting pitcher; the Astros were completely out of the race and veteran lefty Claude Osteen was near the end of his career and therefore expendable. The Astros traded Claude for a "player to be named later." That player turned out to be Cruz, and Jose went on to become the Astros MVP five times. His durability and excellence prompted the Astros to retire his number in 1999.

Conversely, the most infamous deal the Astros ever struck was made just after the end of the 1971 season. In it, Joe Morgan, Denis Menke, Jack Billingham, Cesar Geronimo, and Ed Armbrister went to the Cincinnati Reds in exchange for Lee May, Tommy Helms, and Jimmy Stewart. The Reds got four front-line players in the

trade and the Astros got two. The Astros got better—they moved
from fourth to second in the standings in 1972. But the Reds really
brought a fresh batch out of the oven that year, moving from fifth
to first, kick-starting the Big Red Machine.

I may have accidentally had a hand in that deal. One evening
during the 1971 season, Doug Rader and I were enjoying a cock-
tail with Reds super-scout Ray Shore in San Francisco. Doug and
I maintained that Joe Morgan was a better hitter than Tommy
Helms; Shore argued for his own player, but I'm sure he gained a
new appreciation for Morgan after hearing what we had to say. We
even made a bet with Shore that Joe would hit for a higher average
than Tommy that year. Looking back, we lost both battle and war:

			HR	RBI	R	BB	SB
1971	Helms	.256	3	52	40	26	3
1971	Morgan	.254	13	56	87	88	40

Helms's batting average was slightly better than Morgan's,
but Morgan was clearly the better offensive player. At that time
Helms was one of the best defensive second basemen in the league
and Morgan had stiff hands and a weak throwing arm. As time
went on, Joe overcame these limitations and won several Gold
Glove Awards—to say nothing of his two league MVP Awards. We
got a biscuit for a bag of flour in that deal. The Reds themselves
didn't know what a good trade they had made, just as the Astros
could not have imagined how good Bagwell would become.

Everyone prefers the flour, but the lure of the playoffs and
World Series can make a biscuit look like a banquet.

Bill Veeck once said, "Sometimes the best deals are the ones
you don't make." Another trade between the Astros and Reds that
could have changed my life more than the Morgan deal was not
concluded. In it, Jimmy Wynn and I were going to the Reds for
Frank Robinson. The Astros were unwilling to part with the flour at
that time and a few weeks later, the Reds traded Robinson to the
Orioles for pitchers Jack Baldschun and Milt Pappas and journey-
man outfielder Dick Simpson. Robinson won the Triple Crown in
Baltimore the next year; Pappas was a good starting pitcher and

Baldschun a serviceable reliever, but because I was a lot younger than Pappas and Wynn could have replaced Robinson, I'm sure the Reds would have preferred the deal with the Astros.

I think about this nondeal occasionally and what it would have been like to pitch for the Reds. With "Captain Hook," Sparky Anderson, at the helm I wouldn't have pitched as many innings and likely would have lasted a few more years. I probably would have won a few more games and played in the World Series; I would have pitched to Johnny Bench and benefited from the horsepower of the Big Red Machine. On the other hand, my roots in Houston would have been torn loose while I was still a sapling. Staying in Houston throughout my career has been a rare blessing. If I had gone to Cincinnati, I may not have been offered a job in the broadcast booth or written a column for the newspaper. It is likely I wouldn't have written this book and it is certain I wouldn't have had my number retired.

When I finally was traded, after the 1976 season, I wasn't worth near as much. Shoulder troubles had taken a heavy toll. In early September, less than two months after pitching a no-hitter against the Expos, I threw my shoulder out during a bullpen session in Atlanta. I heard a clunk as I released a pitch and it felt like my whole shoulder musculature had shifted over to the right about an inch. The Astros' team doctor told me that the biceps tendon had come out of its groove. He said it would heal over the winter, but it felt like more than that to me and I wasn't so sure it was going to get better. It kept popping out for a couple of weeks and to get it back in I had to reach my arm up and twist it counterclockwise. I had already beaten the Cardinals four times that year and they obviously had a high opinion of my worth. Somehow they didn't notice that I didn't pitch that September.

Toward the end of the season, Bill Virdon called me into his office and told me that the team would like to trade me. He said that the Astros were going to rebuild and give the young pitchers in the organization a chance to get established and that he couldn't promise me a spot in the starting rotation. I was the top winner on the team that year, had won more games than any pitcher in Astros history, and was still only thirty years old. But I was injured and

I'm not sure the doctor told Astros general manager Tal Smith the same story he told me. Virdon's words were troublesome: There was no question I would be the number one starter on the team the next year if I were healthy, so I knew it had to be more about my injury and my salary than the youth movement. Because I had more than ten years in the major leagues, I had the right to refuse a trade, but I sure didn't want to pitch for a team that didn't want me. Tal asked me to waive the clause, and in exchange for a two-year contract extension, I gave him a list of places I would be willing to go. I got a little extra money out of the deal but I never got over the injury.

The Cardinals had seen me at my best that year and St. Louis was on the list. They ended up getting a burned biscuit.

I guess the Astros were pretty proud of themselves. They got a starting catcher, Joe Ferguson, for me. I pitched about forty ugly innings for the Redbirds the next year and was released the following spring; Ferguson didn't do much more for Houston. Often trades work out that way: You trade your problem and find out the guy you get in the deal has a problem too.

Generally speaking, trades are good for the sport. They enable teams to deal players who are superfluous for players they really need. Moreover, they stimulate fan interest and provide fodder for talk shows. It used to be that the only way to change the nature of your team was to make a trade or bring up a player from your farm system. There was no way for a veteran player to become a free agent back then. Dealing at the major league level was the only way to get proven talent. As a result, players didn't move from team to team as much as they do now.

Lately I have heard a lot of complaints from people my age about the movement of players. Fans say, "I can't even keep up with the players on our own team. Back in the old days, we knew every player on the team, their batting averages, everything. Now they go back and forth before you can ever get attached to them."

Excuse me? Are you saying that you would like to follow a last-place team with the same players year after year? Or are you saying you remember a time when your team won and you knew all the players? *Winning*, not player loyalty, is the name of the game in terms of fan attraction.

One thing I can say without reservation is that avid fans like trades and free agent signings. It gives them something to get excited about, something to get furious about, and, simply, something to talk about. If you hear somebody say that they don't like sports any more because they can't identify with the players, I'd bet the person is over fifty years old. I would also bet that fan does not have any tattoos and does not make a million dollars or more a year. What older fans can't identify with is the young generation of athletes. I have a little trouble myself, but it's not about trades or free agents. It's about being a curmudgeon or being hip.

Most of the time, fans don't like the trades their teams make. They want to get a prime-time player when one of the regular players on the team is dealt, but a lot of times they get a player they've never heard of. In Houston, Larry Andersen was a popular player. A lot of fans wondered how the Astros could trade him for a Double A ballplayer named Jeff Bagwell. "Bagwell? Who the hell is he?" Sometimes the Jose Cruzes and Jeff Bagwells of the world are obtained in what look like minor deals. And sometimes what looks like a blockbuster deal like Dierker for Ferguson fizzles like cheap champagne. Trades can be risky. They can backfire and topple the whole house of cards; they can turn a contending team around and send it packing to the second division; or they can get you over the hump and into the playoffs.

Whenever top players are traded or lost as free agents there is a public relations backlash. I'm sure there were a lot of Mariners fans that didn't want to part with Randy Johnson, Ken Griffey Jr., and Alex Rodriguez. It might be hard to find these fans now—most of them would have a convenient memory lapse because Seattle has become a better-balanced team with the young players they obtained in the trades. Fans can fondly remember players on winning teams, even when they may only play with the club during one winning season. I can name every player on my winter league team from 1967 because we won the championship; I can also remember almost all the players who wore the Astros uniform with me for twelve years. But I can't remember which years which players were together because we never won the pennant.

Now, the rich teams, like the Yankees, can sign free agents. Since they can afford the added salary and don't have to part with any big league players, they have virtually no risk: The Yankees can make a bad deal and just swallow the salary and buy another player. However, a team like the Royals can't do that. These days, if you have the money, you have an ace in the hole. You can afford to make a few mistakes. When paid admissions provided the lion's share of revenue, the playing field was almost level, but now that broadcast revenue is more of a factor than ticket sales, market size is of paramount importance. The Yankees have New York; with the coverage of superstations WGN and WTBS, the Cubs and Braves have fans all over the country and advertisers lined up to send their commercial messages to these fans. The Cardinals have much of the Midwest and the Red Sox have New England.

Yet, even with the money, there is risk. The Cubs have tended to eliminate the risk by keeping their payroll under their revenue, and consequently, they have not won a pennant since Hitler retired. The Braves and Yankees have paid more for talent and hit the jackpot, but remember the Yankees didn't win their division from 1981–1993. They spent a lot of money but they didn't develop many players in their farm system. The modern Yankees are solid up the middle at the most expensive positions with players they developed themselves—Derek Jeter, Bernie Williams, Alfonso Soriano, and Jorge Posada. Similarly, the Braves have developed many of their own stars like Chipper Jones, Andruw Jones, Javy Lopez, and Rafael Furcal.

The Dodgers and Orioles have spent a lot of money too, but they haven't grown their own key players like the Yankees and Braves and, as a result, they haven't won nearly as much. I cannot write a formula for success, even with unlimited funds: It takes an owner who is willing to gamble, a general manager who can see the difference between Joe Morgan and Tommy Helms, and it takes a lot of good scouts and a good farm system. Even the best teams aren't two-deep at every position. Consequently, it takes a little luck in the injury department.

It also takes players who can work well together. In my years managing the Astros, I benefited greatly by having Craig Biggio and Jeff Bagwell—they played hard every day and set the tone. The only year we had a problem was in 2000 when we had a couple of new players who were like turds in the punchbowl. No matter who your manager is or who your team leading players are, you cannot win a championship without heart, and too much bad blood can ruin the old ticker. This is where trades come in again. Many managers have said that the easiest way to improve a team is to excise the boils; this is what we call addition by subtraction. The only problem with that type of trade is that you will have trouble trading with that team again. The Astros and Tigers traded a lot when Tal Smith was the president of the Astros and his son Randy was the general manager of the Tigers. The two teams made several deals but after the last one, with Brad Ausmus and Nelson Cruz coming to Houston and Mitch Meluskey, Roger Cedeno, and Chris Holt going to Detroit, there probably won't be another Astros-Tigers trade soon. Randy Smith got the ax in Detroit—Tal is still with the Astros.

In the end, I think most teams hope that their trading partners are happy with the players they obtain. The best trades make both teams better, and they make it a lot easier to trade with that team again.

CHAPTER 10

Cheating

*The tradition of professional baseball always has been agreeably
free of chivalry. The rule is "Do everything you can get away with."*

—HEYWOOD BROUN

IN THE EARLY DAYS of the last century, professional baseball
players were held in low regard. They were then perceived to be
just about as noble as lawyers and used car salesmen are today. In
those days, pitchers routinely spit tobacco juice on the ball to make
it darker and thus harder to see; they roughed up the hide of the ball
to create movement on their pitches and waxed the hide for the
same reason. Some of the players, like Hal Chase, were suspected of
being in cahoots with gamblers. At that juncture in the history of
the sport, players earned low wages and had to work during the off-
season to make ends meet. These circumstances don't offer an excuse for consorting with gamblers, but they do suggest a reason.
That association eventually dealt the sport a mighty blow in 1920,
when eight White Sox players confessed to conspiring with gamblers to throw the 1919 World Series to the Reds for a modest fee.
This event became known as the Black Sox scandal.

Things are a lot different now. Most major league players
work out during the winter, but few are gainfully employed. The

specter of gamblers controlling the outcome of a game was briefly in the news when Pete Rose was accused of gambling on baseball in the 1980s. We may never know if Pete gambled on games he could have thrown. The deal Pete made with commissioner Bart Giamatti silenced gambling accusations that appeared in the *Dowd Report* compiled by John Dowd, an ex-marine and attorney hired by Major League Baseball to investigate Pete's gambling activities. Pete agreed to accept a lifetime suspension from professional baseball, and it appeared he had given away his plaque in the Hall of Fame. I know Pete's gambling activities started when he was quite young. In fact, I still recall running into him while having breakfast at a restaurant named Wiggins, which was right across from the Netherland Hilton where we stayed in Cincinnati. I was still a teenager and I was having breakfast with one of our veteran pitchers, Jim Owens. Pete only had a few years in the big leagues at the time, and he came over with a *Racing Form* and asked Owens if he wanted to get a bet down. I was fascinated, but declined the opportunity to place a wager.

Gambling, it seems, is an integrity issue; drugs are personal. At least that is the way it looks at this point in time. There is one player in Cooperstown already who got caught with drugs. I imagine there are a few more who did not get caught. I'm talking about illegal drugs. Meanwhile, legal drugs are causing quite a stir these days too. If there's a reason to cheat now, it is to excel, win, and get paid for it. The age-old ploys of doctoring the ball and corking the bat are still part of the game, although it is mostly talk. In the five years I managed, I only suspected a few players of altering the equipment, and I wouldn't have bet a single bob on it. We even *encouraged* a few pitchers to throw spitballs or scuff-balls, but they wouldn't do it. They would practice it in the bullpen and get the intended result, but when they got into the game they were afraid to use the illegal pitches. The guys who actually do cheat are the tip of the iceberg; what lies beneath the surface is the entire universe of professional baseball. It is my opinion that more than 95 percent of that iceberg is underwater.

Still, the pay divide between a part-time player and a star is the width of the Grand Canyon. If you can crack the starting lineup and stay in it for a few years, you can retire from the game and never need another job. The stars can save enough money to set themselves up for life while the lesser lights will probably have to face the real world when they finish playing. What was once a penny-ante game is high-stakes poker now. This scenario is not an excuse for cheating either, but it does offer a reason.

My grandfather Al Keller was a semipro catcher in the 1920s. He used to tell me that he would teach me the emery ball (a fastball that tails or sails depending on the side of the ball the scuff is on when it's thrown; the ball tends to move away from the scuffed side because of the added friction on that side of the ball). When I was in high school my grandfather said that I still didn't throw hard enough to throw the pitch. I may not have been artful enough either. It is difficult to scuff the ball with everyone watching, and the movement of the ball is so dramatic, people would be watching every pitch. When I played, it was much more likely to see a pitcher throw a spitball than a scuffed because it is easier to get a slick substance on the hide of the ball than it is to scuff it. The spitter is held on the smooth hide of the ball and it squirts out with very little spin, like a forkball, but with much more velocity. After my rookie season with the Colt 45's, I asked my granddad if I threw hard enough to use the emery ball yet. "You don't need it now," he said. My problem was that I went rather quickly from not having it to the point where it wouldn't have helped me if I had. Would I have tried it? You bet. I certainly prefer chivalry to deceit, but I favor supporting my family over chivalry.

I *think* doctoring the ball came first. Corking the bat by drilling a lengthwise hole in the business end and filling it with a light and bouncy material came next. Cork was used to soup up the bats at first; I've heard now some players use Super Balls. During my playing days, the starting pitchers usually had a contest with the relief pitchers to see who could hit the most home runs in batting practice. I corked a few bats for use in these games but I couldn't tell if the cork added distance to my fly balls. The regular players insist that it works. I believe them, but I don't think the corked bats have more spring. I just think they're lighter and that the players can obtain a slight improvement in their bat speed.

The whole thing is silly, except for the intrigue. The light bats that the players favor these days explode all the time. A guy would really have to be desperate to use a corked bat. Getting caught, like Billy Hatcher did ten or twelve years ago using a bat he said belonged to Dave Smith, would almost be a sure thing if a player used an illegal bat for even a week. When the bat exploded, the cheater would be caught red-handed, with the contents of the barrelhead scattered on the infield. The bats they use these days are so light, they're like corked bats to begin with. Who would take the chance, knowing that he could hit the ball out of the park with a legal bat?

It is a little harder to cheat these days, under the scrutiny of four umpires and five television cameras. In the early days of the sport, each game had only one umpire. When this lone arbiter ran toward the foul line to see if a ball was fair or foul, some base runners cut inside a bag by ten feet or so while the umpire was looking the other way. Now, with four umpires, they can't get away with it so they don't even bother to try. What was considered fascinating in the roaring Twenties is reprehensible now. It seems like the doors to enhanced success by treachery are closing, one by one.

In the recent negotiations between the players and the owners, another door—the steroid portal—had apparently been shut. *Apparently.* The procedure now is to test many of the players for steroids at spring training, and the rest during the course of the season. If less than 5 percent of the tests prove positive, testing will be eliminated. Since testing will also reveal chemicals that mask steroid detection, it should provide a good assessment of the problem. I'm not the least bit worried about a steroid scandal. I think the game is in good shape and we are making a mountain out of a molehill both in terms of drugs and equipment.

The door to muscular might through the miracle of modern medicine is a topic of great interest. But in my opinion, it is a door that is seldom opened anyway. I don't know how many players have taken drugs or supplements to grow bigger muscles, but many players, including Sammy Sosa and Barry Bonds and Mark McGwire, have bulked up to prepare for battle and it shows. Still, Bonds won a few MVP Awards before he added the muscle mass, and McGwire hit forty-nine home runs as a rookie, long before the bodybuilding trend of the last few years. I saw Sammy hit one to the back of the pavilion in the Astrodome before he looked like Hercules.

When Ken Caminiti admitted to taking steroids to gain a competitive edge, he opened Pandora's box and all sorts of demons burst forth. Jose Canseco seems determined to keep the box open by writing about it. Caminiti won the National League Most Valuable Player Award, in 1996, abusing himself from within and without, slamming his body to the ground in pursuit of ground balls and ingesting drugs that made his already strong body even stronger, and Canseco did about the same thing. Whether they will regret it remains to be seen. If the after-effects are not severe, Caminiti will likely conclude that winning the MVP was worth it. Considering the problems he had with amphetamines and alcohol before '96 and with other illegal drugs afterward, his story, along with Darryl Strawberry's and that of a few others, could be dismissed as addictive behavior, which is found in nonathletes all over the world. I feel particularly bad about Caminiti's case because I consider him a friend. As a competitor his instincts were practically flawless. Off the field, his instincts betrayed him. Throughout his career with the Astros, he was one of the most popular guys on the team. He would give you the shirt off his back and, if you needed it, he'd give you his pants too.

Everyone knows that athletes have taken drugs to improve their performance. In the Olympics, where competitors are tested for illegal drugs, some have failed the tests. There is no drug testing in Major League Baseball, but there is drug testing in the minors. It is not uncommon for a minor leaguer to get busted for drugs, but the only ones that know about it are the athletes and their teams. If a no-name guy is caught with marijuana in his blood, it is a non-story. The industry seems to have adopted the Clinton administration policy for gays in the military—don't ask, don't tell. Still, it is only human to ask: Is this a pervasive problem or just a manifestation of the underbelly of twenty-first-century American culture? Do professional athletes succumb to addiction more readily than people who don't make their livelihood in the spotlight? Or is the drug problem in professional sports just part of a societal problem?

I don't know how many baseball players medicate themselves in order to improve their performance. I do know that steroids are only part of the problem and, I think, a smaller part than other drugs. In March of 1999, our team doctors presented a lecture on strength-enhancing supplements. At that time the poster boy for strength products was Mark McGwire. McGwire admitted to using androstenedione, which is not an illegal drug—it is considered a dietary supplement. In effect, it fools the body into making more testosterone. It has been banned in the Olympics but you can still buy it over-the-counter at your local vitamin store along with watered-down versions of diet pills and anti-inflammatory medicine. Because of McGwire's great strength and his setting of a new single-season home run record, andro was big news. During spring training several years ago, our doctors spoke out against steroids because they have documented evidence of deleterious effects. They did not condemn the supplements, but did warn the players that they could become dehydrated and encouraged anyone who used them to drink a lot of water. The doctors also speculated that problems could occur when the current users of andro and creatine got a little older. Creatine causes the body to add weight and, when combined with weight lifting, it enhances the development of muscle mass. These supplements are so new that they have no long-term history. If you use them, you're taking your chances.

This presentation got the players' attention. They are literally on the battle lines where terms of engagement are critical. When your body is your profession, you tend to look at the question of enhancing it from all possible angles and each player has to decide for himself whether the gamble is worth the risk. I wouldn't be surprised if I learned that some players tried steroids without any appreciable improvement in performance, and then quit taking them.

Toward the end of the 2000 season, at Shea Stadium in New York, another doctor spoke to the players at the behest of the commissioner's office and the players association. The intent of this presentation was to dissuade the players from experimenting with the steroid family and its relatives. The doctors said that there was some evidence that steroid users started losing body hair and grew boobs. The drugs could also affect sleeping habits and lead to aggressive behavior. When I got back to the coaches room, I told my staff that someone must have been giving me steroids. I had all of the symptoms.

I suspect that there is more drug abuse among our entire population than most of us realize. And I also suspect that the numbers are even higher among professional athletes. But suspicion is not fact—it's only a guess. There is such an emphasis on athletic performance in our society that even the high school kids are bulking up. I know because the father of one of my son's friends sells "safe supplements," or so he says. We have advised our son, Ryan, not to take them, but what if he gets to Triple A ball and just needs a little more juice to get to the majors? What will we say then, when he's an adult? If we say anything at all, we would likely encourage him to resist the temptation, but would he listen? Not if he's like I was. I didn't have a high opinion of my parents' wisdom at that age. I just did what my teammates did—that is, drink. I also tried an amphetamine one time when I wasn't feeling well on my day to pitch. I felt like King Kong when I took the mound—I think I had about eight strikeouts and six walks after five innings. I wasn't pitching; I was just throwing like a madman. After the effects of the drug diminished, I was able to go on and get the win. I didn't strike many batters out after the fifth, but I got them out. After that experience, I decided that my mental faculties were more important than my physical strength.

If the baseball-loving public didn't already know there was a lot of boozing in Major League Baseball, it found out when Jim Brosnan, a Reds relief pitcher, published The Long Season in 1960. They learned that many players also used "greenies" (amphetamines) a decade later when Jim Bouton wrote Ball Four.

Marijuana and cocaine got some play in the 1970s and early 1980s; crack is still around. I don't think any of these drugs, starting with alcohol, have been eradicated, but some seem to be less prominent now in the age of steroids. In fact, the players usually follow their peers and the unwritten code of behavior that is prevalent on their team. Some feel the pressure and are looking for escape, some are seeking enhanced recreation, and some of it is done to improve performance. In some cases, mostly with steroids, body sculpting seems to be an incentive.

Last summer, after Caminiti held court, I heard an interview with Curt Schilling. Schilling said that Brian Jordan and Deion Sanders, both of whom played baseball and football professionally, told him that the MLB schedule was more grueling than the NFL's by far. It's the daily grind that gets you. Baseball players seldom suffer severe injuries like broken bones; what wears them out is the little dings, scratches, and pulled muscles that won't go away. Every time they play a game they aggravate the injury. Some guys never want to miss a game. If they don't feel good on a particular day, they find a way to lift their spirits. It's one thing to get up for one game a week, it's quite another to do it six or seven times.

When I was pitching, I always had a few beers after a game. I didn't need to get up for the game because I only pitched once or twice a week and usually had to control my adrenaline rather than create it, but in the aftermath of the competition I was so wound up I had trouble settling down and going to sleep. Besides, almost every time I pitched, I had a reason to either celebrate or forget. I still drink more beer than I should but have found it hard to break the habit.

It is even more difficult for the everyday player. Most I have known have found reasonable ways to deal with the physical and emotional demands of the schedule, but what's dangerous is the cycle. It can start innocently enough; you show up at the park and you have a cold. You have to go against a real tough pitcher; you decide to take a greenie and then you go out and play like crazy, swinging for the fences and diving after balls you cannot possibly reach. Afterward, you're all wound up; you have a few beers to settle down. Then you wake up feeling bad the next day and it all begins again.

At one point, I thought about having a heart-to-heart meeting with the players, even though I didn't think we had many offenders. I was pretty sure that the guys who might be cheating would let my message pass through their system like an enema anyway. Maybe I should have said something nonetheless. It wouldn't have made a bit of a difference but at least I could have said that I had done my part.

The one thing that focuses attention on steroids is the appearance of the athlete. If he drinks or takes greenies, it is not readily apparent; if he spends his off-season bulking up it's obvious the first day of spring training. I don't have to mention any names— if you are a serious baseball fan, you can fill in the blanks. So many players have pumped iron over the winter that it would be difficult to compile a list without leaving someone out. It would also be irresponsible to single players out by virtue of their appearance. The strength-enhancing drugs simply enable an athlete to work out harder and more often. Who is to say that a guy couldn't do this himself?

The one conclusion I have arrived at is that strength helps hitters more than pitchers. Jeff Bagwell and Craig Biggio lift weights so much during the off-season that they look like Charles Atlas when they get to spring training. They don't lift near as much during the season and they gain flexibility as the season unfolds, but on the first day each spring, they have almost no elasticity in their bodies. At the beginning of each workout we would stretch and throw to loosen up for drills. While most of the pitchers and players throw about ninety feet, Bidge and Baggy play catch about fifty feet apart. They laugh at themselves because they can't throw. To me, though, it's not that funny. If a pitcher pumped iron like some of the players, he would become muscle-bound and would not be able to throw as hard. You may be able to muscle a ball over the fence but you cannot muscle a pitch up to the plate.

Some analysts have speculated that bodybuilders like Mark McGwire and Sammy Sosa have led an offensive surge in baseball that is directly related to subsequent drug use among other players, who are willing to go to extremes to keep up with the power hitters. That may be part of it, but I don't think it is just the drugs. Some say the ball is juiced and I don't think it's that either. If equipment is involved in the game's run-scoring binge, it is likely the bat. Most players these days use bats that are shorter and quite a bit lighter than the players of my era. When I was playing, it was a rare sight to see a bat broken into pieces—bats broke, but they didn't come apart. Now bats break with a crack and the pieces fly in all directions. I think the bats are weaker and the players stronger. A lighter weapon results in more bat speed; more bat speed produces more home runs and more broken bats. The folks at the Louisville Slugger company must love it.

I certainly don't endorse cheating, but I'm not going to lose any sleep over it. Most of the time, ballplayers remember their playing days as the zenith of their lives. They don't think the guys who came before them were as big and strong and they're right about that, but bigger and stronger doesn't necessarily mean better. I try not to compare and contrast players of different eras: Generally speaking, I think there are more good hitters now than when I pitched, but I'm not sure if they are really better or just look better because the pitching is worse. I know Babe Ruth and Lou Gehrig could start for any team in baseball today. I would guess that the role players of that era were less adept than those of the current crop.

One thing is certain, however: The modern players look more athletic. They actually wear the uniform the way it should be worn, like a comfortable, well-tailored suit. In the early part of the last century, the uniforms were so baggy that it would be hard to tell whether a player was muscular or not. In my generation (1965–1977) we wore the uniforms skintight, which, in many cases, looked terrible.

The quality of major league baseball is as good as, if not better than, ever. And I don't believe it is so much a matter of steroids, but a result of bigger, stronger, faster athletes who practice a lot. Cheating isn't a big issue in baseball but it sure does make for sensational headlines. In 1986, the Astros played the Mets in the League Championship Series and the Mets cried like babies about Mike Scott scuffing the baseball. (Gary Carter was the biggest whiner of all.) The only player who didn't complain was Keith Hernandez. He said, "The strike zone is not that big and we're major league hitters. We're supposed to be able to hit the ball no matter where it is in the zone even when it's moving. Mike Scott is a great pitcher, but we can hit him." As it turned out, they couldn't hit him at all and I think the only player who got more than one hit off him in two games was Hernandez. Think about it like this: Everyone knows that Gaylord Perry threw a spitball; he won 314 games and a place in the Hall of Fame, he also lost 265 games, almost all of them to guys who didn't throw spitballs.

To succeed in major league baseball, you have to have talent and use it effectively. There have always been pitchers who doctor the ball and hitters who doctor the bat. It doesn't matter if the bat is supercharged unless it meets the ball, and it doesn't matter if the ball is dancing the Texas two-step on its way to the plate if it's not a strike. I believe the whole issue of getting an illegal edge is vastly overstated. When you cross the lines and play the game, you accept the challenge of the opponent and of motivating yourself to play your best under the circumstances of that game. Give me a team of talented players who never take medicine or use illegal equipment and I'll beat a team of cheaters almost every time.

Sure, Caminiti won an MVP award looking like Superman, and Bonds, Sosa, and McGwire have performed better after getting bigger. But when these musclemen go out there against little guys like Greg Maddux or Pedro Martinez they don't look so strong. I wish I could say that there are no drugs in the game, but I can't. I can say, however, that drugs don't win MVP Awards, Cy Young Awards, or pennants. Players do.

CHAPTER 11
La Vida

In baseball, you're supposed to sit on your ass, spit tobacco,
and nod at stupid things.

—BILL LEE

I SUPPOSE IT IS THE NATURE of the male of the species to deal in dirt. Sexual and scatological affairs are a part of the culture where men are drawn together in the absence of women. I found this to be true not only in baseball, but also in the National Guard. A left-handed pitcher by the name of Fred Scherman once told me that he would go all winter without cursing and then start up again like a drunken sailor on the first day of spring training. A lot of guys start chewing tobacco and dipping snuff when they put the uniform on, but do neither of these things in the winter.

I wasn't a choirboy even in the winter months, but my language changed too once the season got underway. While it may have been baby blue in January, it was royal blue in July. The baseball culture brought us together for a few beers quite often and after tipping a few, the language got loose. Players were less inhibited back then, but about half of the players on the teams I managed were regulars at baseball chapel on Sunday. Some of them hit the sauce après game, but most did not. These guys go with "Dag nabbit," "Jimminy Christmas," and other inoffensive epithets. It must be difficult for the religious players to hear the Lord's name taken in vain every day. Some of them, like Al Worthington many years ago, have been righteous, always on a crusade, trying to save the game from the real opponent—the devil. Some, like Tom Griffin and Craig Reynolds, found ways to separate their faith from the vulgarities of their chosen profession. I think the game is cleaner now than it used to be, probably due in part to the presence of female reporters in the clubhouse, but I doubt it will ever be lily white.

Still, the trend toward responsible behavior seems to be gaining momentum. Some of the players carried a paper sack with two or three beers from the clubhouse to the bus and up to their rooms to watch ESPN highlights when we were on the road. During the 2001 season, I caught Lance Berkman with a paper sack. This seemed so out of character that I said to him, "What have you got in the sack, Lancelot?"

"Just some water," he said, opening the sack to show me.

This type of nonconformity would have begged censure in the old days. It may have led to a fine in kangaroo court for conduct unbecoming a ballplayer.

I was a conformist for most of my playing days. In other words, I was a renegade. Thirty years later, I had to remind myself that I was the author of the bawdy songs that we sang on the bus in the late 1960s and early 1970s. There were no women on the bus at that time, but we did impugn the coaches, manager, and trainer in a way that I could not have endured if our players had done the same thing to me. In fact, as a manager I had my limits: In 2001, I fined one of our players for using the intercom on the airplane to broadcast a comedy tape that was so obscene that I could hardly look our female travelers in the eye when they got off the plane and onto the bus. When I talked with the culprit the next day, I got the impression that he was surprised that anyone, male or female, could be offended by the tape. I really felt old when he left my office.

Of course, I am old in the eyes of the players, and I'm a different person now. I go to church and I seldom find smut amusing, but I remember how farting or talking about farts brought forth outbursts of laughter when our kids were young. That humor was usually directed toward me, and I laughed at their laughter. It was contagious. The question is where do you draw the line, as a parent or a manager? The answer is not a matter of right and wrong so much as it is a matter of taste.

When I was managing, I tried to remember that I was young once too. All I had to do was recall some of the things I did or saw one of my teammates do and I could more easily understand our players' shenanigans. As the years went by, I slowly learned more and more about the game. This progression of knowledge is inevitable when you stay tuned in for many years. Connie Mack, after managing the A's for more than fifty seasons, said that he learned something new about baseball every day. His claim was exaggerated but it makes a point; we do not come to the major leagues as finished players, expert in all phases of the game. Instead, we come as experienced athletes with many more experiences yet to come. Oftentimes, one of my coaches would express disbelief when one of our players did something stupid. I tried to gently remind him that he didn't know as much when he was a player as he knew as a coach.

It is interesting to me that the same player can seem both thoughtful and thoughtless depending on when and where you encounter him. For example, Brad Ausmus was on first with two outs late in a game in 1997. We were a run or two behind and the pitcher was at bat. I gave Brad the steal sign because if he made it, I was going to pinch-hit for the pitcher, and if he was thrown out, the pitcher could work one more inning and then I could pinch-hit leading off the next inning. On the first pitch, Brad did not steal, so I put the sign on again; again he stayed at first. Now the count was 0-2 and there was no point in running. When I talked to him afterward he said that he saw the sign but assumed it was given by mistake. "I didn't think you would want me to go because if I got thrown out, we would have to lead off with the pitcher in the next inning," he said. His reasoning would be valid about 99 percent of the time. This was the other 1 percent. When I told him what I was thinking he grasped it immediately.

In 2001, when we clinched our division on the last day of the season in St. Louis, we had a big celebration in the clubhouse with champagne flowing freely. Brad got up on a chair about ten minutes into the hilarity and yelled for everyone's attention. Order was restored for a moment and Brad asked that we observe a moment of silence for the victims of the September 11 attacks. I was stunned—he actually had the snap to put our triumphal glory in historical perspective in a way that made us all more circumspect. I don't know how he could have thought to do that and not thought about the ramifications of trying to steal second base. I have to surmise that we are all subject to moments of thoughts both lucid and blurred for no particular reason, other than our nature as human beings.

One thing, though, is patently clear: As a team, we rarely see things in concert for any appreciable length of time. At least three players I have encountered over the years were offbeat most of the time. One of them was Doug Rader. Doug possesses three qualities in abundance: intelligence, strength, and lunacy. And this combination is highly combustible. Take, for instance, this bizarre turn of events involving Doug and the San Diego Padres.

When Ray Kroc bought the Padres prior to the 1974 season, he was flush with success. McDonald's made him a millionaire, and now if his new team could just win the pennant, he would have a golden ring to go with his golden arches. But things didn't start well: The Padres' first three games were in Los Angeles and the Dodgers pounded them mercilessly. The Padres limped down the coast to their home field, Jack Murphy Stadium, and things didn't go any better. Kroc was enflamed when the Astros swept his team in the first home series of his reign, and he let everyone know about it on the public address system.

"This is Padres owner Ray Kroc," he said, during game three, "and this is the worst ballplaying I've ever seen. If these guys don't do any better, I'll get some who can!"

After the game, Rader was highly indignant. "Who is this guy?" he asked, loudly. "He must think his players are a bunch of fry cooks!"

This quote got into the newspaper. The outburst by Kroc provoked censure from Commissioner Bowie Kuhn and it was not taken well by Padres players. But after things settled down, the Padres' marketing staff thought it might be fun to stir fryers when the Astros returned.

The next time we went to San Diego, any fan who wore a chef's hat and apron was eligible for free tickets to the game of June 28. About 2,500 disgruntled chefs showed up early, ready to give Rader a raspberry soufflé.

Rader was surprised but by no means beaten. "Before the game, when we were taking batting practice, these people who had been given free admission to the ballpark if they wore chef's caps were all over my case," he said when I talked to him about it years later. "So I had the clubhouse guy go out and get a chef's hat, an apron, and a skillet, and I took the lineup card out in the frying pan. That got 'em off my back. It was just a case of quick thinking on the part of yours truly."

Though Rader's quick thinking may have mollified the fry cooks it didn't shut them up completely. They acted as if Rader, not Kroc, had belittled their players. They were especially vocal when Rader committed an error early in the game and then struck out with men on base. In the eighth inning, with the Astros behind 5–3, Rader led off with a line shot to right.

"I hit it off the wall in right field," Rader recalled. "I thought I had a double easy. But Dave Winfield was playing right field and he threw me out by about ten feet. I can't remember if we won or lost the game, but the chefs were on my side at the end, I know that."

As it turned out, the Astros could have at least tied the game if Rader had stayed at first. Instead they lost 5–4, much to the delight of the 2,500 short order cooks who had come out to roast the Rooster (Rader's nickname, because of his wiry red hair). And the raspberry soufflé was a stunning success—everyone at Jack Murphy Stadium on June 28, 1974, agreed that Doug Rader had gotten his just desserts.

When we traded for Lee May in 1971, Rader finally had an equal on the team in terms of sheer physical strength. Rader and May were both front-line players and they became the best of friends. The Rooster, with his bully-of-the-barnyard personality nicknamed May "Grouper," when he came over to the 'Stros. May

couldn't have cared less about being a bully. There was never a hint
of bad blood between them, only mutual admiration. But in 1974,
the Astros traded for another player with legendary strength,
pitcher Jerry Johnson. J.J. liked to strut his stuff and Rader liked to
tease him with lines like, "She doesn't want to get her uniform
dirty today." I'm pretty sure Doug didn't want to fight Jerry but he
tiptoed to the precipice of confrontation many times. Jerry wasn't
nearly as bright as Rader, and Doug was wont to agitate him constantly. Since Jerry was new to the team and not nearly as important a player as Rader, he didn't want to cause a scene, but he was
highly aggrieved when his manhood was impugned in front of
the whole team. I think Doug intentionally provoked him when a
lot of other players were around for two reasons. One, he wanted
everyone to know that he was still the head Rooster in charge; and
two, if a fight broke out, he wanted it broken up. Over the course
of the season, Doug and Jerry became friends. Doug maintained
his position of dominance, not by overpowering Jerry but by out-
smarting him.

The same thing happened in San Diego, according to my
friend Bill Greif. "Rader got into it with Dave Winfield," Greif recalled. "At one point Doug said, 'Ain't nothing between me and you
but air and opportunity.' " I doubt Winfield was afraid. But he
didn't want to take it to the next level.

One spring, I made a trip to Orlando to pitch against the
Twins. I don't know what I was complaining about, but I know I was
bitching about something. Since I was a starting pitcher, I didn't
have to make many trips but Doug had to make most of them. He
snapped and challenged me then and there, right in front of everyone in the locker room.

"Why don't you make a trip or two before you start whining
about everything," he said. "In fact, why don't you just take your
sorry ass back to Cocoa. We can find someone around here to pitch
the game."

He was right, and I was still embarrassed. Embarrassed to be
put down and to have to back down. I wasn't nearly as strong as
Jerry Johnson but I was at least as smart. Better to be embarrassed
than to be embalmed.

It didn't take me long to learn not to play pepper with Doug. When he had the bat he would tap the ball back to the fielders in the standard fashion. But just when he had you lulled into a slow rhythm, he would take a sharp swing at the ball and smash it right into your ankles. He was also a terror in the clubhouse: Our digs in the Dome were spacious, but they were not as large as a driving range. Doug didn't seem to care. More than once, he teed up a golf ball and smashed it across the clubhouse. Mercifully, he gave warning in time for us to throw ourselves into our lockers behind our clothes. And luckily, he never hit anyone, though it was a distinct possibility. I have also seen him take slap shots with a hockey stick and puck—and he could slap it hard. When he was in college, he played semipro hockey under the aliases of Lou D'Bardini and Dominic Bulganzio.

One might think that a guy with a psychotic personality like Doug's would scare the death out of a tender rookie, but it was just the opposite. The Rooster would take the kids under his wings in spring training and make sure nobody messed with them.

In 1968, Minnesota Senator Hubert Horatio Humphrey was running for president against Richard Nixon and George Wallace. One night, we flew into St. Louis just as Humphrey was flying out. We were about as successful in our campaign as he was that year. We finished tenth in a ten-team race; he finished second in a three-man race.

There is no mistaking an athletic team in an airport. They're the ones who walk down the concourse in a herd, looking like prime beef. There was no mistaking Humphrey and his entourage that day either; he was in the middle of a coterie of supporters and security men. But Rader spotted him anyway.

"Hey, it's Hughie," Rader yelled. "Hughie, how you doing? Are you going to be the next president, Hughie?"

Humphrey looked at Doug, waved and smiled as he continued along the concourse. A couple of security men slid over to the left to put themselves between their leader and our nutcase. At this point, everyone on the concourse was watching the exchange.

"Hughie, aren't you going to tell us what you are going to do for us when you're president?"

Humphrey kept walking. As his entourage passed by us, he was still waving and smiling.

"Okay, Hughie, I'm sorry for bothering you. Good luck. And toodle-ooo."

Doug did the same thing at the Astrodome one night. The PGA had a tour event in Houston and two players, Ray Floyd and Ken Still, came out to the ballgame to put on a pregame exhibition. For some reason, Lawrence Welk was with them. The two golfers, and Welk, along with Rader and me, went out to center field and hit wedges in a closest-to-home-plate contest. Rader greeted Welk like a long-lost friend, grasping his hand in a death grip. "Boy, this is an honor," he said, as Welk grimaced, trying to wrest his hand free.

"If my mom could see me now," Rader continued. "Larry Welk, the world-famous Larry Welk. I can't believe it."

I couldn't believe it either. Doug kept calling him Larry as the rest of us stifled laughter. Welk didn't hit his wedge shot very well. How could he?

Another great practical joker in Astros history was Larry Andersen, who did some of his best work in the airport, where we all spent entirely too much time. For example, we were in Pittsburgh late one summer in the mid-1980s when our plane had a mechanical problem that forced us to wait at the gate for a couple of hours before boarding. Some of the guys stayed by the gate and read books or newspapers. Some drifted off to the bar for a couple of drinks. After an hour or so, the drinkers came back to find out when the plane was going to leave. It seemed like we would be boarding soon, so instead of going back to the bar, Andy dipped into his bag of tricks and came up with a retractable dollar device. This little gizmo housed a thin fifteen-foot monofilament line that attached to a bill. In this case, Andy was going for the big fish, so he used a $20 bill. The concept is to place the bill on the ground, and then when some innocent passerby reached down for it, you simply push a button and the bill whips right back to you like a measuring tape.

Six or seven guys sat on the floor of the concourse with their backs leaning up against the wall. When there was a lull in the pedestrian traffic, Andy would place the bill in the middle of the

walkway and feed the line out as he returned to his group of con-
spirators. When an unwary traveler reached down for the bill,
whoosh, it skittered across the floor right back to Andy and everyone laughed heartily. This went on for an hour or so and before
long the whole team was nearby watching. The scene provided
great comic relief in a time of need—I think most of the guys would
rather have been watching Andy than flying to the next city. I
couldn't believe how well it worked. Seldom did more than three or
four people pass without someone falling for it. Under any circumstances, it would be embarrassing, but with a whole team of players
laughing and rubbing it in, the victims were absolutely mortified.
I would guess that he tricked twenty people with it and each time
the reaction grew louder. One hefty gal had her arms full of pack-
ages and she had to put them all down on the floor in the middle
of the concourse while a bunch of people moved to and fro around
her; when she reached for the bill and it whisked away from her, she
stretched for it and fell down; the team erupted and she turned
blazing red. She got up and loaded her bags again and walked off
muttering.

Although Andersen was an accomplished prankster, the Astros
spent a long time waiting for another character of Rader's dimen-
sion—thirteen years to be exact. Doug was traded to the Padres in
1975; Casey Candaele joined the team in 1988. Casey came from
a baseball family: His mother, Helen, played in the All American
Girls Baseball League just after World War Two—she stole over
350 bases. You have to be tough to do that wearing shorts. Helen
brought all the Candaele boys up to be ballplayers, hitting them
fungoes and throwing batting practice. Casey was the runt of
the litter but he was the only one who made it to the big leagues.
Rader was a large man, 6'4" and 210 pounds; Candaele was small,
about 5'8" and 160. But they both had that devilish twinkle in their
eyes.

When we were in Kissimmee, playing the Royals in spring
training, Casey went up to the batting cage when the Royals were

hitting. "Where's Bo Jackson?" he said in mock anger. Someone told him that Jackson didn't make the trip.

"That figures," Casey said. "He's afraid of me. I didn't like the way he looked at me the other day at your place. I told him I was going to kick his ass and now I'm going to have to wait. You tell him when you get back that I haven't forgotten. I'm still going to kick his ass."

When the team traveled to Montreal, each player had to claim his own baggage off the carousel and take it through customs. Everyone threw in a dollar as we waited and then the guy whose bag came out first got the money. Well, Casey had played in Montreal and had apparently made a friend at the airport. When the conveyor started turning to bring the bags down the ramp to where we would pick them up, everyone looked to see which bag would come first. Casey's did, of course, because he was carrying it as he came through the hole in the ceiling and rode down the ramp ahead of the rest of the luggage. It was worth the $1 price of admission.

Casey was a California guy who grew up surfing the wild Pacific. Fact is his balance is so good that he can stand up on one of those big exercise balls and do a squat. It may not have been as difficult to surf an airplane, but it was much more impressive. He used the laminated safety information page in the seatback pocket for a surfboard and he never could have pulled it off if he had big feet. As it was, he could get both feet on the plastic page and when we were taking off, he would get right up where the curtain separates first class from coach (the coaches and manager were in first class), and Casey held on to the side of a seat until the plane took off. Then he released his grip and went zooming down the carpeted aisle in his best surfing posture. When he got to the back of the plane, he stepped off his surfboard, grabbed a beer, and went back to his seat, casual as you please.

One night we were in Cincinnati for the last game of a road trip. The players were a little jittery because a hurricane named Chantal was in the Gulf of Mexico. It was supposed to make landfall in Galveston about the time we were supposed to land in Houston. If the hurricane stayed on course, we would have to land somewhere farther inland and take a bus. Players got word from their wives that the stores in Houston were running out of flashlight batteries and masking tape, which was used to tape windows to keep them from breaking. So when we got to the locker room, a lot of the guys had batteries and masking tape. The phone on the clubhouse wall was in constant use (this was before players started carrying cell phones).

That's when Casey took center stage in the buff. He started gesticulating wildly and pacing up and down, shouting like a street corner evangelist.

"What are we going to do?" he asked. "Chantal has us by the balls. Our wives and children are right in her path and she's a big bad momma. Pretty soon all the trees in Houston will be knocked flat and the downtown skyline will be leveled. What the hell good are a bunch of batteries and masking tape going to do? We're screwed! She's going to knock our houses down and steal our loved ones.

"Do you hear what I'm saying?" he said as he jumped up on a table in the middle of the room. "Our little kids are going to be flying through the air! Big Chantal is going to rush right through Texas and Oklahoma and keep on coming north, mowing everything down! Pretty soon our airplane will be whipped around and heading for Canada. Tomorrow we'll be playing for the Blue Jays."

There wasn't a dry eye in the room and nobody was crying. We landed in Houston without more than a wayward breeze and no rain.

Casey specialized in nude scenes. He was known to take batting practice in the indoor batting cage in the Astrodome without a stitch of clothing. He could do a lot of things to help you win a ball game. He could play all the positions and play them well, and he was a switch hitter and a pretty good bunter. He'd go out and warm-up a pitcher between innings, and he was always hustling.

"I can have a bad day on the field," he once told me. "But I never have to have a bad day hustling. That's up to me."

More than anything else, Casey was a nut. He could make you laugh when you felt like quitting. One day, I was traversing Florida and thinking about him when a tune popped into my head:

The Utility Man

He'll get the ball in play, they say
He'll try to make you balk
Be careful with the bases loaded
He's gonna try to get a walk
He's not going to hit a home run
No, he's never going to take you deep
But if you don't watch out for that pissant, buddy
He's surely gonna make you weep

He's just a bench-sittin'
Switch-hittin'
A typical utility man
He's a playin' hit-and-run
And he's a crafty and a cunnin'
He's a heckuva utility man

He can really run and throw, you know
He can pick the infield clean
He'll cover the outfield like the morning dew
He pitches better batting practice than the pitching machine
He's not going to hit the long ball
No, he's never going to go downtown
But if you play back at third base you better
Watch out 'cause he's gonna lay one down

He's just a back-slappin'
Hand clappin'
A typical utility man
Yes, he's a warmin' up the pitcher
Not a whiner or a bitcher
He's a heckuva utility man

He's gonna steal your signs sometimes
He'll try to psyche you out
He's always talkin' to the umpire

Tryin' to get the benefit in case there's any doubt
Well, he's not gonna hit the long ball
No, he's never going to reach the fence
But he is gonna try to find some way to beat you
If it's only screamin' at you from the bench

He's just a connivin', contrivin'
A typical utility man
Yes, he's a stayin' out late
And he's a commiseratin'
He's a heckuva utility man
Yes he's a heckuva utility man
And he's doing the best that he can

Naturally, the banjo is the key instrument in the song.

In the weeks leading up to spring training, many teams send a group of players on a bus tour of the organization's key outer markets. I was a member of this contingent when I was a young player. I didn't mind speaking at a luncheon or dinner and, after a winter away from baseball it was great to see a few teammates again. The typical contingent was the manager or the GM, a broadcaster, a publicity man, four players, and a bus driver. Before we traveled a single mile, the bus was loaded with chips and nuts, beer and soda, and a couple of boxes of photographs that we would attempt to sign and foist upon Astros fans, young and old.

We would leave Houston on a Monday morning and stop for lunch in Beaumont. After lunch we'd go to Lake Charles, Louisiana, check into a hotel, and then move on to a dinner program, which was exactly the same as the one at lunch. The announcer would get up, say a few things about the team, introduce the head table, and then bring us up one by one to make our short speeches. The last one to speak was always the manager.

After Lake Charles, our tour would move on to Lafayette and New Orleans the next day. The first time, I couldn't wait to see the Big Easy and I saw it—well, for at least a few hours. After that it was kind of a blur: The next day we went to Alexandria and Shreveport, then we would work our way back to Houston, hitting a few small Texas towns along the way. Most of the time, the groups we spoke to were service clubs, Rotary, Lions, and Kiwanis clubs, and so forth. By the time we finished, I had recited the Pledge of Allegiance twenty times and knew most of the groups' songs. After a short breather for the weekend (thank goodness the service clubs didn't meet on the weekend), we would head back out through Austin and San Antonio and then work our way down to the Rio Grande Valley and come back through Corpus Christi and Victoria. It was a lot of traveling, speaking, and signing, but I enjoyed it. We had the music going on the bus and played cards most of the time. After the dinner program we went out looking for trouble and were able to find some occasionally.

The one thing that really makes the caravan drag, though, is the speeches. For the interested fan, this type of program is fine, but for us, ugh; we not only had to make the same speech twenty times, we also had to listen to each other just as many times. One year, we had Rusty Staub on the trip and our manager was Grady Hatton. The last day, I got up at lunch and said that I was tired of making the same old speech and I was going to speak for one of my companions instead. I did Grady Hatton's speech, going over the whole team and all the prospects. Grady is a Texan and he pronounces the word "help" as if it were "hep." So I said things like, "At third base, we have Doug Rader, a young man who is a great fielder and has a lot of power. I think he can really hep us." I went through the whole team that way and Grady was fit to be tied. I had not only used all his material, but I had called attention to the flaw in his speech. When he got up, he had to try for a different spiel, but it didn't go so well. He also said "hep" four or five times and each time, the crowd laughed louder. That night, we made our last stop and I did the same thing to Rusty. I stole all his material and also his speaking flaw, which was to say "you know" all the time. I bet I said "you know" fifty times while I went through the routine. Then Rusty got up and tried to speak without saying "you know" but he couldn't do it. Every time he said it the audience laughed. By the time he was finished, they were howling.

One other year, we had a young man named Lew Temple along. Lew worked in the minor league end of the operation and if anyone had questions about our prospects, he could answer them. Of course, nobody had ever heard of our prospects so Lew basically had nothing to do. Determined to make himself useful, he decided that he would take responsibility for procuring an item from each stop we made. In Austin, he nabbed a sign that said, "Quiet, Legislature in Session," from the Texas Capitol building. In Temple, Texas, he grabbed the brass bell that the Kiwanis Club used to call the meeting to order. He started ringing it and yelling at everyone to sit down so we could get started. (After we departed Temple, Lew still had the bell.) At one hotel along the way, there were some rubber cones on the floor with a sign that said, "Caution: Wet Floors." When we left, a cone left with us. In San Antonio, we spent two hours at a mall, signing autographs. Since Lew didn't sign, he was free to roam. When we got back to the bus we had the sign that was used to direct shoppers to our location. It said something like, "Astros Autographs in Front of Sears," with an arrow to direct the flow of traffic. By the time we got back to Houston we had a gavel, a pair of pantyhose, a cowboy hat, and a few other items.

Lew was crazy, too crazy even for baseball. He eventually got fired and became an actor, but not before he got his boss, Fred Nelson, into a whole heap of trouble. Lew and Fred were walking down a hallway in the business office at the Astrodome. One of the secretaries, a bovine creature, was walking along about fifty feet in front of them. Lew spotted a side door in the hallway and with a devilish grin, let out a loud moo that sounded just like a cow. The secretary turned around with a look that could kill—just after Lew had slipped through the doorway. When she turned around, the only one she saw was Fred.

One thing I doubt the marketing department of the team considered was the effect that a raucous week of travel would have on the players. If you were lucky, you would only gain five pounds, and, no matter what you did, you would be in no shape to start spring training.

In the early 1990s we decided to crank the caravan back up, mostly, I think, because our owner, Drayton McLane, wanted to put on a show in his hometown of Temple. In 1992, we were on a press caravan prior to spring training and one of the great practical jokers of all time, Luis Gonzalez, came along without the dress shirt and tie that was required at a dinner in Alexandria, Louisiana. Gonzo picked up a cheap polyester shirt and tie combo at Wal-Mart and made the appearance, complaining that his new outfit was crawling all over his body. Afterward, we decided to go out to a country and western club and Gonzo changed into more comfortable clothing. He came downstairs with the shirt and tie in his hand and we called a cab. While we were waiting under the porte cochere of the hotel, he hurled his formal attire onto the pavement and set it on fire. Because it was made from synthetic fibers, it burst into a flaming inferno. Our public relations director, Chuck Poole, was worried that we would get into trouble and that the story would get back to his boss. So what did he do? He leapt into the fire, attempting to stomp it out. The problem was that Chuck's penny loafers had more than a few coats of liquid polish on them and, instead of putting out the fire, he ignited his own feet. Chuck is portly and nearly bald. He's a funny guy without any props, but with flaming feet he was hilarious. The manager of the hotel stormed out of the lobby, asking, "Who is in charge here?"

Chuck was dancing like an Indian on the warpath as he said, "I am."

That was in 1992 and ten years later, as Chuck retold the story, he mentioned that we had given out a lot of autographed balls on that caravan. "If anyone saved them, they've got a lot more than they expected then," he said. "Not only did they get your autograph and Gonzo's. We also had Curt Schilling with us that year."

One year, Gonzo was on one leg of the press caravan with me, while Chuck Poole was on the southeastern leg to Beaumont, Lake Charles, Lafayette, and New Orleans, where he had honeymooned the week before with his new wife, Laura.

"Laura and I went to Pat O'Brien's, a bar made famous by its signature drink "The Hurricane," and told the bartender that I would be coming back the next week with some major league ballplayers and he said 'Oh sure.'

"We were in Beaumont the next day after my honeymoon and

I was partied out," Chuck recalled. "I had made up my mind that I wasn't going to go out on the town. The guys kept pestering me about it but I stuck to my guns. Later that night, full of spirits, Jim Deshaies, Larry Andersen, and Barry Waters, our traveling secretary, called me and asked me to meet them. I hung up on them. I just wasn't going to go out. Well, in the wee hours of the morning, I heard this banging on my door. Apparently, they had gone for some late night snacks and thought I would like a plate of nachos. When they came to deliver them, I didn't answer the door. When they finally stopped banging on the door, I heard this tapping, but I ignored it.

"Well, the next day, I woke up feeling fine and proud of myself for staying in. When I went to open my door to get down to the bus, I couldn't get the door open. I tried and tried but even though I could turn the knob, the door wouldn't open. Finally I called the front desk.

" 'Is the door unlocked?' they asked.

" 'Yes, it's unlocked,' I said.

" 'Well, then it should open,' they said.

" 'I know.'

"Finally they said they would send up someone from engineering. At that point I was starting to panic. What if the bus left without me? How would I get to New Orleans?

"When the engineer came up he asked me if the door was unlocked and I told him that it was. He tried to get it opened but could not. Finally he said, 'Stand back.' I was afraid he was going to crash it down, but instead, he sprayed some WD 40 through the keyhole, filling the front of the room with an oily haze. 'It still won't open,' he said. At this point I started thinking about going out the window. Would they have a ladder long enough? I was in a state of panic.

"Then he said, 'Hey, did you know there was money in your door?'

" 'Money?'

" 'Yeah, there's money in the jamb,' he said. Then he got a screwdriver and popped two quarters out of the jamb and the door opened. 'Is this your money?' he asked.

" 'It is now,' I said, as I stepped over the plate of nachos. I rushed down to the lobby with my bags and was breathless when I got to the counter to check out. I saw the guys standing by the front door, innocent as babes, as if nothing had happened, even though it was already past the time the bus was supposed to leave. When I joined up with them to get on the bus, they broke out laughing. Needless to say, I went out the next two nights and when I took the guys to Pat O'Brien's, the bartender stared at me in disbelief."

Gonzo is a perfect gentleman when women are around. When they're not, he can cross over to the caveman mentality in a nano-second. One thing that always broke the angst of a losing streak was his fake dong. The thing was huge, at least two feet long and three inches in diameter. It was as realistic as an exhibit in the wax museum and it had a belted harness that allowed him to strap it on. Whenever things were a little dicey and the team was in danger of going into a funk, Gonzo would slip it on and wrap a towel around his waist so that the pecker head was hanging out about even with his knees. This always got the desired result—a lot of laughter. It almost always loosened things up on the field as well. One time when we were really struggling, Drayton came into my office prior to game time. He liked to come down to cheer me up and show support when times were bad. On this occasion, he was still in my office when it was time for me to go to the dugout with the lineup card. "I gotta get down to the field now," I told him. "All right, let's win one," he said. "I'll go out with you."

I saw the dong hanging down when I turned the corner toward the door that led to the dugout at the Astrodome, and I didn't know whether to laugh or cry. The provocative appendage was taped to the wall above the door and hanging so low that I had to go around it. Because Drayton is about 6'4" himself, he had to sidestep it as well. Above the door was a sign that said, "Squeeze the dong for good luck." I scurried through the door, turning left, and Drayton took a right. He didn't say anything about it later and you can be sure I did not bring it up either. My only regret was that I didn't squeeze it. When we lost the game, I knew it was my fault.

. . .

A few years ago, the veteran members of our team started an initiation ritual: They would get some garish-looking clothing and shoes at a resale shop and put them in the rookies' lockers during the game on getaway day. When the rookies came back to shower after the game, the outrageous outfits were the only garments there. They had to wear these getups or go naked. Then they had to serve food and beverages on the plane. Most of the guys took it the way it was intended—as a rite of passage—but a few of them were really embarrassed and upset. This is a good way to find out what a guy is made of. There are so many ways to look foolish in baseball; if you can't shrug it off and move on, you will never make a go of it. I liked the ritual when I was managing because it gave me some insight into the mental makeup of the guys I didn't know very well.

It's one thing to pull a prank, but it's quite another to put your life in danger for the entertainment of the team. Pirates announcer Bob Prince was known for many things, but one thing that is not generally known about him is that he dove into a swimming pool from the window of his room on the sixth floor of the Chase Park Plaza hotel in St. Louis to answer a dare and win a bet. Prince spent his last season as a broadcaster in Houston and he told me that he wasn't the least bit afraid. "I was a diver in college," he said. "I knew I could make it." Others were not so sure—there was an apron of concrete about fifteen to twenty feet wide between the building and the pool.

Count Dave Roberts among those willing to risk his neck, literally, for his teammates' amusement. Dave was a rookie third baseman with the Padres when he took a similar dare. He said he could dive into the Chicago River from the bridge at Michigan Avenue in downtown Chicago. About midnight that night he took the leap of faith, executing near perfect form on a gainer from at least sixty feet above the water.

In 1986, Mike Scott won the Cy Young Award and he did it in style. He won the clinching game with a no-hitter and we floated in the bubbly effervescence of glory. Naturally, Gonzo provided the Cuban cigars. Three relievers, Dave Smith, Charlie Kerfeld, and Larry Andersen, provided the comic relief. Andy had obtained rubber Conehead masks for the occasion. They were perfect, fitting over the head, which prevented champagne from getting into their eyes, but the main reason for the masks was simple humor. Yogi Berra was a coach with the team that year and when he saw Smitty, Charlie, and Andy in the lunchroom, he said, "You guys make a helluva pair." No kidding, that's exactly what he said.

Most people doubt that Yogi actually said everything that has been attributed to him, but I don't. During his first spring with the Astros, he was talking with Mike Scott. Yogi had played golf at Lake Nona the day before and it was a course a lot of us played the previous November in a golf tournament arranged by owner John McMullen.

"How was Nona yesterday?" Mike Scott asked.

"It was all right," Yogi said. "Except for one thing. They were marinating the greens."

A few days later, Scotty was talking to Yogi about playing with a group of major league all-stars in Japan.

"Did you see Don Ho over there?" Yogi asked.

"Don Ho?" (He's a Hawaiian recording artist.)

"You know, that guy who hit all the home runs."

"Oh, you mean Sadaharu Oh. Yeah, I saw him."

On the first Saturday of the season, it was my job to do the Yogi Berra show, a pregame interview segment. The Astros had started the season with two wins and two losses, even though two of the best players on the team, Terry Puhl and Jose Cruz, were out of the lineup with injuries and we had to open with two rookies, Eric Bullock and Tony Walker.

I started the interview by saying, "I know you've just seen the team at spring training and a couple of games during the season and I know it is too early to make any real judgments, but what do you think of the team so far?"

"Well, Larry," Yogi said. "I'm very impressed with the team, especially the injuries."

• • •

I have always had a fondness for Wrigley Field. I got my first win there, and though the day games always came too early in the city that Billy Sunday couldn't shut down, the atmosphere around the ballpark was terrific. I have been there in five different decades and that's just the half of it. In ten more years, Wrigley will celebrate its one hundredth birthday. I have heard some talk about a new stadium for the Cubs, but I doubt it will come to that, as Wrigley is in a great neighborhood. Even though the Cubs haven't won, well, much of anything, the old park is full of fans almost every summer day. Sometimes the wind blows in off the lake; sometimes it blows out. It can be a great park to pitch in or a bandbox depending on the direction and the force of the wind. The wind in the Windy City isn't much stronger than the wind I have noticed in every other ballpark around the league, but it is more persistent. Sometimes, in April, May, and September, it is cold enough to numb the fingers and chill the bones. I would guess that it is too cold for comfort in about six or eight games a year. Perhaps it is too hot three or four times each season.

The rest of the days and nights are luminous with the memories of years gone by. Only the style of clothing has changed. You don't see many fedoras these days. Cigars are out of the question. When a pitcher takes the mound he is working on the same hill where Fred Toney and Hippo Vaughn pitched the only double no-hitter in major league history. Bare-chested Bleacher Bums still sit where Ernie Banks hit his 500th home run. Did Babe Ruth really point to center field before hitting a home run there off Charlie Root in the 1932 World Series?

Several years ago we spent a stormy day at Wrigley. The game was delayed by rain several times and the ninth inning bumped up against the sunless penumbra of dusk. I could almost see player-manager Gabby Hartnett circling the bases after his "Homer in the Gloamin' " put the Cubs in first place on September 28, 1938.

All of these things come to mind when I think about Chicago, but the one thing that stands out above them all is the statue of

General Sheridan astride his vaulting steed, which the team bus always passes on the way to the ballpark. When I was a player, it was said that if you looked at the horse's balls you would go hitless that day. Jose Cruz called it the "Balls Horse." "Don't look the Balls Horse," he would scream as the bus rounded the turn from Lakeshore Drive to West Belmont Avenue. "You gonna take an o-fer every time." Then Cheo would look around to see if anyone was taking a peek, and if he saw someone he would chastise him. "You gonna take a o-fer, Cliff Johnson, I'm telling you! I saw you look the Balls Horse! Now you get no hits today, maybe the whole series. I saw you look you big donkey!" This act produced great paroxysms of merriment that carried us the final mile to Wrigley Field.

Over the years, the tradition changed. Players started taking cabs and there were fewer players on the bus. The horse was still a legend, but it was a horse of a different color. Over time the ritual was to have the rookies on the team climb up to the base of the statue under the veil of darkness and paint the horse's balls with the team colors. The Reds would paint them red and then the Dodgers would come to town and paint them blue. There was a policeman that worked at the ballpark who participated in a mock arrest. He would come into the locker room after batting practice and ask to see one of the rookies. He would tell him that he was being arrested for defacing public property. I saw this enacted several times. At first, it was funny. The last time, about four or five years ago, I actually felt sorry for the kid who fell for the ruse hook, line, and sinker. The policeman told him to change into his clothing because he was going to have to take him to the police station. I can't recall who it was, but he seemed on the verge of tears as he took off his uni and started putting on his civies. He was almost completely dressed before the first sputter of laughter cut the air and led to a fusillade of guffaws that left the kid feeling somewhat relieved and absolutely mortified.

In 1992 the Republican National Convention was held in Houston, forcing us to take the mother of all road trips, a month-long sojourn to almost every city in the National League. The last game of that trip was played on a Sunday afternoon in Philadelphia. At the time we were staying in the Hershey Hotel, right across Broad Street from an opera school. Long about 8:00 A.M. an aspiring diva took the stage for rehearsal and she was so loud she awakened many of the players and staff of our ball club. Jim Deshaies was the last player to get on the bus. "Well," he said. "They say it's not over till the fat lady sings, so I guess this trip is finally going to end."

CHAPTER 12

The Big Seize

Open up a ballplayer's head and you know what you'd find?
A lot of little broads and a jazz band.

—FORMER MANAGER MAYO SMITH

THE ONLY DIFFERENCE BETWEEN a ballplayer and a former ballplayer turned announcer, turned manager, is that by the time they opened the latter's head, the little broads had departed of their own accord and the tenor sax was meandering in and out of a sweet, sad refrain of bitter glory.

If I were to mention the names of Bucky Dent, Carlton Fisk, Kirk Gibson, Joe Carter, Bobby Thomson, or Don Larsen almost every avid baseball fan would immediately conjure the thought of a specific moment in baseball time. A game-winning home run, a perfect game—the ephemeral stuff dreams are made of. The exclamation point at the end of an epic adventure—a championship won, a hero crowned.

In my case it's different. During my thirteen years as a major league pitcher I experienced almost everything except the final victory. Mention my name and perhaps a few fans would recall that I pitched against the Giants on my eighteenth birthday. Some may remember the no-hitter I pitched against the Expos. I did, however, have a defining moment that most fans would think of immediately, even though I don't remember much about it.

It happened at the Astrodome on Sunday, June 13, 1999, in the eighth inning of a game with the Padres. I had been having mild headaches for several days. They weren't splitting, migraine headaches, and they seemed more a nuisance than anything else. I was able to knock them out with a couple of Advils.

At the time, the Reds were our closest competitors. They were playing on TV that day and I was watching the game in my office as the start time for our game with the Padres drew near. When Mike Hampton came into my office and asked if I was going to come down to the dugout for the game I was surprised. I looked up and it was about 2:00 P.M. Our game started at 1:35 and was already in the second inning. When I slid into my seat alongside my bench coach, Matt Galante, he laughed.

"I don't know what happened," I explained. "I was watching the Reds game and somehow I just lost track of the time."

"That's all right," he said. "Nothing has happened yet."

Little did he know, something big was going to happen—something really big. As I recall, we took the lead on a home run by Derek Bell. The ball was hit down the right field line and barely cleared the fence. I remember getting out of my seat and moving to the edge of the dugout to watch the play. That was my last clear memory. Moments later I had a grand mal seizure right then and there on national television. I lost consciousness and started flopping around on the floor of the dugout. It must have been pretty scary, but I wouldn't know. I didn't feel a thing. That was my defining moment: I became a national news story. I was on the front page of the *Houston Chronicle* for four days running.

I was lucky that the event occurred when it did. There were emergency medical people on hand, including our team doctor, and the famed Houston Medical Center was just ten minutes away. If it had happened at night on the road, as it did with Darryl Kile, I probably wouldn't be around to tell the rest of the story.

• • •

The next three days were a blur.

I am told that I came to on the way to the hospital but I don't remember it. I don't know if I was under sedation but I certainly was not wide awake. I told my wife, Judy, that it was nice of Jeff Bagwell and Craig Biggio to come by to see me after the surgery on Wednesday. She told me that they came to the hospital the day before the surgery on Monday.

I remember a glass wall between my room and the next. The television in the other room was visible from my position in bed and I asked one of the nurses if she could turn it a bit so that I could watch the game. She did and I watched, though I can't remember who won.

I remember the doctor, Rob Parrish, telling me that they had found the source of my problem and were confident they could repair it. He told me that I cracked him up on the way to the operating room when I said. "You know how people always say, 'It's not brain surgery . . . ' But this *is* brain surgery."

The operation lasted just over five hours and was deemed a success. Dr. Parrish told the reporters that the seizure was caused by a tangle of blood vessels that was called an arteriovenous malformation, an AVM. He said that the rupture of vessels in my skull precipitated the event, and that the pocket of blood that was causing the headaches and prompted the seizure was larger than a walnut but smaller than a melon. "It was about the size of a lime," he said. "Or maybe a really large jalapeño."

I was really lucky. The event occurred in the right frontal area of the brain, the one area that can be invaded without doing major damage. If the AVM had been located in any other part of the brain, it would not have been possible to remove it without compromising a bodily function such as eyesight, or motor skills. Dr. Parrish explained that the surgery was performed in a noneloquent part of the brain. Afterward, he told me that he had taken the dumb part out. I suppose he could have said that I would no longer say stupid things because only the eloquent part of my brain remained but I have proven this assumption to be untrue.

The morning after the surgery seemed like the day after the

seizure to me but it was actually the third day. When I woke up I knew that I had undergone brain surgery, and as I swung my legs around to get out of bed, I wondered if I would be able to stand up or if I would be completely off balance. I tentatively put my feet on the floor and slowly put weight on them. They held and I was able to stand up without holding on to anything. With that, I breathed a sigh of relief and took a step—no problem. It was really nice to know that I was ambulatory. I was one happy camper as I strolled to the nurses' station to get a cup of coffee. When I felt the warmth of the cup and smelled the aroma of the beverage, I knew that I had my eyesight, my sense of touch, and my sense of smell. I noticed a newspaper and asked if I could borrow it. There I was on page one, and I could read it! This sequence of events took only five minutes or so, and already I knew that the surgery was successful.

They really spoiled me in the penthouse suite of Methodist Hospital. I could order food from an extensive menu at any time of the day or night; I could watch videos; my room was spacious enough for me to get some exercise walking back and forth. And with the block paneling and mahogany furnishings, I could have been in the Ritz-Carlton Hotel. I stayed in this room for three days. During that time, I visited with several prominent guests including Bob Lanier, the former mayor of Houston.

When I was released, Dr. Parrish told me that I could walk for half an hour each day, but I would not be allowed back in the dugout for a month. I walked the first day I was home. The next day, I called the doctor and said, "If I can walk for thirty minutes, why can't I hit a bucket of golf balls?"

"You probably can," he said. "If it bothers you, just quit and go home."

It did not hurt—just the opposite. It felt great. I thought that if I could hit a bucket of balls, I could play. So the next day, without asking permission, I played eighteen holes of golf. I didn't play as well as I normally do, but I was able to generate just as much power as ever. From that day on, I lived my life as if nothing had happened. Sure, it would take a few months for my hair to grow back, but I wasn't concerned about that at all.

At this time, the Astros were in Cincinnati. They lost the series to the Reds, and then they went to Arizona and were swept. Our comfortable lead was gone just that fast. I left my bench coach Matt Galante with a tough assignment—hold the lead while playing two of the best teams in the league on the road. The road trip was a bust, but we started winning again when we got back home. I went out to the ballpark to say hello to everyone and to let the guys know that I was feeling well. I showed off my scar that ran from one ear straight over the crown of my head to the other ear. I was like a warrior coming home after winning the war. I sensed the players were nervous but I quickly broke that spell by joking around. I joined the announcers for an inning in the television booth and had a great time. I longed to get back to work but was forced to wait the whole month.

While I was recuperating, I answered my mail. I got about 1,000 get-well cards, many of them from AVM patients and their families and friends. It took me almost the whole month to respond to all of them, but I didn't have anything else to do and I found it therapeutic. The e-mail messages were a lot easier. I wrote a letter in response and sent it out to 4,000 fans simultaneously. Reading the letters really informed me as to my own good fortune. Many of those who wrote had lost eyesight or hearing; some were unable to walk; a few said that they had a lot of pain but that the doctors told them the AVM was in a part of the brain that rendered it inoperable.

After I got back in the saddle, we started winning at a furious pace. In early September we ran off twelve straight wins, a club record. Still, the Reds stayed right on our tail. We only gained one game on them during the winning streak and didn't clinch the division until the last day of the season when we won our ninety-seventh game. I think the doctors were worried about the effect the stress of competition would have on me, but if stress was going to bother me, it already would have. We lost so many players to injuries that season that during September I had infielders Craig Biggio and Billy Spiers playing in the outfield. If not for our playoff collapse against the Braves, our last season in the Astrodome would have been perfect.

After I came back to manage I was interviewed in every city, sometimes more than once. At one point I said that I would be glad when we finally made the rounds of all the teams so that the "Larry Dierker Freak Show" would finally end, but it never did. Even now, people come up to me like supplicants. When I see the look of concern in their eyes I know they are about to ask me how I am feeling. On the one hand, this can become tiresome. On the other, it is gratifying, as it shows me how much they care. But the ultimate sign of caring came right after the seizure when the whole team formed a huddle in front of the dugout and prayed for my recovery. A photo of that scene appeared on the front page of the newspaper the next day. This really meant a lot to me because I knew a lot of the guys in the huddle were not religious. I led the league in prayers that year, but even prayers couldn't overcome the Braves' pitching staff.

EPILOGUE
Out of It

IT TOOK NEARLY FOUR HOURS and a succession of big shots
to capture me. First, I met with Tal Smith, the Astros president,
then general manager Gerry Hunsicker, and finally owner Drayton
McLane. We had a press conference the next day and I became the
thirteenth manager of the Astros after spending thirty-one years
with the franchise. It took five minutes to set me free. The hiring
meeting took place at a posh office tower in the Galleria; the firing
was at Gerry's house. Actually, Gerry gave me the choice of retiring
with full pay or getting fired with full pay. I played the game like
the good soldier I had been for thirty-seven years. I guess the se-
mantics of "stepping aside" as opposed to being forced out made
everyone feel more comfortable. It didn't make any difference to
me as long as I got paid.

Gerry came right to the point and I chose the retirement option just moments after sitting down in his study. He was circumspect about it and I was too. I felt that we had maximized our talent
in 2001 to come up with ninety-three wins. Vinny Castilla and

Moises Alou were key players in that championship season and both were going to be free agents.

"I don't think Drayton is going to approve much more payroll," Gerry said. "That means we will probably lose both Mo and Vinny. It may be a long year."

I didn't think the loss of these two players from the lineup would kill the team, but I knew it would force two young players into the lineup and weaken the bench. The offense and fielding figured to be about average and the pitching staff, though loaded with young talent, was short on experience. Roy Oswalt and Wade Miller were way above average in 2001. Lefty Carlos Hernandez was great in a short sample of three starts and eighteen innings of pitching. His season ended when he dove back into second base and jammed his left shoulder. Even though a full recovery without surgery was likely, I was concerned that he would lose a little zip and that little zip was his trump card. I thought Shane Reynolds would give the team 200 good innings, but I did not think he would pitch like the staff ace he had been before back surgery. Dave Mlicki, the fifth starter, hadn't been a winning pitcher for several years and he appeared to be near the end of his career. Tim Redding would get another chance to compete for a starting job—he had an impressive season in the minor leagues in 2001, but did not perform well in the big leagues. The team would likely do well with a lead, as Octavio Dotel and Billy Wagner promised to be as good as any one-two bullpen punch in all of baseball. But with Mike Jackson and Mike Williams going elsewhere as free agents, the middle relief appeared to be shaky. At that point in time, I thought it would be hard to finish first again. The team would be too young for the most part, and too old at first and second base, where Jeff Bagwell and Craig Biggio were still good but starting to show signs of aging.

Leaving the dugout at this juncture ensured me of going out on top. I would have to give up my lifelong goal of going to the World Series, but I couldn't foresee a World Series in Houston any time soon. If I worked all year to have a .500 season I would be considered a failure. I would probably get fired and would have to endure another season in the pressure cooker to make the same amount of money. Sure, I was sensitive about it, but I was also realistic. I thought we had done an excellent job playing the cards we were dealt. My tenure lasted longer than I thought it would when I took the job, and I was just about set for retirement with the money I had saved.

The next morning, there was a press conference to announce my retirement. I didn't expect to be sentimental about it but I did get a little teary-eyed. I still managed to interject some humor by wearing one of my signature aloha shirts and expressing concern for everyone in the room who had to keep working. "You guys better get on back to your stations and get back to work," I said. "As for me, I'm going to play golf. I'm on vacation."

I did play a lot of golf in October and November. I thought I could get my handicap down into the single digits but I was wrong. I got worse instead of better, snap-hooking one shot after another. When I started throwing clubs and cussing, I realized that I needed to take a different approach to the game. If I could just accept the fact that my handicap should be about 14, I could compete. But I couldn't accept it. I kept playing to a 10 and losing money. Thank goodness I wasn't playing a high-stakes game.

I followed the off-season baseball news, particularly with regard to the Astros. When Mo and Vinny signed with the Cubs and the Braves respectively, and Gerry re-signed only super-sub Jose Vizcaino, I was just about certain that the Astros would drop back in the standings. It looked like a .500 ball club to me. I was surprised when Jimy Williams got my old job. Usually, when a soft-spoken, players' type manager is fired, a hard-nosed disciplinarian is hired to replace him, the thinking being that the team is too complacent and needs a spark to catch fire again. Eventually the players rebel against this type of leadership and another calm, steady type of guy gets the job. I didn't know Jimy well, but his managing record was excellent and I knew he wasn't a fire-and-brimstone type manager.

As spring training approached, I thought I might feel a little tug—I did not. I had been going to Florida every spring since 1965. After thirty-seven straight pilgrimages, I thought there would be some sadness—there was not. When I was young, healthy, and free-spirited, I started itching for spring training just after New Year's Day. After I started having shoulder trouble, I knew I needed every day of the off-season to get my arm ready for the new season. I began to realize that it was going to be a long, long haul and that there was no need to rush into it. Most of the second half of my career I was lonely in Florida. Our children were in school and I only saw my family during the week of spring break. Pitchers and catchers usually report to camp in mid-February. As a broadcaster I didn't have to be down there until the games started two weeks later. Either way, I would have only one day off. In baseball, the worst part is the first part.

In 2002, I wouldn't go to spring training at all. I thought I would be happy to miss it, but I wasn't sure until it happened. When I saw a picture in the newspaper of players doing their stretching on the first day of camp, I was elated. I never understood why the early days of camp were such big news. After all, we would not start playing games for two weeks, and even when we did play we wouldn't be playing to win. Meanwhile, the Rockets would be in fierce competition for a playoff spot and we would force them to the second page of the sports section. When I saw a clip of Astros camp on television I felt smug. Thank goodness, I'm not down there, I thought. They can have it. In 2002 the Rockets didn't have a chance to make the playoffs, but because they were playing real games, I followed them more closely than the Astros. I had a mild interest in the Astros and read most of the stories coming out of Kissimmee, but I didn't listen to a single game on the radio. In 2003 it was exactly the same, except this time the Rockets were fighting to get into the playoffs, and since I have gotten to know their coach, Rudy Tomjonovich, I had even more interest in basketball.

Now as the weather warms up and the trees sprout blooms and leaves, I plant flowers and play golf. At spring training, I could usually get nine holes in after our workouts. Every so often I could play eighteen. Now I can play all day if I want. One day, I played sixty-three holes. I kept up with the bill paying and fan mail, spent some time evaluating investments, and still had ample free time. I could remember coming back from Florida in April and having a Himalayan heap of correspondence on my desk. In all those years, I had to file my income tax late. Now I am right on time.

In mid-March of 2002, my daughter Ashley came in from

London to visit her mother-in-law in Naples, Florida. I met her there and spent a couple of days. Then I headed north to Clearwater to spend two days with my old broadcast partner Dewayne Staats. The next day I traveled to Jacksonville to play in a golf tournament. On the way, I stopped by the Astros' spring training headquarters in Kissimmee and it was really hard to get out of the car. I knew my presence would create a stir, but I also felt that it was the right thing to do since I was in the neighborhood. The first person I saw was the Astros' irreverent equipment manager, Dennis Laborio. Dennis's face lit up with a broad smile. After that, it was easy. I visited with Gerry and some of the players. I talked for a few minutes with Jimy Williams and he was most gracious. Now, *he* would have to explain why the team lost this game or that one. It is a tough assignment to take over a team that has finished first four of the last five years. But Jimy did a good job, and the Astros finished 84-78 in second place.

I felt like a lightning rod as I stood by the batting cage. A lot of players and many of the coaches came by to say hello. They approached me like they would the bed of a relative with a dread disease. I was able to put to rest the notion that I had been cast overboard into a stormy sea against my will. I particularly warmed to Burt Hooton, who had done a marvelous job with our pitchers in 2001. He had lost a brother and a sister-in-law that year. "Hey, man," I said. "This is nothing compared to what you went through last summer."

While I was there, I saw Billy Wagner, Octavio Dotel, Wade Miller, and Roy Oswalt throw on the side. After watching my son's high school games, the Astros' pitchers looked un-hittable. These four guys alone could prevent the Astros from having a bad year, if only they could stay healthy. I played terribly in the golf tournament after pulling a muscle in my back the first day. A month later, Wade Miller pulled a muscle in the back of his neck, after several ineffective starts in the regular season. Wade was put on the disabled list as the Astros stumbled out of the gate. Craig Biggio appeared to be guess-hitting all the time and guessing wrong. Jeff Bagwell went cold after a sensational spring.

About that time, Drayton contacted me about having my number retired. I was excited about it, but was worried about how the fans would take it if the Astros weren't playing well. The team went on a six-game road trip to Philadelphia and Pittsburgh and after they lost the first five games, they were wallowing in fourth place with a record of 14-21. Luckily for them and for me, they started a seven-game winning streak, which was ongoing as of May 19, when my number was retired. Although this did not put them in first place, it did prove that they were capable of contending for the flag again. The winning streak improved everyone's spirits. I would have felt awkward accepting my retired jersey if the team was on a losing streak and in last place.

Actually, I felt more than awkward when the number 49 first came into my life. I was twelve years old and my brother, Rick, was nine. It was just after dinner and we were lying on the bottom mattress of our bunk bed when Rick started chanting "49" and I couldn't make him stop. "49, 49, 49," he droned.

"Shut up," I said.

"49, 49, 49."

"Shut up!"

"49"

"Shut up!"

(Pause)

"49."

Rick was lying on his stomach and I on my back. To emphasize my demand I lifted my right leg and brought it down forcefully with my heel digging into the small of his back. Rick wailed and then started to cry. Dad came in and I got a spanking. His injury was severe enough that he had trouble walking the next day and stayed home from school. From that day until this we have told and retold the story until the repetition of the "49" has become a memorable chant.

In November of 1995, Rick, Dad, and I were playing golf in Hawaii when a feeling rushed through me like a favoring trade wind. "I think 1996 is going to be my year," I said.

"Every year is your year," Rick replied.

"No, I'm serious," I said. "Look. I just turned forty-nine.

Forty-nine was my number. It's also seven squared. What could be luckier than that?" Honestly, that was the first time I ever thought about the number forty-nine as something special.

Rick is a great believer in luck and karma and all things working out for the best. He makes Norman Vincent Peale look like a cynic. He bought my logic with a knowing nod. My golf game was peaking in the broadening sunset. I was firing pars and birdies, hitting the ball like a pro. At that moment, I was, as they say, full of myself. I told Rick that I would probably be notified about getting a Fox broadcasting job by Christmas.

Christmas came and went. I didn't get the gift I was eagerly anticipating. When I went skiing in late February, the only thing I knew was that I would be doing Astros radio and television again. Not to worry, it could still be a great year. The team figured to contend for a championship, I felt fantastic, and the Fox deal was still a possibility.

Then came the first clue that my fortunes were changing. I was skiing with my son, Ryan, when he looked down a mountain of moguls as we stopped for a breather. "Can we do that run?" he asked. "Yeah, I guess so," I said, grudgingly. Ryan took off and I fell in behind. He tumbled a few times while I was slip sliding slowly along. After he got pretty far ahead, I decided to go for it. I started to get a rhythm and felt somewhat inspired. Hey, I can do this, I thought. That's when it happened: Out of the corner of my eye, I saw Ryan fall, and suddenly I was catapulting headfirst. I landed in a heap, with a sharp pain in my right thumb. I didn't know it then, but this incident would render my forty-ninth year decidedly unlucky.

I had detached the ligaments from the base of my thumb, but I didn't know it. I went to spring training, and the pain persisted. I could play golf, but my thumb hurt when I opened a car door and when I turned the ignition key. I finally had it checked and had surgery just before the start of the season, emerging from the operating room as a left-handed broadcaster. I have the score sheets to prove that it can be done and that it doesn't get much better in six months. My score sheets from that year are easy to read, but they look as if a third-grader penciled them.

In late April, I started experiencing pain in the back of my neck and under my left shoulder blade. One night in New York it got pretty intense and I was short of breath. The next day I had it checked out and there seemed to be no serious problem. I took some anti-inflammatory drugs and the pain all but went away. But when it resurfaced I went in for tests and while I was at the doctor, my heart started doing gymnastics. I was rushed to the emergency room and had surgery for pericarditis (an inflammation of the lining of the sac that contains the heart) that night. I may have been close to dying—I was afraid to ask.

Lucky me. I awoke in the intensive care unit with a plastic pear-shaped device stuffed down my throat. I couldn't speak and I thought my broadcast career was over. I must have looked like a sad case to the rest of the heart surgery patients. They were twenty or thirty years older than I. But I was the only one wearing a cast.

I got the cast off my hand in May and my thumb was swollen and ugly. The rehab exercises were painful and the swelling kept getting worse. After a couple of weeks, the doctor did another test and found a bone infection. I had to have surgery again to gouge out the infected end bones and fuse them together, top and bottom, eliminating the joint. Then I had surgery again to insert a catheter into a vein near my heart so that I could give myself intravenous antibiotics morning and night for six weeks. During this time, my prednisone dosage was declining—thank God for that. Finally, on September 23, the day after my fiftieth birthday, the cast was removed from my hand and replaced with a removable splint. The worst part was over for me, but not for the team. For them, the best part was over. A nine-game September swoon dashed all play-off hopes and put a damper on designs for a new stadium in downtown Houston. I thought about the tragic flaw of hubris—excessive pride—and decided that the next time I felt giddy about my prospects I would hold my tongue.

My forty-ninth birthday led me nowhere but to the hospital; my fiftieth brought good health and a new challenge. The team limped to the finish line in 1996, finishing second, and I got the cast removed from my right hand and forearm. Two weeks after I traded my cast for a splint, I became manager of the team. This bizarre turn of events put me in the position of doing more with the number 49 than I had done as a player. I inherited a good team and got lucky, capturing the Central Division the first year with only eighty-four wins. The next year we vaulted to 102 wins, a team record. I won the National League Manager of the Year Award. In the last year of the Astrodome, we were tormented by injuries and dogged by the Cincinnati Reds. We managed to capture the Central flag for the third straight time, this time with ninety-seven wins. I managed better that year but did not win the award. And, as usual, we lost in the first round of playoffs.

This was the last hurrah for the Astrodome as a ballpark and what a way to finish. We won the last game to clinch the division. Then we celebrated—not just the year we had but major league baseball in Houston. A team-of-honor was chosen and paraded out on the field. At this point, I was fifty-one years old and never felt better.

We stunk the first year at Enron and finished fourth with a record of 70-92. Then in 2001 we won again, this time with a weaker team and fewer victories (ninety-three). Four championships in five years is quite an accomplishment, and combined with four straight exits in the first round of playoffs, it got me fired. I finished with a record of 448-362 for a .553 winning percentage. My 448 wins are second on the all-time Astros list behind Bill Virdon, who managed the team for eight years. The winning percentage is first on the all-time Astros' list and better than that of many Hall of Fame managers.

All told, my pitching record (139-123, .531, 3.30 ERA) is about halfway good enough for enshrinement in the Hall, and my managing record is about the same. The combination, along with eighteen years as your friendly broadcaster, was good enough to stir some talk about retiring number 49 and Drayton picked up on it— funny how that works.

I don't know whether I could have done anything differently to win in October—nobody knows—but the Astros obviously thought that it would be easier to advance with a different manager. I believe they were correct in that assumption because the monkey on our backs would have grown into a gorilla if we got a fifth chance. In fact, I may have become a hero by "retiring" at the right time. I could have been a goat again by managing the last year of my contract. Instead, I wrote this book and played golf, knowing that no Astros player, coach, or manager will ever wear 49 again. I went on the ESPN telecast on the night of my number retirement and told Joe Morgan that I didn't think I deserved a demotion but that the team was probably better off without me. The Astros lost the game to the Pirates that day. You be the judge—blessing or curse?

Either way, I have to admit I was shocked when I had lunch with Drayton just before the start of the season and he told me about retiring my number. In an ironic way, it may have been that the sports talk show hosts (some of whom were on my case and may have contributed to my dismissal) encountered a backlash of calls from Dierker fans, defending me and putting the blame on the players, and that got the ball rolling. I know my friend Kenny Hand mentioned it when Judy and I spent an hour on his radio show in the spring. When Drayton told me of his plans, I was thrilled, but I was also scared by the enormity of it all. I didn't want to be teased and disappointed. He asked me when I wanted to do it, and I said as soon as possible.

"If the team doesn't start well, you aren't going to want me standing out at home plate reminding everyone of our championships," I said.

I don't think he picked up on what I said. The thought of losing seldom enters his mind.

Until a date was set and a public announcement made, I wasn't going to start celebrating. I was afraid the whole affair would disappear like a coin in the hand of a magician, but it did not. To Drayton's credit, he picked May 19 and announced it a month in advance. This gave me plenty of time to marshal family and friends for the big event.

On the day the press conference trumpeting the retirement of my number was held, I played golf and had three or four beers. I felt more like taking a nap than making a speech, and if I sounded subdued it was because I was just plain tired. I'm not sure I would have said or done anything differently if I were full of energy. The honor was in recognition of excellence over time; I likened it to the difference between the way I felt after my twenty-win season in 1969 and my no-hitter in 1976. The no-hitter was cause for jubilation, but I am more proud of my performance during the '69 season. Still, it is hard to celebrate something like that unless it is tied to a world championship. Even if we had won the World Series in 1969, we would have celebrated one event—the last game.

At the press conference I mentioned that I had accomplished almost everything I wanted in baseball except for going to the World Series and making the Hall of Fame. Lots of players of middling talent have gone to the Series. In that sense, I suppose having my number retired could only be surpassed by enshrinement in Cooperstown. When I learned that only 130 numbers have been retired by all of the teams in baseball, and I looked at the names that go with those numbers, I felt aglow. It was like fatherhood. You don't jump for joy, but you enter the land of contented dreams when they tell you the baby is normal and your wife is resting comfortably.

A few weeks later, I was talking with Larry Yount, my contemporary and Robin's older brother. We all went to Taft High School in Los Angeles and Larry told me that the only thing Robin really wanted was to have his number retired by the Brewers. He got that, and went to Cooperstown too. I wonder how many high schools can boast two major league baseball players whose numbers have been retired?

In the two weeks that followed I learned that I would not make a good secretary. I always suspected that the traveling secretary was the toughest job in baseball. Now I know for sure. Trying to arrange tickets for everyone and coordinate travel schedules and hotel reservations was challenging. My family arrived on Friday and I took them all out to dinner. It was my first dinner check for more than $1,000.

Many of my family members and friends gathered on May 18. We had an open house, with fifty or more people showing up. We went through several cases of soda and beer along with quite a few bottles of wine, and I could tell they were less enthused about the Astros winning streak than I was. I still didn't think the team could win the division, and was happy that my appearance the next day would be salutary, a day for sweet, not sour, grapes. As it turned out, the team lost on May 19 and did not win again until the 26th. My day couldn't have come at a better time. Even the weather was perfect.

We arrived at Astros Field at 5:30 on that day, an hour and a half before game time. The team had set up a reception area behind home plate, with drinks and hors d'oeuvres. At least twenty of my former teammates were on hand along with many players from my broadcasting years in the 1980s and 1990s. The team found the perfect vehicle for my coronation parade—a 1948 Chrysler Town and Country convertible woodie. What a beautiful car: Drayton said that he was going to buy it for me until he found out that it was worth $100,000. Then he said, "Larry's still getting paid and he can afford it if he wants it." (I bet he just about choked when he heard the price, but I didn't. I have been looking for the right woodie for years and knew what a choice convertible would bring. I'm looking for the station wagon, though—the back-to-the-future SUV.) I suppose Milo could have bought it for me but as he said when I brought it up on the air, he was much too poor.

When we started our tour of the warning track from home plate all the way around, I was waving to the fans. A guy with an aloha shirt, standing behind the Astros dugout, was giving me the *mahalo* sign, which translates loosely to "God bless you" in Hawaiian. The funny thing is that this Hawaiian hand sign is precisely the sign that a manager gives the home plate umpire when he comes out of the dugout to do a double switch with a pitching change. You hold your right arm up and point outward with your thumb and little finger, twisting your hand, more than waving it. When Rick first saw me do this on TV, he said, "That's cool the way you give the umpire the *mahalo* when you change pitchers."

Anyway, I went with the *mahalo* sign with both hands after that. I did not feel so exultant as proud as I cruised around the field. I noticed that about half the seats were taken, which really pleased me because I was afraid that the crowd would be sparse on a Sunday night an hour before game time. By the time I got around to home plate, my former teammates were seated along the first base side and my family was opposite them. I sat down next to Judy and they announced six different players from Ryan's high school team, each wearing a different version of the No. 49 jerseys I wore as a player and manager. When the kids circled around behind me, I said hello to them, trying to loosen them up. They marched out tight-lipped and stiff, like mummies. I wasn't sure what I was going to say, but I knew I wasn't going to say much. More isn't always better and attention spans for on-field ceremonies are short.

Still, I wanted to say something in a nice way, offer thanks, that sort of thing. I almost panicked halfway through Drayton's introduction because his speech was reverberating and with my high-frequency hearing loss, I couldn't make out a word he was saying. I turned to Judy and said, "Tell me when he calls me up there. I can't hear him." She said later that she couldn't hear him that well either but she did give me a nudge when it was time.

I think the unrehearsed speech went fairly well. I acknowl-edged my family and my extended family of teammates. I made a friendly overture toward the fans even though I still felt the sting of the lash they gave me the previous October. The one thing I re-gretted was that I forgot to finish with the first thing that came to mind when I thought about what I wanted to say—"Aloha." I wanted to start with it and end by saying, "Most people know that 'Aloha' means both hello and goodbye in Hawaiian, but many do not know that it also means love. And so I say as I leave the rest of the story to the guys in the dugout, 'Aloha, everyone.' "

Well, as the perennial fifteen-game winner once said. "I don't want to win twenty. If I do they'll expect me to do it every year." I would rate this ceremony as a fifteen-game winner. One word, "Aloha," would have made it better. The gift of the woodie would have been nice as well. But the real gift is the symbolic immortality that comes with a retired jersey number—that's the gift that keeps on giving. Along with the brick engraved with our family's names outside the stadium, it signifies the roots that have taken so long to grow here in Texas in the gumbo clay of the coastal plain.

The next day, Rick and I played golf and I was duck-hooking everything, playing like a duffer. I thought about our golf game six years ago in Hawaii. Back then I thought playing well was the foreshadowing of a career advancement that would take place the next season. Now I know that it was simply a golf game, nothing else. This time, I didn't worry about how golf would affect my future. I just kept changing my stance, changing my grip, searching for the right tempo. I never got it together that day, but I didn't blow a fuse over it. Perhaps that round was a harbinger of a future failure, but I doubt it; perhaps Rick was chanting "64." I don't care.

After the number retirement, I only went to the ballpark four or five more times, usually for a specific reason. I followed the team closely on radio and television and found it more satisfying than visiting in person. The team started playing better but still floundered in the middle of the pack. The All-Star Game was played to a tie and the Astros remained five to eight games back until they got hot toward the end of July. By August 7, they were 59-53 and only one game behind the Cardinals.

Until that point, I was charitable in my feelings for the team. When they approached first place, I found myself pulling against them. It was an odd, ambivalent sort of feeling. I wanted the individual players to do well because I liked them, but I didn't want the team to win too much. If they went on a second-half surge like the 1986 Astros, they could win the division and win more than the ninety-three games we won the year before. I still didn't think this would happen but I began to worry about it. If the Astros played better without Alou, Castilla, Jackson, and Williams, it would make me look bad. I didn't want my departure to look like the end of a bad experiment. I wanted it to feel like it did on the day of my number retirement. I wanted the team to do well for the players and the fans, but when they lost a game, it didn't upset me.

As the season turned to September, the Astros were four games out and they never got closer. They went 3-4 against the Redbirds down the stretch and finished 84-78, the same record that won it for us in 1997.

The summer was gone and there would be no October baseball in Houston. You can't lose in the first round if you don't get into the playoffs. I must admit, I wasn't unhappy with the way it turned out. The team got good work out of some young relief pitchers and Oswalt and Miller were nails in the second half (Roy lost his bid for twenty wins on the last day of the season).

In the spring of 2002, I wrote an article for *Texas Monthly* and ended it by saying that one of the things I had always wanted to do but was never able to because of baseball was to go rafting down the Colorado River through the Grand Canyon. I finally managed to do it. The whole family made the trip and we had a wonderful time. We were trapped together in isolation—we had to get along and did happily. Laughter was the common denominator of the trip.

(Our guide told us that he was in the Canyon on 9-11 and that he didn't know about the attacks until September 14. That, more than anything, made me realize how small we really are. You could have put the World Trade Center buildings in that Canyon and they would look like toys.)

I had another great family experience on October 5: My mother turned eighty and we had a big party in Los Angeles; Ashley even flew in from London. The old gal was pretty spry, which gives me great hope. I went for a walk with her the day before the party and didn't bother to change from thongs to shoes. She made me pay by going three miles at a pace where shoes would have served much better. We had about seventy-five guests at the party and I was really proud of my mom. Of course she threw me a strike for the ceremonial first pitch on the day of my number retirement, so I wasn't really too surprised that she looked better than most of her friends.

The thing that surprised me more than anything was that I wasn't contacted about several managing vacancies; our beat writer, Jesus Ortiz, called to tell me that my name had come up with regard to the Kansas City job, but the Royals never spoke with me. I had been careful not to say that I would never manage again. I didn't think I would, but I could envision a circumstance where I might throw my hat in the ring. After the season, there were many openings, and still no calls. Maybe all the general managers thought the four division championships were a fluke, and maybe they're right. I know it didn't happen just because of my leadership.

I finally received a call about managing in early November

2002. At that time, the Brewers, Cubs, and Mariners were still looking for a skipper. Alan Nero, who negotiated Art Howe's deal with the Mets, wanted to know if I was interested in getting back in the dugout. I didn't have any interest in the Brewers job because I didn't think they stood a chance of winning. The Cubs appeared to have enough pitching to make a run at it. I studied the Mariners and I was convinced that they had a good chance to beat the Angels and A's in 2003. I told Alan that I would consider those jobs, but I never heard back from him. I still don't know if I threw my hat into the ring too late, or if they just weren't interested.

I was grateful for the sabbatical last summer but one thing concerned me: I figured I would get plenty of broadcast offers, but I ended up doing two mid-season games for Fox, and that was it. I watched a lot of games and listened to a lot of former ballplayers doing analysis, and frankly, I was nonplussed that I didn't get any more assignments. I'm not sure I can out-manage the other skippers in the major leagues, but I am certain that I can provide better commentary than most, if not all, of the color men who were working the games.

One thing I have found in my post-playing years is that the world of business is less orderly and rational than the world of athletics. In business, the quality of a person's performance is often a subjective judgment—a matter of opinion. In baseball, it is patently clear if a guy has talent—statistics speak volumes. When I hear players talking about how they got screwed or how unfair it is, I have to laugh. Wait until they get out there in the world and see how they like it. You can lose an executive position to the boss's son no matter how hard you work or how deserving you are. But the boss's son cannot take your job on the field. Sure, there are times when players get demoted or benched when they should be playing, but for the most part, life on the diamond is fair. It can be cruel, no doubt, but it is usually rather obvious if you are a real player or just a reasonable facsimile. There were disappointments in my baseball life, but whether on the mound, at the mike, or in the dugout, I know I succeeded on my terms and without losing my mind. After all, this ain't brain surgery.

Writing this book has been a great avocation. It brought back many good memories and even helped me refine my own perspective on the sport I have been married to all my life. Yes, the honeymoon is over, the separation all but complete. I still have plenty of energy, however, and I will be looking for reconciliation this summer.

Last December I was talking with my oldest daughter, Ashley, and she gave me the ultimate Christmas present by telling me she was pregnant with our first grandchild. It was a gentle reminder that some things are more important than baseball.

About the Author

LARRY DIERKER has spent nearly his entire adult life with the Houston Astros in one capacity or other. He made his major league debut with Houston on his eighteenth birthday in 1964, striking out Willie Mays in his first inning of work. In his fourteen-year pitching career (thirteen with Houston), he was the Astros' first twenty-game winner, a two-time All-Star, and pitched a no-hitter. He is still the franchise leader in starts, complete games, innings pitched, and shutouts, and is second in wins. From 1979 until his appointment as manager, Dierker was the club's principal color analyst on radio and television, made several network television appearances, and for several years wrote a column that appeared in the *Houston Chronicle*. A surprise choice as manager in 1997, Dierker led the Astros to first place in the National League Central Division in four of his five seasons as manager. An avid reader, cigar smoker, and connoisseur of fine Hawaiian shirtwear, he lives in Houston, Texas.